IMPRISONMENT
IN
WESTERN AUSTRALIA

Evolution, Theory and Practice

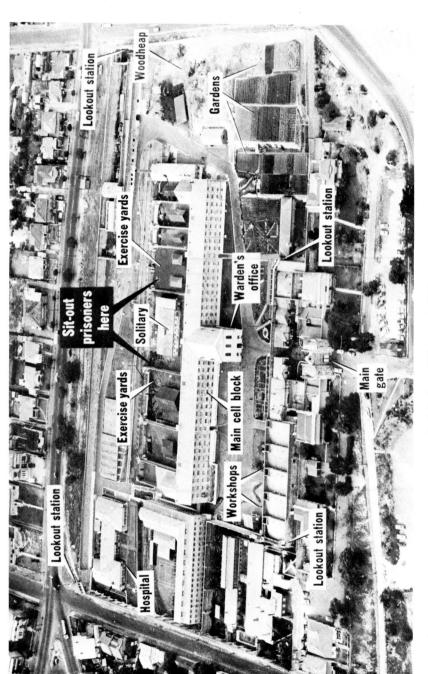

Aerial view of Fremantle Prison

IMPRISONMENT IN WESTERN AUSTRALIA

Evolution, Theory and Practice

J E THOMAS
AND
ALEX STEWART

UNIVERSITY OF WESTERN AUSTRALIA PRESS
1978

First published in 1978 by
University of Western Australia Press
Nedlands, Western Australia

Agents: Eastern states of Australia and New Zealand: Melbourne University Press, Carlton South, Vict. 3053; United Kingdom and Europe: International Scholarly Book Services (Europe), 8 Willian Way, Letchworth, Hertfordshire SG6 2HG, UK; USA and Canada: International Scholarly Book Services, Inc., Box 555, Forest Grove, Oregon 97116.

Thomas, James Edward, 1934-
Imprisonment in Western Australia.

Index.
Bibliography.
ISBN 0 85564 132 0

1. Punishment—Western Australia—History.

2. Correctional institutions—Western Australia—
History. 3. Penal colonies. I. Stewart,
Alexander, 1916-, joint author. II. Title.

364.6'0994'1

Photoset by University of Western Australia Press. Printed by Wescolour Press, a division of West Australian Newspapers Ltd, Fremantle, Western Australia and bound by Printers Trade Services Pty Ltd, Perth, Western Australia.

For Simon and Philip—remembering Australian kindness

Dyret pan vynnych kymer awelych
agwedy delych tra vynnych tric

Acknowledgements

We are grateful to the then Chief Secretary of Western Australia, M. E. Stephens, and to the then Director of Corrections, Colin Campbell, both for giving permission for this research to be carried out and for granting Alex Stewart leave for this purpose. Similarly, the granting of study leave by the University of Hull is much appreciated.

To Dr Trevor Williams, Professor Richard Harding, both of the University of Western Australia, and to Bill Kidston, formerly Assistant Director, Corrections, and now Assistant Director, Community Welfare, we owe a special debt. To Trevor Williams goes the credit for conceiving of the idea, and mooting it, in England, on a convivial occasion. Richard Harding and Bill Kidston worked hard at ensuring that practical difficulties, such as office accommodation, and the attraction of finance were overcome. Dr C. T. Stannage of the Department of History was of great help, frequently discussing general aspects of the history of Western Australia in very generous and erudite fashion. Our gratitude to these four, in these particular respects, and for much encouragement and interest, is considerable.

Thanks must go to the Australian Criminology Research Council for financial assistance, which was especially valuable because it enabled extensive visiting of prisons to be carried out. The Imperial Relations Trust in London, which has done so much to foster Commonwealth links, especially between Australia and Britain, was most generous through the provision of an air fare.

The Faculty of Economics and Commerce, and the Law School at the University of Western Australia were hosts to J. E. Thomas during study leave. But the staff of both were much more. They were hospitable, generous, and helped with transport, and with secretarial assistance. The production of this book owes a lot to the support of these departments. Within the university too, Vic Greaves, Manager of the University of Western Australia Press, has always shown great interest and support.

We owe an especial debt to Mr P. D. Wilson, Queensland State Archivist. As will become clear, it was extremely difficult to obtain information about a Royal Commission of 1911. Mr Wilson went to a great deal of trouble to marshall such information as there was—and very crucial it turned out to be.

Five people in Australia helped to type the manuscript, at a difficult time because of the end of the academic year, and other pressures. The speed and cheerfulness with which they did so, struck us as truly remarkable. We are most grateful to Susan Davies and Margaret Bond of the Law School, University of Western Australia, Lesley Ridler of the Department of Commerce, University of Western Australia, Val Clewley and Mona Cotton of the Department of Corrections. We are grateful too for much assistance with typing to Anne Gardham and Karen Petch of the Department of Adult Education, Hull University.

We hope that this will be intelligible to staff and prisoners past and present, and not only in Western Australia. Without their experiences, which they were happy to discuss, we might have given a less than human account. To them, above all, we are indebted.

Contents

Tables

Graphs

Illustrations

Introduction

With the considerable exception of T. A. Williams's unpublished thesis, 'Custody and Conflict', noted in our bibliography, nothing of any length has been written about imprisonment in Western Australia. Our book is an attempt to set out the multifaceted chronicle of an important part of the social history of the state. Although basically this is a historical account, it is not only that; nor is this simply a local history. It is becoming clear that the similarities between prison systems are greater than the differences, and the history of the Western Australian system is in a sense the history of modern prison systems.

Any first account of a prison system must be eclectic, drawing on several disciplines if it is to give an overall picture. As well as writing a history, we have examined penological, administrative and organizational aspects of the system. The book should therefore be of interest to a wide variety of people. The whole is an attempt to show how present practice has evolved. This cannot be understood without a thorough grasp of its historical antecedents.

This leads to another problem: the question of deciding at what point discussion of a given topic should be halted. For example, in discussing Aboriginal imprisonment there is a temptation to review the whole field of native policy. Again, the reasons why a settlement was made in King George Sound are complex and go beyond the fact that convicts were sent there. But we have had to concentrate on prison policy and administration. When we have felt that we are straying into matters further afield, we have generally stopped.

We begin with a description of the prison system in the infancy of the colony. There is a certain amount of plain, narrative description here, as in the rest of the book. This is because, while we have tried to put Western Australian practice into a broad theoretical context, there is room, we feel, for setting out in accessible form details of such episodes as the first judicial execution which took place. We then go on to outline those features of the convict era which are relevant to the main theme of the book, the evolution of the system. There is, incidentally, a need for a major analysis of the many aspects of transportation to Western

Australia. The only scholarly account, which confines itself to a
limited period, is that by Gertzel, noted in the bibliography. That
unfortunately has not been published.

Then follows a consideration of the one major inquiry which
has been made into prisons: the Royal Commission of 1899. From
this period onwards we trace the beginnings of the modern period,
especially the introduction of indeterminacy in sentencing, which
in the form of parole is still controversial. We also recount the
especial provision made for Aboriginal prisoners, and discuss the
issues raised by their treatment. The last part of the book deals
with recent policies. Since these policies are still new, and since
their consequences are still to some extent speculative, we have
not gone into a great deal of detail, which would quickly become
out of date. Instead we have tried to discuss in broad organizational and penological terms the implications of such developments. Such an assessment must naturally be preliminary only,
since the situation does not have the stability which makes other,
more historical situations, susceptible to examination.

The Western Australian prison system has always been divided
into three segments. There are first those prisons which *de jure*, as
in the case of Rottnest Island, or *de facto*, as in the case of
Broome at the present time, contain mainly an Aboriginal population. Then there are the other country prisons, generally small and
with a mixed or predominantly white population. The expansion or
contraction of areas of the state has been followed by the opening
and closure of such establishments. In 1899 for example, the Royal
Commission pointed out the pressing need for a prison at Coolgardie; in 1975 a prison was opened at Roebourne—both being a
reflection of mining patterns. At the centre is the third segment,
Fremantle. Because of its size, its different origins, its traditions
and its persistence as a prison, Fremantle will feature prominently
in this book. However, although it has always dominated the
prison scene in Western Australia, the system comprises more
than just Fremantle, a fact which non-Fremantle prison officers
have always been fond of pointing out. Part of the task of this
book is to look at the general, common denomination which links
these three broad parts of the prison system.

This book sets out therefore to collate wide-ranging facts about
imprisonment in Western Australia, to set out the most interesting
and significant of these and to place developments in a historical-

penological context. To this end there is much discussion about the history of penal treatment. It is intended to be a preliminary account and by no means exhaustive of the Western Australian system. We hope that more developed and sophisticated analyses may be built upon it.

Increasingly the attention of the historian is turning from a consideration of major political events and personalities to a new interest in the history of ordinary people. People sent to prison are usually very ordinary. The idea of prison is distasteful, but the treatment of men and women in Western Australian prisons is an important part of the history of the state. Moreover such treatment is a measure of the maturity and humanity of the society which decided, and continues to decide, what that treatment should be. We hope that this book will encourage an interest in less-known areas of the state's activity, and that there may be topics with which we can only deal briefly, but which will encourage further research.

In 1979 Western Australia will be celebrating its 150th anniversary. It is hoped that this book will be an appropriate and timely addition to the knowledge about the state.

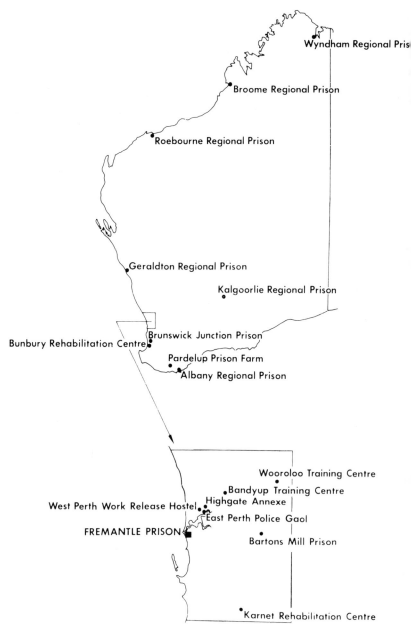

1   Locations of institutions and police gaols in Western Australia

xvi

1

Early Imprisonment

King George Sound—The first prisoners in Western Australia—A prison hulk—Fremantle Round House—The first prison rules—The Parkhurst boys—The first legal execution—Early prison legislation —New prisons—Rottnest reformatory

In the light of what was to happen in respect of transportation to Western Australia, it was a paradox that amongst the earliest settlers to arrive in the colony were convicts from New South Wales. The annexation of Western Australia arose because of the concern of the British Government about potential French expansion in the area. This concern was, it occurred, due to 'certain false rumours',[1] but at the time British fears seemed justifiable enough. By March 1826 fears of French ambitions were so great that the British Empire builders pondered over maps, and the focus of their interest increasingly became King George Sound, a stretch of deep water in a promising harbour on the south coast, on a coast-line which had repelled earlier explorers both because of its bleakness and because of its unsuitability for shipping.[2]

General Darling expressed the view that King George Sound was unsuitable even for a penal settlement—the intention being that 'convicts, reconvicted of lighter crimes at Botany Bay might be sent'. In spite of Darling's objections three ships sailed from Sydney on 9 November 1826 to settle points along the south coast of Australia.[3] So it was that a state, which thirty years later was to be the subject of so much controversy over the question of transportation, numbered amongst its founders a party of prisoners from New South Wales. The party consisted of twenty-three prisoners under the command of a Major Lockyer, and they arrived on the brig *Amity*. She dropped anchor in Princess Royal Harbour in King George Sound, at what was to be the town of Albany, on Christmas Eve 1826. The party landed a few hours later.

The building of a prison was not regarded as a priority, probably because the two great potential crises which always alarm prison officials were absent. These are riot and escape, the two components which signify loss of control and consequently failure. In respect of the first, the prisoners seemed to have been reasonably

well-behaved, a factor which was no doubt taken into consideration when they were selected. They continued to behave well and
were rewarded. In October 1829 their good conduct resulted in a
notice that labour would cease on Saturdays at eleven o'clock.
The second fear of prison officials, escape, was highly unlikely.
To the south there was the sea, to the north, east and west there
was wild country, harbouring a formidable number of dangers,
both natural and human. The only precaution which seems to
have been taken was that when ships put in, care was taken to
ensure that convicts did not stow away. In spite of these apparently
insurmountable obstacles to escaping, it would have been a very
odd group of prisoners which did not contain somebody who
would not try. In February 1830 eight made for the bush and one
was never recaptured.

As late as 1831 a return of buildings in the district does not list
a gaol, although a prison built later, in 1836, was 'to replace the
original prison of the New South Wales regime at Residency Point
referred to as the 'Black Hole'.' This building is likely to have
been a punishment block of some kind. By the time a prison was
built in Albany in 1836, formal possession had been taken of the
colony by Captain Fremantle in 1829.

The King George Sound settlement had not prospered, possibly
because of its extreme isolation from the eastern settlements, and
possibly because the soil was either not productive, or was misunderstood and mishandled. The idea of a penal settlement was
abandoned by proclamation dated 7 March 1831,[4] largely because
it was intended to establish a settlement on the Swan River. One
of the conditions laid down, which as has already been mentioned
will concern us in discussing transportation, was that no convicts
would be sent to the Swan River. Since the area around King
George Sound was intended to be part of the new penal colony, it
followed that the convicts would have to go, especially since Governor Stirling expressly wished to attract colonists to the southern
region.[5]

Although the imperial convicts left, the Albany district soon
found plenty of use for its prison. The social life of the district
was being disturbed in particular by drunken seamen, and in addition the natives were constantly in conflict with the authorities.
The latter utilized two punitive devices from the Middle Ages, one
of which was used for black offenders. These were chained to a

large staple, which was driven into a large peppermint tree near the prison. The other mediaeval relic was the stocks, to which criminals were consigned in the 1830s. These were the adjuncts to 'Spencer's Gaol', as it came to be known locally, until it was demolished in the 1880s when the railway arrived.[6]

Meanwhile the new settlement on the Swan River took an inevitable step forward toward maturity by realizing that the community needed a prison. Since building prisons is a very time-consuming and, especially if they are to be secure, a very expensive business, a short-term solution had to be found. The answer, familiar to the penal administrators of the day, was to establish a prison hulk. Hulks, which were the shells of old ships, had been used in England since the end of the previous century. Originally they had been found necessary because of the difficulty of finding enough colonies to which convicts could be sent. This difficulty was compounded by the fact that until 1821 the British central government had no prisons of its own.

The hulks were authorized by the Hulks Act of 1776 for a period of two years. They were squalid, unpleasant, devoid of any merit whatever, and were the subject of a great deal of criticism from reformers, whose case was given a boost by the writings of authors such as Dickens. Although no one, not even the authorities responsible for them defended their use, and in spite of all efforts to have them abolished, they were in use in England at the time of the settlement of the Swan River Colony, and indeed would continue to be used for another forty-five years.

Penal history is replete with examples of 'temporary' expedients which became very permanent indeed. The hulks are a very good example. When the last of them was closed, they had been used by the English government for ninety-nine years. The very last hulk to be administered by the English government was at Gibraltar, and this was closed in 1875.[7] Since they were familiar enough to the administrators of the day, it was not surprising that the new Swan Colony should establish one as a means of punishing its embryonic criminal population.

In August 1829 the *Marquis of Anglesea*, carrying general cargo, and ten soldiers of the 63rd Regiment, four women, and two children, one of whom had been born on the voyage, arrived in the Swan River from England.[8] In September the captain of H.M.S. *Sulphur* reported that the *Marquis* 'drove with three anchors ahead in a gale of wind, in Gages Road and went onto the rocks, was bilged', and he feared could never be got off.[9] The wreck was ideal for the purpose and was promptly taken over.

After the first Quarter Sessions in the colony, held in July 1830, the chairman compiled a list of prisoners who had been sent to the *Marquis*. From this it can be seen that the distinction of being the first colonial, as opposed to imperial prisoner in Western Australia, went to one Edward Chapman, committed by the lieutenant-governor in 1829. His offence was noted as 'misconduct as an indentured servant', and for it he was put on the hulk for twenty-eight days. He was the first of twenty-seven prisoners there between December 1829 and July 1, 1830.[10] It appears that some rules had been drawn up for the governing of the hulk, but these have not survived in their entirety. One which has, was an instruction in July 1830 that the prisoners' diet was to be reduced.[11]

The chairman of the Quarter Sessions in the report (mentioned above) expressed dissatisfaction with the hulk, mainly because it was difficult to find boats to take the prisoners out to it. Since there was nowhere to lock them up in Fremantle, which 'occasioned much difficulty and embarrassment of the constables', he supported a proposal by the chief constable that a 'secure lock-up house' should be built for 'riotous or suspected characters', for those awaiting trial and for those awaiting transfer to the hulk.[12] This was the proposal which led to the erection of the first purpose-built prison in Western Australia: the Round House at Fremantle.

Plans were drawn up by a civil engineer, H. W. Reveley, and work on the new prison began on 1 September 1830. It was completed on 18 January 1831 at a cost of £1603 10s, had stone walls, a weatherbound roof, and contained eight cells.[13] The building, which has survived, is in a high part of the town at Arthur's Head, and its twelve-sided design makes it not only the oldest public building in the state, but also one of the most distinctive. The new prison was able to accommodate both men and women.

A set of rules was drawn up for its management,[14] and this first set of rules for the administration of prisons in Western Australia is of great importance, since, as is often the case with prison rules, they set a precedent upon which the later style of prison management was to be based. The rules showed that the intention was that prisons in the state should be administered according to the English model. This was not the English pattern, which is familiar, of a highly-structured centralized organization to administer prisons, developed in the last quarter of the nineteenth century. Like much administration in England before this centralization, authority was to be vested in the local magistrates.

In England the magistrates had controlled the majority of prisons since the Middle Ages. Each group of magistrates were responsible for those in their district. The argument for giving such authority to powerful local people is obvious enough. Theoretically, they know what is going on in the community, and they shape its development. They ought therefore to have a substantial degree of control over what happens in respect of criminal behaviour as well as everything else. However, there are considerable disadvantages in such a system. The principal one is that local lay administrators are generally accountable for community money. This has always made them very reluctant to spend, most especially on groups as unpopular and as powerless as prisoners. Lay local administration of prisons in England is one of the most squalid aspects of the history of public administration. More generally, it may be noted that an important role of the central government has always been to protect minorities from the excesses or lack of interest of local rulers. Not only has this been true of England itself, but has been an important component of administrative attitudes in the British colonial empire.

Already in England in the mid-nineteenth century magisterial control over prisons was being questioned. This was due basically to the increasing intervention in local affairs by the central government, which culminated with the Whig government of 1832 and which was

> dominated by two leading assumptions—the value of uniformity of administration throughout the country and the impossibility of attaining this uniformity without a large increase in the activity of the central government.[15]

But there were reasons connected with the prisons. Not only was there dissatisfaction because of the extremely unsatisfactory way in which they were being administered, but central government was itself becoming more and more involved in prison administration. It had been forced into this situation at the end of the eighteenth century, when transportation became difficult after the achievement of independence by the American colonies. The discovery of Australia went some way to relieving the situation, but even Australia was unable, and increasingly became unwilling to cope with the large number of prisoners who had been sentenced to transportation in England.

Under pressure from reformers the British Government eventually built their first prison, Millbank, London, which was opened in 1821. At the same time there was further pressure from reformers for closer examination of what was done in the local prisons in the charge of magistrates. A succession of Acts, most of them abortive, culminated in an Act of 1835 which set up an inspectorate.[16] In the years afterwards the inspectors described in fine detail the inadequacies and cruelties of the system. It was their criticisms that led eventually and substantially to the demand for the centralization of prison administration in England, which took place in 1877.[17]

In Western Australia in 1831, when the first set of prison rules were drawn up for the Round House, all of this was some way ahead. Following the English tradition, it was decided that the Quarter Sessions was to be the body which administered the prison, the preamble to the Act stating that the laws of England were to apply to the local situation as far as was possible. It was stated, emulating the English system, that the superintendent was to report regularly to the Quarter Sessions, and that visiting magistrates were to inspect the prison at least once a month.

The rules contained many of the reforms which had been advocated as a result of English experience in the previous fifty years. The basic criticism made by European prison reformers, around which all their proposals revolved, was that there was too much freedom in prisons. There was too much freedom for prisoners to drink, too much freedom for them to have visitors of dubious standing, and in general too much freedom for them to 'contaminate' others, a word which is frequently used in the writings of the reformers. To offset this, the rules proposed that no drink should be allowed into the prison, that the prisoners should be made to keep themselves and their environment clean, and that there should be no visitors except when a member of staff was present.

The reformers were not only concerned about the freedom of inmates to misbehave; they were even more concerned about the freedom of staff to ill-treat prisoners. This was reflected in the rules which ordained that there should be a regular report made to the Quarter Sessions, that any use of irons was to be reported to them, and that there should be a proper record kept of deaths. Two English practices of many hundreds of years standing were also forbidden. The first of these was the payment of fees by prisoners. It had always been traditional in English prisons that a prisoner upon arrival in the prison should pay a fee, and when he left he should also pay a fee, even if he had been remanded and subsequently found not guilty of the offence with which he was charged. The rules also stipulated that under no condition should a member of staff allow prisoners to leave the prison not 'even in company with the gaoler himself'. This again was a traditional English practice, which originally enabled debtors to 'go abroad', that is, to be freed to try to find money to pay their debts.

In essence these rules showed awareness of an absolutely crucial priority in the formulation of prison regulations. It is that there should be vigilance on the part of representative members of the community, about what is done in the community's name within the necessarily confined space of a prison. It may be argued that while such rules take away a great deal of freedom from the prisoners, they do at the same time try to ensure that the capricious cruelty of the more casual regime was no longer possible. Later, when native imprisonment in Western Australia is considered, it will be seen how regrettable it was that such rules were not formulated in respect of those institutions to which natives were consigned.

Soon after the issue of the 1831 rules a new criminal group was injected into the evolving society of the colony. Juvenile immigration to Western Australia began in August 1834, when fourteen boys and four girls arrived on the *James Pattison* in the charge of Stirling himself. After disembarkation these youngsters were allocated by a local committee to settlers, as were thirteen others who followed shortly afterwards.[18] Juvenile immigration is best known though for the systematic removal of boys from Parkhurst prison— which is on the Isle of Wight—between the years 1842 and 1849.

Parkhurst was one of a growing number of penal institutions set up by the British Government in its attempt to cope with an increase in the prison population occasioned by the progressive reduction of transportation to Australia. It was specifically converted from a military hospital to try to establish a reformative regime for juveniles.[19] At the time of the settlement on the Swan the English prison system comprised two parts. The local justices continued to be responsible for a network of county and municipal gaols, to which were consigned offenders who were generally not convicted of serious offences. The serious offenders, sentenced to transportation or penal servitude, spent their time on hulks, waiting for a ship to take them overseas, or in a convict prison of some kind, in both cases in the charge of the central government. Parkhurst, which was and continues to be a conventional Victorian prison in design, took the juveniles in the government system, and it was from amongst these that boys were 'encouraged' to migrate. Strictly speaking then, the first experience that the new colony had of the English criminal was when these young men arrived on the Swan River.

After an abortive Act of 1839, which was refused the royal assent, an Act was passed in 1842 which sought 'to regulate the apprenticeship and otherwise to provide for the guardianship and control of a certain class of juvenile immigrants'.[20] The provisions of the Act were simple enough. A 'guardian of government juvenile immigrants' was to be appointed, who would supervise the 'moral, religious and technical instruction, the health, comfort, and general treatment' of the boys. They were to be apprenticed for a period of between two and three years, and *inter alia* there was provision for the channelling of mutual dissatisfaction when it arose between master and servant.

The first guardian was John Schoales.[21] His first group of eighteen lads arrived in August 1842, and they were soon put out as apprentices to butchers, carpenters and other tradesmen. In his first annual report Schoales pronounced the scheme a 'complete success', although some of the boys had to be withdrawn because of lack of proper care on the part of their masters.[22] The total number of boys brought out was 231, of whom a small number came from Millbank Prison. The last fifty-three arrived on the ship *Mary* in 1849, and the settlers, who had previously expressed satisfaction with the boys, complained that some of the *Mary* contingent were badly behaved. Indeed, one lad was an idiot, presenting a serious problem since there was as yet no asylum in the colony. After this contingent Wittenoom, who had succeeded Schoales in 1847, reported that numbers were now too high, and that no more should be sent for two years.[23] In fact the *Mary* contingent was the last, and a *Government Gazette* notice of February 1852 announced the ending of the scheme.

On the whole, as far as can be judged, the scheme seems to have worked reasonably well. Many of the boys, like their fellow-convicts in later years, settled down and contributed to the development of the colony. But also as in the case of their fellow-convicts the stigma of their origins was not easily shaken off. When a petition for licensed premises in Toodyay in 1851 was presented, for example, it was opposed by some people on the sole ground that one half of the twenty-nine signatories had been Parkhurst boys.[24]

The guardian, whilst generally expressing satisfaction, occasionally reported unsatisfactory behaviour. In 1843 for instance, a boy called Neale was very troublesome. One episode especially displeased Schoales, when the lad had charged his master 'with the commission of an offence not to be named'. Whether the charge was justified or not is uncertain, but it seemed sufficiently convincing to the master's neighbours for the latter to treat the alleged offender very coolly.[25]

Sooner or later, in the life of the colony, it was inevitable that a judicial execution would take place. The first white prisoner to be hanged in Western Australia was one of these Parkhurst boys, John Gavin. Since the event has some regrettable distinction, it is worth recording something of the circumstances as recounted by Schoales.[26]

According to Schoales, Gavin had decided to murder the wife of the man to whom he was apprenticed. The reason he gave for this was that for some time she had found more fault with him than he thought he deserved. Instead, in a moment of haste, he killed her son George Pollard, because he believed that if the boy were still alive, he would be a witness to his mother's murder. He confessed as much to Schoales, who for his part, according to a letter which he wrote to the governor, tried unsuccessfully to have the death sentence commuted. In April 1844 Gavin was literally carried to the scaffold by Schoales, who said goodbye at the foot of the ladder. After the boy had been hanging for an hour, they gave his body to Schoales who 'at 4.00 p.m. . . . laid him without a rite of church in the sandhills southwest of the gaol.'

Even then Gavin was the subject of controversy, since Schoales was accused of preventing the boy from having access to a Roman

Catholic priest, which he fervently denied. Schoales expressed his thanks to the high sheriff and his assistants for their 'excellent arrangements and hearty acquiescence in any suggestions proposed for the amelioration of the boy's suffering', adding: 'I trust that my lot, nor theirs, be so cast as to subject us to the repetition of such an awful duty.' By an odd coincidence, when the execution took place at the Round House, Fremantle, the boy and the colony were both fifteen years old. As for Schoales himself, the end of his life was unhappy enough. He was accused of swindling and, according to Erickson, began to drink heavily and died in 1847 aged thirty-seven.[27]

The very first *penal* Act passed in the colony was not strictly concerned with prisons, but only noted that existing imperial arrangements for the treatment and execution of convicted murderers would apply in the colony.[28] The first major Act in respect of *prison* administration in Western Australia was passed in 1849.[29] This Act began by regularizing the status of the institutions in Perth, Fremantle, Rottnest and Albany, declaring them 'legal public gaols and prisons'. Unfortunately for the native prisoners on Rottnest that institution was excluded from the detailed regulations for management which followed.

This Act, which was to be the principal source of reference for prison administrators until the end of the century, gave important enabling power to the executive council to make rules in respect of prisons. Like the hand-written rules of 1831, the Act drew heavily upon English precedent, even where this was irrelevant or even meaningless. The best features, however, embodied much of what was valuable in the English experience, and much of what reformers such as John Howard, Elizabeth Fry and Thomas Buxton had fought for. Some of the more notable of these provisions were the separation of males and females, and an insistence that females should be supervised by females 'where practicable'. Such great hopes of the Victorian penal reformer as the curative power of education are reflected in statutory provision for teaching. Attention was even paid to minutiae such as the provision of scales, so that prisoners could observe the weighing of their food.

The Act shows that its architects were aware of the great issues of penal debate which were going on at the time. The most important of these was the relative merits of the 'silent' and the 'separate' system. The silent system allowed prisoners to work in association, but in complete silence. It was popular with those authorities who wished to avoid having to build expensive cellular facilities, or who felt that association was more humane than segregation. The silent system has been known as the 'Auburnian' system, after the prison in New York State, where early in the last century it was rigidly enforced with the whip.[30] Indeed one of the reasons why it lost the battle with the separate system was because of the difficulty of enforcing it. In England, at Coldbath Fields Prison in 1836 for example, there were 'no less than 5,138 punishments for talking and swearing'.[31]

The separate system meant that a prisoner would eat, work and sleep in his cell on his own. Its proponents believed that it would be more effective in preventing 'contamination' than the silent system, and gradually it was adopted as a policy all over the world. The separate system is not, in theory, the same as solitary confinement. A distinction was made by an English prison chaplain who wrote that under solitary confinement the prisoner has no contact with anyone. Under the separate system however 'he is only kept rigidly apart from other criminals but is allowed as much intercourse with instructors and officers as is compatible with judicious economy.'[32]

Whether these subtle distinctions were as clear to prisoners as to the chaplain is arguable. Those who formulated the Act of 1849 were aware of the distinction and legislated for it. They ordered that separate confinement to prevent contamination be given for a limitless period by the sheriff or the visiting justice. Solitary confinement could also be awarded as a punishment, but only for restricted periods of time.

There was unfortunately a certain amount of ambiguity in the wording of the Act, which in later years was to be exploited. One outstanding example of this was the provision that an offender against prison rules might 'be punished by close confinement, in or without irons, for any period not exceeding one calendar month, and . . . be kept on bread and water for any portion of that time not exceeding seven days'. Eventually it came to be the practice that prisoners in Fremantle who underwent a bread and water punishment, invariably did this in the dark cell. And in succeeding years there was much juggling of these punishments, so that the maximum inconvenience was caused to the prisoners. This was a matter which was raised by the Royal Commission of 1899 and which will be discussed more fully.

The tendency of prison legislation to lead to the fossilizing of traditions and practices may be seen in the provision that the maximum period a prisoner could be sentenced to bread and water was seven days. This continues to be the case in Western Australia. In Victorian England on the other hand, three days was considered to be the maximum, and until the recent abolition of dietary punishment this maximum was adhered to.

The trouble with the Act, as is often the case with prison legislation, was that its good intentions were not fully implemented, and that major defects were not removed in the light of experience. The most notable of these, it later became clear, was the sheriff's control over the prisons. This again was an ancient English precedent and problem, but what the Western Australian legislators had failed to do was to take into account English experience. This was that sheriffs were not very good at running prisons, and that they were usually in conflict with other people who were involved in penal administration. The Royal Commission of 1899 was to show how ineffective the sheriff's supervision of the gaols was. Again, as is common in casually-supervised prison systems, the few modifications that were made to provisions in the Act in later years tended to increase severity of punishment.

The next Act affecting prisons was passed in 1850.[33] It was designed 'to provide for the due custody and discipline of offenders transported to Western Australia'. The most important and far reaching provision in this Act was that which stated that:

> The term of any sentence passed in this colony on any convict shall be in addition to and not concurrent with any former sentence passed on the same offender, who shall be detained until he shall have served the full term and time of all such offences, and so on as often as he should be convicted.

This initiated the 'cumulative sentence' which is a feature of prison legislation in Western Australia. It is a sentence which was to be of concern to the Royal Commission in 1899, and in spite of its falling into disuse after the Commission has been, as we shall see, resurrected in recent years. It is an especially severe feature of Western Australian legislation.

In 1856 the sentence of transportation was abolished in Western

Australia,[34] and in 1860 an Act replaced that sentence with penal servitude.[35] During the same period several Acts enabled governors to declare premises as legal gaols, authorized the transfer of colonial prisoners from one gaol to another, and gave the governor power to make rules for the colonial prisons.[36] 'Trafficking', which is the passing of unauthorized articles to prisoners, in the strict sense by staff, was legislated against in 1857,[37] and again in 1879.[38] In 1887 authority was given for prisoners to undertake public works, and on those occasions for them to be 'kept at such work in chains or otherwise secured'.[39]

How far the problem of escaping prisoners was confined to imperial convicts as against colonial prisoners is not clear, since under the Act of 1850 convict could mean both if the man had been sentenced to transportation. A sentence of transportation could be imposed locally under the provisions of the Act of 1849, and the fact that the 1850 Act was 'to apply to offenders sentenced therein to transportation' indicates that this was done. Certainly the problem was serious enough as early as 1854 for an Act to be passed which sought to cope with 'convicts illegally at large'.[40] Death was prescribed for a number of offences—robbery for example—and the killing of a convict who resisted could be defended as 'justifiable homicide'. A further Act of 1868 elaborated.[41] This noted that the 1854 Act was deficient in the sense that it had been established that if a convict shot at someone and missed, he was not technically guilty under the Act. Therefore levelling a weapon and discharging it with or without bullets was now deemed an offence. So, Western Australia proliferated its penal legislation.

As such new contingencies arose, new laws were passed to cope with them. But in general, prison administrators in Western Australia during the first sixty years of the life of the colony were not faced with any major problems. The prisons were small, and the prisoners, like most prisoners in rural societies, were relatively placid. It was a far remove from the rigid, stratified society of England which had as its inevitable offshoot a criminal subculture, where a criminal status originally achieved became ascribed as the prisoner was progressively labelled. There was nothing in Western Australia to compare with the large English prison acting as a receptacle for an embittered dejected group which Victorians commonly described as 'the criminal classes'. So the business of imprisonment seems to have been carried on with little fuss until the 1890s.

Nevertheless as time went on, the system expanded. A gaol was opened at Perth in 1856, which reflected the growth and importance of the town. By 1882 this gaol was the cause of some concern to the authorities. It was described as having twenty-six cells and seven association wards. In 1881 there was a daily average population of seventy-eight prisoners, most of whom were in association. This revived the old dread of the reformer, 'contamination':

> This constant association tends I fear, to nourish vicious propensities, preventing that reflection which separate confinement is supposed to engender. The average number of punished prisoners for the last three months has been 90, and consequently this evil has increased.[42]

A few years before, in 1878, a commission, whose business was to enquire into certain public service departments, visited Perth Prison. The commission expressed the opinion that it was a very satisfactory establishment, but that prisoners ought to work, for example, on making footwear for inmates of other institutions. The concern of local people about expense is reflected in this recommendation, and also in the governor's hope that Fremantle would be handed over by the imperial government, but that the prospects were 'very remote'. Money, he considered, would inevitably have to be spent on Perth Prison. One further idea which he liked, and which was to be resorted to in later years, was that some lockups would be declared gaols and expensive transfers would thus be spared.[43] However, Perth was actually closed in 1888.

In 1879 four new gaols were proclaimed: at York, Newcastle, Bunbury and Busselton.[44] Further establishments were brought into being at Roebourne in 1881,[45] at Derby in 1887,[46] at Wyndham in 1888,[47] and at Carnarvon in 1890.[48] The opening, and later closing, of prisons reflects in very interesting fashion the development, or contraction, of areas of the state. This is a process which continues up to the present time.

The most important event in prison administration during this period was the transfer of the Imperial Convict Establishment at Fremantle to the colonial government. Fremantle was then, and still remains, by far the largest prison in the state. It must have been obvious that as the colony moved towards independence, after the cessation of transportation, this transfer would be inevitable. The question had been discussed before Governor Broome formally suggested the move in August 1883.[49] In a letter to the English home secretary, Harcourt, he reported that there were only seventy-five convicts left in Fremantle. It had become 'a department which is now a husk without a kernel'. Harcourt in his reply conceded that the transfer was desirable, but that failure to agree between the respective governments had prevented this being done before. Broome proposed that the colonial government would be satisfied if four points could be satisfactorily resolved. These were:

1. That a grant of £45 a year should be made by the imperial government for each convict maintained by the colony and that the amount agreed for lunatics, which was £42, should be implemented.
2. All the imperial property, including the stores, should be handed over to the colony free of cost.
3. That all buildings should be put in good condition before the handover.
4. All officers employed by the imperial government should be pensioned at once, regardless of whether or not they were going to be re-employed by the local government.

Broome described these terms as 'by no means over liberal'. They were clearly very generous to the colonial government. The imperial government then suggested that it might be possible for imperial inmates of Fremantle Prison, the invalid depot and the asylum to be concentrated in one building. To this Broome replied that it was impossible, for the very sound reason that it is unreasonable to put anybody except prisoners in a prison. Amongst other reasons he advanced for swift action was the danger of the imperial buildings falling down. Eventually, after an unsuccessful attempt to set up a select committee of the Legislative Council to consider the question, the prison, the asylum and the invalid depot were handed over on 31 March 1886.[50] The imperial government assumed responsibility for sixty-two convicts and fifty-two invalids. Fremantle, like the other colonial prisons, now became the responsibility of the sheriff, at this time Roe. He predicted that

The majority of the prisoners frequenting the gaol being as usual

the vagabond portion of the ex-convict class who know no home
excepting the gaol or the depot, who spend most of their time in the
gaol or the depot . . . no doubt will be a burden on the colony to
the end.

The last years of the century saw also the beginning of a debate
which in Western Australia has never been satisfactorily resolved,
i.e. a debate on separate treatment for juvenile offenders. By 1880
the need for an establishment for the reception of juvenile offenders was recognized, and it was announced that it had been
decided that a reformatory should be established on Rottnest
Island. At that time juveniles were concentrated in Perth, and once
again it was observed that their association with adults was undesirable, 'there being great objection to their associating with this
class of prisoner'. The intention was that on Rottnest they would
be supervised by a tradesman.[51] The reformatory was duly established and in 1881 the superintendent, who was also the superintendent of the native prison, reported that there were ten boys
there. The view was expressed at the same time that the length of
time for which they were normally detained was not long enough
to effect any substantial training. A uniform at the time consisted
for the winter of a suit of moleskin, and for the summer a duck
jumper and trousers. In the next year, 1882, it was reported by the
colonial secretary to the superintendent:

the doctor has represented to me that the health of the boys in the
reformatory is suffering from over confinement. You will direct the
officers in charge, that on two days in the week, they are to have
from three to six hours for recreation and exercise about the island.
They must not of course go alone, but must be accompanied by the
officer in charge.[52]

A little later in the year the colonial secretary in a mild rebuke to
the superintendent wrote that the officials should be told when
boys were released so that help could be offered towards finding
suitable employment. The superintendent was also directed to
interest himself more actively in their after-career.[53]

Until it was closed at the beginning of the twentieth century, the
establishment remained small, and life in it on the whole was
fairly uneventful. The year 1893 seems to have been an exceptional
one in that the conduct of some of the boys was so bad 'as to

necessitate special reports and severe punishment, which had the desired effect'.[54]

In the last years of the nineteenth century the establishment was quite crowded, but this was because industrial school children were being sent there. The superintendent expressed the view that it was wrong that 'these neglected waifs should be condemned to associate with young criminals'. In the same year three of the boys were sent to gaol as 'incorrigibles'.[55] Finally, after a recommendation from the inspector of industrial schools, the reformatory on Rottnest was formally closed in 1901. The few remaining inmates were transferred to the senior industrial school at Collie, which was organized by the Salvation Army.[56]

Very little of the material described so far has been recorded by penal or social historians. This is because the story of imprisonment in Western Australia has been dominated by the question of transportation. This is understandable. Transportation was, and in some respects still is, a world issue of the greatest importance, and Western Australia's preparedness to perpetuate it was of major concern to the eastern colonies, to Britain and to historians who have since traced the growth of the state. It has been regarded rightly as a much more important historical issue in the early development of the state than the treatment of relatively small groups of local, colonial prisoners. It is appropriate now to trace and review the main outlines of the relatively brief period of transportation to Western Australia, and to trace the impact of the phenomenon on the developing prison system.

2

British Convicts in Western Australia

Crisis in the new colony—The question is raised—The first convicts—Sapper officers—Henderson—Du Cane—The convict career—Governor Hampton—Opposition from the east—Fenian escapes—Pressure for cessation—The convict contribution to Western Australia

When the Swan Colony was formally proclaimed in June 1829, one of the linch-pins of its foundation was a resolve that it would never become, as some of the eastern colonies had been, a receptacle for convicts from the mother country. It was a proud but, as events turned out, an over-optimistic ambition. By the early 1840s the situation economically and socially began to look bleak. The total white population was only 3853 in 1843, and in 1844-5 there was an excess of emigration over immigration of 1852. At the same time the price of stock began to fall, the value of imports exceeded that of exports and interest rates were high. The causes of the mounting crisis, and possible solutions were the subject of much argument between the imperial government and the settlers, the favourite point of disagreement being land regulations. But in reality the troubles were manifold. The surveyor-general, John Septimus Roe, who had grown up with the colony, gave it as his view that many of the settlers were themselves unsuitable for the task which confronted them.[1] The relevance of these broad issues to a discussion of imprisonment is that the continuing deterioration of the economy led directly to the decision to send convicts to Western Australia.[2]

Although there was a slight improvement in 1847, partly because of an increase in imports and partly because of some success in mining exploration, the fundamental problem remained: an obvious chronic shortage of labour.[3] Several possible solutions were discussed, ranging from a suggestion that Chinese from Singapore on three years' contracts should be introduced, to a hope, unfulfilled as it transpired, to emulate South Australia, which had been a focus of German immigration.[4] In 1848 there were only 514 more men than there had been in 1843. Without an increase in the supply of labour not only was development impossible, but the

18

very existence of the colony was in jeopardy.

Already in 1844 some of the settlers had discussed convict labour as a way out of their difficulties. The proposal of York Agricultural Society that a petition for forty convicts should be submitted did not meet with much support. It was highly probable that the absence of a convict and ex-convict population was one of the reasons why many of the settlers had chosen the Swan River as their new home, and the proposal to import convicts did, after all, seriously undermine the basis of the colony's foundation. During the next few years the discussion continued, with the advocates of convict labour gaining ground. In 1846 a W. S. Stockley initiated a petition urging their import,[5] and a memorial in the *Perth Gazette* in the following year showed how support was growing.[6]

Meanwhile the subject was being discussed in England and there was official correspondence about it between London and the colony. Towards the end of the decade Grey, the colonial secretary, asked Governor Fitzgerald to discuss with the settlers the desirability of approaching the British Government with a request for adult convicts. Fitzgerald reported that the idea was welcome, and in October 1848 made specific recommendations in a lengthy minute.[7] The colonists, it appeared, wanted seventy men with their families and thirty single men. Ideally, they were to be from the rural areas of England and would include agricultural labourers, blacksmiths and coopers. It was also agreed that the numbers of convicts sent would be balanced by an equal number of free settlers. The governor expressed strongly the view that he should be responsible for the convicts and that a protector should be appointed as had been done with the Parkhurst juveniles and with Aborigines.

Fitzgerald wrote again in March 1849 reporting a very gloomy state of affairs. There were simply not enough people to develop the economy, and trade had slumped. Large numbers of people were leaving for South Australia, and those who stayed did so only because they had no choice. Fitzgerald confessed himself somewhat baffled by the ambivalent attitude of the settlers towards the convict immigrant. In a memorandum, which he enclosed, they expressed 'great regret and alarm' at the prospect, but the situation was desperate and they *did* want them. Actually the cause of their 'alarm' was uncertainty about the concomitant financial arrangements. They wanted to be assured that the cost of the penal settlement would be borne by the imperial government. This apprehension was natural enough, but in fact the British Government was to be extremely generous during the convict administration. The matter now moved swiftly to its conclusion. Grey wrote, enclosing an Order in Council dated 1 May 1849, which formally established Western Australia as a penal colony.[8] One set of arguments was at an end, but others were to begin.

Transportation had always had its critics in England.[9] It had been used since the early seventeenth century, and before that had its roots in the mediaeval practice of abjuration, that is, leaving the country consequent upon resort to sanctuary. America and the West Indies received the earliest transportees, but the volume leaving Britain increased after the discovery of Australia. From 1788-1850 Shaw estimates that over 72000 men were sent to New South Wales alone.[10] On several occasions more were sent in one year to New South Wales than were sent to Western Australia during the whole eighteen years of convict administration.

During the early part of the nineteenth century many eminent people expressed concern about transportation. They objected to its questionable legality, to its extreme nature as a punishment and, as a volume of experience built up, to the cruelties associated with it. It is possible to detect, as always in debates about crime and punishment, an inevitable confusion which gave rise to emotional and contradictory claims about its effectiveness. For although some people were concerned about its brutality, others objected to its laxity.

Captain Alexander Maconochie, who had distinguished himself through his easing of the tyranny on Norfolk Island, to which incorrigibles were sent, was especially appalled by the practice of 'assignment'. This was a system whereby convicts were hired out to settlers, generally with inadequate pay or no pay at all. Maconochie was one who believed that English convicts were worse off than negro slaves.[11] Against this there were others, such as Governor Arthur, who approved of it. So the arguments raged until the Molesworth Committee of 1838 condemned assignment together with every other aspect of transportation.[12]

The eastern colonies were dismayed at developments in the west. They had had enough of convicts and wanted to try to shake off the image which they had brought with them. Out of the convict system had developed a number of traditions, all of them, it seemed to contemporary observers, being undesirable. These included the legendary dissolute and corrupting behaviour of convict women, and the practice of bushranging, in later years to be romanticized but at the time a cause of some concern. It was this kind of experience which led from the outset to implacable opposition to transportation to Western Australia, an opposition which while ultimately effective, was to sour relationships between the east and west.

The British Government, which as an institution is very slow to learn from colonial experience, had learned a good deal in respect of transportation. The caution which derived from that experience is the keynote of Grey's directives to the colony, in June 1849, about the organization of the convict system.[13] Above all there was to be no assignment. When a convict gained his ticket of leave, which he could after good behaviour in prison, he was free. There were only three constraints on his behaviour: that he was confined to a specified district, that he had to report regularly, and that he could have his ticket revoked. That being so, the need for a protector was obviated. The ticket-of-leave man could arrange his employment and could negotiate with employers to that end. The law would admonish and protect him as it did everybody else.

While the negotiations were being completed, a selection was made from eligible convicts in England. These were then transferred to Portland Prison. This establishment, which is still in use as a borstal institution, has the distinction of being the scene of no fewer than three of the eight murders of English prison staff, which have taken place since the nucleus of a centralized prison system was established in 1850.[14] Grey reported that there were enough married men, who happily combined agricultural backgrounds with good prognoses, to make up the seventy asked for by the settlers. He had therefore added another five bachelors to the party.

Almost before the colonists could reflect on the momentous change in the life of their home, let alone prepare a suitable reception, the *Scindian* had left England. On board the latter were 75 convicts, 50 'enrolled pensioner' guards, 42 women, 78 children and 14 immigrant girls. On June 1, 1850 the *Scindian* arrived at Fremantle. The convicts were given new prison numbers. The first two to be numbered, when they came ashore, were two prisoners called Samuel Scattergood and John Patience.[15] Western Australia came of age at the same moment that it became a penal colony.

On board this ship was an army captain, Edmund Yeamans Walcott Henderson, who was to establish the penal settlement and make a considerable impact both on the development of Western Australia and on its emerging prison system. He was assisted in the creation of the new penal settlement by officers and men of the Royal Engineers, the sappers, some of whom like Henderson were to become men of distinction in public affairs. Because they were so important in moulding the penal history of the world in the second half of the nineteenth century, and because their general influence in early Western Australian affairs was so wide-spread, it is appropriate now to review the background of these soldiers and their role in prison administration. This is especially necessary because so little has been written about them. The more important of them are entered briefly in various biographies, but only one, Du Cane, has been the subject of a biographical study.[16]

The most important feature of their contribution to prison administration was an insistence on the rule of law being paramount. This was one manifestation of a high degree of integrity, which is evident in their work, and was probably the most important single reason why the convict experience in Western Australia was so much less brutal and squalid than it had been in the eastern states. Although the crucial contribution they made to avoiding a repetition of that brutality has not been boldly acknowledged, there is plenty of contemporary evidence to show that people appreciated this fact. They received praise not only from superior officials, who, as will be shown in respect of Aborigine imprisonment, tended variously to condone, excuse, ignore or support blatantly outrageous behaviour by subordinates, but from people below them. Opinions of underlings are not only rarer, but are often more truthful. One comment on Henderson, for example, appeared in a letter to the London *Star* in 1867 from 'an old West Australian convict screw'. The subject was allegations of cruelty against Governor Hampton and his son, which the 'screw' thought highly likely, and to which we will return.[17] In his letter he wrote that 'Henderson's plan has always been to win the men back by kind treatment rather than brute force.' One of the lamentable features of the post-convict prison period in Western Australia from 1870 to 1900 was that the insistence on correct, legitimate treatment for prisoners was not carried on. Henderson's momentum somehow was to lose direction.

The second contribution of these engineer officers to prison administration sprung from the same insistence on law. The main feature of prison administration for over 500 years, before the mid-nineteenth century, was a ramshackle staff structure, confused and anachronistic, which specialized in capricious and often devastating cruelty. The whole rotten structure has limped along, first because communities believe that prisoners probably deserve what they get, secondly because prisoners are powerless, and thirdly because of the lunatic state of the law, which, to take one example, insisted that fees should be paid by a prisoner even if he were acquitted at his trial.

Reformers at the turn of the nineteenth century despaired. The engineer officers, who set up centralized prison systems in England and in Western Australia, combated all this through the creation of a cohesive, intelligible staff structure, based on military tradition, carefully supervised, but also, more important, carefully supportive of staff in adversity. It was this model which was being developed in Western Australia and England simultaneously, which was eventually copied by all advanced prison systems.[18]

Henderson may be singled out as typical of a breed in respect of background and technical and administrative skill. He was born in Hampshire, England, in 1821, the son of a vice-admiral. After training at the Royal Military Academy, Woolwich, he was commissioned in 1838. In 1839 he was in Canada, and in 1845 was a member of a board of commissioners appointed to settle the boundary between Canada and New Brunswick.[19]

In 1850 a Board of Directors of Convict Prisons was set up in England, and the chairman was another sapper officer, Sir Joshua Jebb. The latter evidently approved of Henderson, since he nominated him as a successor, as chairman of that board.[20] It is also highly likely that Jebb encouraged Grey to appoint Henderson to Western Australia. The engineers had learnt an important organizational lesson in the old penal settlements. There conflicts had arisen between heads of the convict establishments and the engineers who directed the work. It was decided therefore, as a result of this experience, that Henderson would be in charge both of administration and of work.

Henderson had two periods as Comptroller-General of Convicts in Western Australia: 1850-56 and 1858-63. It was in 1863 that he became chairman of the English convict prisons in succession to

Jebb, and held the post until 1869. He then became Chief Commissioner of the Metropolitan Police, a post he held with considerable success, which was scarcely diminished by criticism because the police could not control some very violent riots in London in 1886. He was knighted in 1878 and died in 1896.

Shortly after arrival in Western Australia, faced with the colonists' demands for labour and for extensive works, Henderson asked for more engineer officers and men.[21] The leadership of the corps at the time seems to have been very highly imaginative, since there was approval of any scheme which utilized the talents of its members, and incidentally increased their experience on civil work in England or abroad. The skill of the Royal Engineers was a source of frequent congratulation. They had, in fact, in 1851 been so congratulated because of their work on the Great Exhibition. It was small wonder that Henry Labouchere, president of the Board of Trade, commented:

> Whenever the Government was in difficulty in finding an officer of high capacity for civil administration, the right man was sure to be obtained among the officers of the Royal Engineers.[22]

The response to Henderson's request was the arrival of three junior officers: Lieutenant Wray and Second Lieutenant Du Cane, who arrived at the end of 1851, and Lieutenant Crossman, who arrived in early 1852.[23] These officers brought with them a total of ninety-five sappers. Wray was stationed at Fremantle, Du Cane at Guildford and Crossman at Albany. All three were appointed magistrates and also visiting magistrates of the convict stations. They began a prodigious work programme before they were recalled, Du Cane and Crossman in 1856, because of the Crimean War, and Wray a little later. Du Cane went on to become the most important and most controversial figure in nineteenth-century prison administration.

Edmund Frederick Du Cane's life was curiously similar to that of Henderson's. Slightly younger (he was born in 1830), his father too was a service officer. Edmund passed out of Woolwich at the head of his term, was involved in work on the Great Exhibition, which was such a signal success, and having arrived back in England when the Crimean War was finished, was engaged upon important work on the fortification of dockyards and arsenals, notably those of Dover and Plymouth, which attracted another commendation. In 1863 Henderson chose him to be a Director of Convict Prisons in England, and in 1869 he succeeded his old chief as chairman of the board. Du Cane's centralizing of the local prison system in 1877 was one of the administrative wonders of the century, and he went on to establish a considerable reputation as a prison administrator. He was knighted in 1877.

Like Henderson's, the end of his career was marked by controversy. It was claimed that the system which he had developed in England, while it had some good features, was too strict—harsh even—and was not effective in reducing crime. These criticisms led to a major review of prison policy in 1895, when the Gladstone Committee reported. He retired soon afterwards and died in 1903.[24] On a more personal level, both men were exceptionally tall: Du Cane was 1.83 metre and Henderson was 1.91 metre. Both were enthusiastic artists and established a mild reputation in their day as such. Du Cane obviously liked Henderson and left a succinct first comment in a letter to his brother on the man who was to have such an influence on his life: 'Met Henderson—handsome, conceited, good sort of fellow.'[25]

When Henderson and his party landed, they ran into an annoying and potentially serious problem. The harbour master explained that there was no accommodation for them. Henderson overcame this by renting a wool shed, which was only partly roofed and had no floor, two large wooden stores, a house, two cottages, stables and a piece of land to serve as a parade ground. This was in the vicinity of Essex Street in modern Fremantle, an area which when the prison was finally built, deteriorated into a series of low-class lodgings.

The career of the Western Australian convict remained, broadly, the same for the whole period of transportation to the colony. A typical and authoritative account is given in Henderson's evidence to the Lords Select Committee on Transportation of 1856.[26] After being sentenced in England, the convict spent nine months in separate confinement—Victorian convicts called this 'doing separates'—usually in Pentonville. During this time he worked alone, and underwent a strict rule of silence which was relieved only by visits from the governor, chaplain or medical officer.

Pentonville Prison, which is in London, had been built in 1842, and was still something of a penological showpiece, since it was the model of the separate system. After nine months the convict would be transferred to a public-works prison such as Portland. If selected, his next move was to Fremantle.

Even if there were not substantial amounts of documentary evidence about the life on board the convict ships,[27] its squalor might be imagined. The journey was long, unpleasant, generally with poor food and rigorous discipline. But in this respect once again the Western Australian convict experience was different because it was later, and because the British authorities had learned lessons from earlier experience.

One of the most important differences was the improvement in the quality of the ships during the period of transportation. The vessels which took convicts to Western Australia were 'beautiful frigate-built ships',[28] rather more comfortable, and of course much faster than the earlier transports. There were still exemplary punishments, including flogging, but this was not inflicted with as much severity or in the same quantity as had been the custom on ships to the eastern states.[29] There was generally more freedom which, amongst other things, inspired the production of newspapers on several of the ships to Western Australia.[30]

When a convict arrived in Fremantle, he might undergo a further period of incarceration. Henderson believed that the practice of allowing men to arrive with a ticket of leave, which enabled them to begin work at once, was disastrous. Nevertheless some of the earliest of the convicts to arrive were entitled to a ticket of leave at once.[31] If during his period in Fremantle his conduct was good, the convict would be awarded his ticket of leave. He was then, within the constraints already outlined, able to look for work. To this end a number of convict-hiring depots were built throughout the west, which acted as labour exchanges, and some of which are still standing. If a man failed to get a position, or was unemployed, he had to work on the public works.

The fact that he was still not free was emphasized in prison rule 30(8) of 1862, applicable to ticket-of-leave men, which stated that 'any man or men reported for idleness will be severely punished.'[32] Finally, at some point after he had completed about half his sentence, he could be given a conditional pardon. This was broadly the pattern throughout the transportation period, although after July 1857 the period spent on public works and on ticket of leave was rather longer, which naturally delayed the achievement of a conditional pardon. The latter entitled the convict to go anywhere except back to England and for some time to the eastern colonies.

At first the settlers were cautious about taking on convicts, but they relaxed when they discovered that they were reasonable, hard-working men, a discovery which was no doubt exploited because the labour situation was still desperate. With regard to the payment of the men, Henderson explained the system to the 1856 Select Committee. The ticket-of-leave man was paid £1 a month, exactly the same as a free man. He was, however, at a disadvantage because he had to pay back his passage money. The amount varied according to the length of his sentence; a man serving ten years, for example, had to pay back £10, while a sentence of fifteen years involved repayment of £15. Paid back at the rate of £5 a year, this left him with only £7 a year nett. The result was that the employers began paying the convicts an extra £5, which was regarded as a form of unjust taxation. Having obtained his ticket of leave, the convict could send for his family. The repayment of his passage money covered the cost of bringing out his wife and two children, but he had to pay £7 10s for each child over fourteen, and half that amount for those under fourteen in excess of two. Since families were often large, this was a considerable obstacle. So, there were many incentives offered to the convict to ensure that he worked hard and obeyed the rules. If he did not, then punishment was severe.

In 1865 a prisoner called Bushell assaulted a warder with a knife—the first time a knife had been used in any assault since the convict establishment had been set up fifteen years before. It was perhaps on this account that the Comptroller-General's Department issued careful instructions about the punishment Bushell was to undergo.

> The convict registered number 5270 Thomas Bushell who at the sessions of the Supreme Court held on the 6th instant was sentenced to death for attempting to murder Warder Hollis will be executed on Tuesday next the 12th instant at 8 a.m., and all the convicted located at Fremantle Prison will be assembled at 7.30 a.m. that day for the performance of the religious, and other services first established on such occasions in the year 1862.
>
> At 8 a.m. precisely solemn pause of five minutes will be made by the Chaplain, during which time the bell will toll, who will inform the men that the sentence of the law is then being carried into

execution; at the expiration of the solemn silence of five minutes the Chaplain will offer a suitable prayer.

After the conclusion of the divine services above directed, the Visiting Magistrate is requested to address the prisoners to the affect that the Government have ordered this service for the purpose of impressing them with the sad consequences that follow violence and wrong, and that however painful the exercise of the power of life and death may be to the Government, it will surely be exercised in defence of all quiet members of the community against those who set the law at defiance.[33]

The only general unpleasantness which was reminiscent of the eastern colonies occurred in the regime of a man who had been comptroller-general of convicts in Tasmania. Dr John Stephen Hampton arrived in the colony as governor in 1862. He appointed his son as acting comptroller-general of convicts, and the two were the subject of considerable public criticism in 1867.[34] The secretary of the powerful Howard Association in London, William Tallack, wrote the to *Star* newspaper enclosing documents, in the form of two letters, one from a Fremantle warder and one from the old 'convict screw' (to which reference has been made), and a petition from some convicts. The warder, who wished understandably to remain anonymous, enclosed this petition, claiming it had been sent to the Legislative Council but that nothing had become of it. He went on to say that the allegations made by the convicts in it were an understatement and that 'the Governor [was] trying to drive those unfortunate men to desperation.'

The prisoners' petition catalogued the alleged cruelties of the governor and his son. They claimed *inter alia* that the number of lashes given for punishment was double that which the law allowed, and that the instrument used to inflict them was illegal; that men were kept in separate confinement for more than nine months and in irons; and that the governor 'takes the trouble to superintend the execution of his arbitrary measures himself'. These and other 'measures', the convicts believed, were a result of his wish

to purposely increase crime towards the close of transportation, so that he could parade it in his returns next year, with a view to impress the home authorities with the necessity of keeping a large protective force in the colony, as the stepping stone to a large subsidy.

Hampton wrote a long letter to the Duke of Buckingham and Chandos denying the allegations. He began with the classic response of the prison administrator to such charges, which is to remind the adjudicator that prisoners have no credibility. 'The sources', he wrote, 'ought to have excited grave doubts regarding the authenticity of the alleged facts.' He then went on to deal with the charges in detail. He denied that flogging was carried out illegally or excessively, noting that he disapproved of it personally, and further, that he had abolished it in Tasmania. He described how some absconders were caught, tried by a resident magistrate, given two years' hard labour in irons, and ordered to be kept in dark cells and put on bread and water until the medical officer ordered their release on health grounds. They were released 'the following month'. This punishment, Hampton noted, was 'neither excessive nor illegal'. In fact even by Victorian standards this award was extreme and in reality illegal. There was no legal provision for ordering an indeterminate sentence of bread and water.

He was correct though, when he said that he did not know of the existence of the petition. It is apparent from the correspondence that the person who received it did not consider any action was necessary, since it was 'only what might be expected from men in confinement', and 'nothing would satisfy these men but to be at liberty to war against their fellow creatures'. Finally Hampton enclosed a number of letters and statements supporting the portrait he had drawn of himself and of his administration. One of the more interesting is a summary of the number of prisoners flogged in the years 1851-67. It is clear from this table that two years after Hampton took over, the number of floggings increased.

Predictably the Duke of Buckingham and Chandos was convinced by his colonial governor's explanations since he concluded his despatch:

> I have much satisfaction in observing the complete replies thus furnished by you to the reflections which were attempted to be thrown on your own personal share, as Governor of the colony, in controlling the administration of the convict system in Western Australia.

This episode demonstrates the characteristics of major difficulties, generic in prison administration, and which will be a constant theme in this account. There is first of all the vulnerability of

Table 2.1

The number of prisoners flogged in 1851-67

Year	No. flogged	No. of lashes	Average no. of convicts
1860	15	880	565
1861	7	408	879
1862	4	236	983
1863	1	100	1347
1864	32	2194	1526
1865	40	2824	1440
1866	17	1105	1713
1867	2	100	1816 (to Sept. 30)

prisoners. They are vulnerable because they are out of sight and may be physically ill-treated with relative impunity. They are vulnerable too because as soon as a sentence is passed, their credibility disappears, since dishonesty, the community believes, now infects everything they do or say. Finally they are vulnerable because the public attitude tends to be that even if they are being ill-treated, they probably deserve it. For these reasons the chances of complaints by prisoners being taken seriously, not to say being acted upon, are very slight.

This is further complicated by the difficulty, even for an enthusiastic and honest investigator, of discovering what the truth is in the prison. He is likely to find access to information blocked, and when it comes to interpersonal relationships, he soon discovers that the social system of a prison is so complex that he makes very little headway. For this reason the most effective agents of change in prison administration have been well-informed, powerful outsiders who simply refuse to accept official apologia.

Therefore to try to evaluate the rival claims for accurate reporting of events in Fremantle in 1867 is almost impossible. Neither Tallack nor the Duke could hope to do so, especially since the highest authority in the colony was the subject of the complaint. All we can do is to observe that whatever may have motivated the prisoners, and more significantly staff, to complain, the allegations are certainly consonant with Hampton's career and character. In the next year, 1868, he was relieved of his post, but not before the imperial government had expressed dissatisfaction with the appointment of his son and replaced him.[35]

During the whole period of transportation the eastern colonies maintained a constant attack upon it. There were two main reasons for their opposition: they were trying to rid themselves of the image which seventy years of transportation had given them, and they were convinced that large numbers of ex-convicts from Western Australia were migrating to the east. Whenever a committee was set up to take evidence on the subject, witnesses came forward from the eastern states to state their opposition. One such witness in 1861 hinted at 'vices too horrible to specify' which were being introduced to his homeland by western convicts.[36] Less emotional observers, including Henderson himself, conceded that there was probably a certain amount of movement as was commonly alleged. To the same committee of 1861 Henderson expressed the belief that 150 ex-convicts had moved to the eastern colonies.[37]

A very significant contribution to the mood of the time was made by Melbourne journalist H. Willoughby. His assessment of the situation is worth pausing over, because it has coloured historical accounts of the convict era in the west. Willoughby's version of the situation was calculated to exploit the confusion of the public, especially in England, about convict administration. And judging from the use that has been made of his account by historians in Australia, he seems to have been quite effective. While some people in England were easily distressed by allegations such as those about Hampton, others were just as easily angered by the news that prisoners were, in a word which is now part of penal lore, being 'mollycoddled'. It was this resentment which Willoughby encouraged in the picture which he drew of some kind of a tropical paradise:

> No-one can say that the convicts work hard, and as far as my experience goes, I have found them remarkably comfortable both as regards shelter and diet. They are always as hospitable as they can be to a visitor. I put up several nights with road parties, and partook of meals with them which any man might heartily enjoy. The meal over, the men would produce their tame cockatoos or opossums, would enjoy a smoke or a stroll, would read books from the prison library, or spin yarns by the blazing fire. After an evening spent thus, we would turn into comfortable beds and be up early

next morning for a wash in the creek. If they do not return thanks
for having their lives cast in pleasant places, the men are a most
ungrateful set.[38]

Even a cursory glance at the punishment sheets for the period
shows that if in fact there were convicts who had nothing to
complain of, they were likely to be the exception. Nevertheless it
is Willoughby's account which influences historians such as Battye,
who, for one, wrote that 'a convict's life was comfortable enough.'
Willoughby also began a tradition, once again intended as propa-
ganda, that the British had broken their promise to send only very
'good' convicts. The reality of this assumption has been examined
by A. Hasluck with the conclusion that the existence of a firm
agreement is very questionable.[39]

It is certainly true that from time to time the 'standards' of
convicts sent out were low. One of the reasons for this was that
Western Australia wanted more public works. To this end men
were sent who were not likely to be given tickets of leave for some
time. It followed that these were either convicts whom the authorities had not 'trained' properly, or were people who were badly
behaved. The imperial authorities were often quite frank about
this. Henderson admitted in 1856: 'Latterly we have received a
very different class of prisoner—the rule is merely to send out the
men that they do not hang.'[40] This last aphorism was seized upon
by opponents, and is another cornerstone of historical assumption.

In spite of Henderson's strictures the British Government continued to send out some unsatisfactory convicts. The *Nile* arrived
on January 1, 1858 with 268 especially difficult prisoners, and
these were singled out for special mention by several contemporary
observers.[41] Although there was concern about some categories of
offender, there is rarely a correlation between length of sentence
and behaviour, a point which then, as now, is commonplace of
practical penal experience. Henderson was one who reflected this
experience when he reported that far from it being true that long-
sentence men were more difficult, quite the reverse was the case.[42]

The Irish convicts were the target of many complaints. Two ships
which arrived in 1853, the *Robert Small* and the *Phoebe Dunbar*,
brought a total of 588 Irish convicts 'many of them enfeebled by
disease and incapable of self control'.[43] As well as sheer dislike of
the Irish, which was already hardening into a general English

attitude as a consequence of Irish political activity, there was a certain amount of distaste of these men because they were Roman Catholics. In Victorian society, where religious affiliation was very important, the settlers preferred having protestant convicts to work for them. A categorical instruction of June 1854 announced that: 'Protestant prisoners only will be selected, except under special cases for reference to the Superintendent, in the selection of prisoners for outstations.'[44]

But once again Henderson, with his experience, tried to correct the stereotype which history portrays of the Irish convict in Western Australia:

> I should wish to put it on record that a good many that were sent from Ireland were about the best convicts that we had. There was a large portion of those that came that were in a very deteriorated condition when they arrived, but they improved very much upon the diet that they got, and the change of air: and I was assured by many people that they were about the best men they had.[45]

His opinion was supported by several settlers, one of whom for example, while admitting that he was Irish himself, believed that Irish convicts were better workmen.[46]

Perhaps Henderson would have been less charitable to Irishmen if he had been asked for his opinion after 1876, since by then on two occasions Irish prisoners achieved what had been believed impossible: escape by sea from Western Australia. The consequence was, as always happens after a sensational escape, that the prison oficials were held up to ridicule. The view of some commentators that Britain and Australia ought to have been pleased to lose such troublesome prisoners was of little consolation in that situation.

The men concerned were all involved in the Fenian movement in Ireland, which had determined on an armed insurrection. It has been suggested by O'Luing that the British Army was heavily infested by active Fenians.[47] The whole plan, however, ended in fiasco, and in the trials of many of the members of the organization in 1866. They were generally sentenced to death, but this was later commuted to life imprisonment. In 1867 sixty-three of them were collected together and embarked on the *Hougoumont*, which was to be the last ship to transport prisoners to Western Australia.

It was believed that Irish activists might attack the ship, and so she was escorted by a man-of-war until she was well clear of

England. Meanwhile in Fremantle the crown solicitor, who had advanced an opinion that an armed attack on the town by ship to release the prisoners was probable, and likely to be successful, was reprimanded by Hampton for interfering in matters which were not his concern.[48] The official was not being as absurd as the governor suggested. One of the plans for rescue which was discussed, but ultimately rejected by those who were organizing the escape, was simply to attack Fremantle by force.[49]

The first prisoner to escape was John Boyle O'Reilly.[50] A man in his early twenties, he arrived in Fremantle with his fellow conspirators in Janury 1868. After working on the road at Bunbury he became a 'constable', which meant that he had a certain amount of independence and authority, as well as the privilege of being allowed to wear his hair long and to sport whiskers.[51] No prison can operate without giving a certain amount of power to inmates. Not only does this enable the prison to function, since it is not possible to employ enough staff to work it, but it happily combines utility with reward for good behaviour. It is a universal feature of prisons, is often justified as a reformatory measure, and is usually abused. Not that a prisoner would regard his actions as abuse, since he is not likely to admit the legitimacy of prison laws which underpin the notion of trust. O'Reilly therefore took advantage of his position to engineer his escape, with the help of priests, notably a Father McCabe of Bunbury. It was arranged that a whaler would pick him up. The ship, the *Vigilant* of New Bedford, failed to do so, but another, the *Gazelle*, took him away in February 1869. He arrived safely in America and became an eminent journalist and a folk hero to his countrymen.

The second escape was altogether more devastating for the authorities.[52] The background to this was that although the Fenians regarded themselves as political prisoners, the English legal system did not categorize them as such. Those who had been in the British Army when they were convicted were classed as criminals. Fifteen of the sixty-five Fenian prisoners were so classed. This insistence on defining revolutionary action as political rather than criminal is still an issue in the treatment of Irish prisoners in England today. In Victorian England it was more than just a matter of principle, because political prisoners had considerable material advantages over their criminal counterparts. This affected the ex-soldiers especially seriously when, after a few years, the political prisoners were pardoned, and the 'criminals' were left in Australia to finish their sentences.

A committee was set up in America to organize the rescue of six men: Darragh, Hassett, Harrington, Cranston, Wilson (alias Mc-Nally) and Hogan. The plan, suggested by O'Reilly now safely ensconced in America, was developed by an American called Hathaway, who had been third mate on the *Gazelle*, and an Irishman called Devoy. The plan was to buy a whaler and sail it to Western Australia. In the meantime in Fremantle the escape was being organized by John T. Breslin (alias James Collins), who arrived in the town and established himself as a businessman. So acceptable was he in the community despite the fact that there was a price on his head in England, that he was shown around the prison by the superintendent, noting afterwards gloomily that it was 'very secure and well guarded'. After a great deal of preparation and a lot of anxiety, such as the delay in the arrival of the rescue ship, the *Catalpa*, in 1876 the six men were taken on board from Rockingham beach. The steamer *Georgette*, suspecting that the prisoners were on board, threatened to fire on her, but was deterred from doing so by the captain of the whaler reminding them that she was an American ship. These men too arrived in America, but not before they had displayed breathtaking ingratitude for the effort made on their behalf, through refusing to co-operate with their rescuers and insisting on landing when and where they wished.

These events provide the material for an interesting case study of escapes. To be successful, there have to be a number of in-gredients. There must, first of all, be reliable outside assistance from people who have resources, intelligence, stability and experi-ence. It was the experience of O'Reilly, and others who had been in prison in Western Australia, which enabled the complex plan to be laid in the first place. Next, the intending escapees must gain positions of trust. Generally a position of trust and a wish to escape are mutually exclusive, since by the time a prisoner is in a position of trust, he is reaching the end of his sentence. If he is not, and wants to escape, he must encourage staff to believe that he can be relied upon. The final ingredient is related to this last. There is always a tendency for prison staff to relax their vigilance. It is after all extremely difficult to remain in a state of tension when all seems remarkably quiet. The monotony of guarding in any prison is calculated to lull, and this is an important ally of the intending escaper. This false sense of security was compounded in Western Australia by the apparent absurdity of any attempt to escape. This has been an important assumption from the beginning of imprisonment in the colony, and nobody was likely to doubt Henderson's accuracy when he said: 'Western Australia is, I may say, a vast natural gaol.'[53] The lesson to be drawn from administrators of prisons, from events in 1876, in a remote part of the world is clear: given the circumstances outlined above, nobody can be sure that escape is impossible.

These escapes, while they are of some consequence to writers of Irish political folklore, were mere episodes in story of transportation. Western Australians were much more concerned with broader issues, such as the opposition from the east to continuance of transportation. Naturally, from time to time Western Australians seemed worried about the character of some of the convicts sent. But although it was suggested that there was 'a strong party' against it initially,[54] it was very muted because of the reality of the situation. Western Australia had no choice; the settlers recognized that, and on the whole they were happy about the arrangement. Their opinions were frequently expressed to the many committees, and commissions of enquiry into the business of transportation in the second half of the nineteenth century. A settler called Burgess expressed an opinion in 1861, which was representative of what many co-settlers said at various times: he believed that convict labour was superior to free workmen because the latter, being in such short supply, could dictate terms to employers; they became, in his word, 'unmanageable'. Burgess also opined that bushranging, of the kind which became the scourge of some eastern states, was unknown and that crime had not increased as much as might have been expected.

At the very time that Burgess was giving his evidence, the one convict who was to pass into Western Australian folklore was establishing his reputation. This was Joseph Bolitho Johns, who arrived in the colony when he was twenty-three years of age. Ultimately he was released on ticket of leave, but was sent to gaol again in 1861 for three years for prison breaking. In 1865 he was given ten years' penal servitude for killing an ox, but this was afterwards reduced to six years. During the next few years he managed to escape from Fremantle prison on several occasions, and continued his escaping career for the rest of his life. As late as 1900 he was given one month's imprisonment for absconding from the Mt Eliza depot. He was at that time seventy-seven years of age. This was the man who has come to be known as 'Moondyne Joe', an interesting character, but hardly to be put in the category of bushranger.[55]

Burgess went on to say that the little crime that was committed was the work of a few convicts from ships such as the *Nile*. His summary of the whole exercise was echoed by fellow Western Australians on many occasions: 'We found the greatest relief and the greatest advantage to the carrying on of our operation from the introduction of convict labour.'[56] It appeared that this feeling was reciprocated by some of the convicts at least. In the petition which complained of Hampton's behaviour, they were careful to note that they 'attach no blame to the settlers of the colony from whom they always received great kindness and encouragement'.[57]

An eminent and well-informed authority, John Septimus Roe, felt equally strongly that the business had been successful. 'Is it your opinion', he was asked, 'that since the introduction of convicts, the colony has greatly advanced?'

'It has increased in population, and it has progressed in prosperity.'

'There is no dispute about that?'

'No.'

Roe did, however, complain about some convicts, especially a 'parcel of lunatics', that Jebb, the English chairman, had sent out. These necessitated the building of an asylum.[58] Jebb, incidentally, defended himself by saying that the imperial authorities had tried to send out the best men they could, but they 'had received a good deal of abuse upon that subject'.[59]

At times the settlers became very angry. On one occasion, for example, a protest meeting was held because the authorities had bought flour from South Australia. If this sort of thing was to continue, they were of the opinion there was no point in having a convict establishment, and stated: '[When] we petitioned for convicts to be sent to this colony we did so with the full impression that they were to enjoy the undisputed right of supplying the commissariat with flour, produce of this colony.'[60]

The settlers really became angry though when the discontinuance of transportation was announced. The decision was the cause of much bitterness because Western Australia believed, correctly, that pressure from the east had been the crippling factor. By the mid-1860s the appeals of easterners for an ending of transportation began to contain threats. A dispatch from Victoria to the other eastern states in 1864 observed:

> It had become painfully apparent to the Government of Victoria that something more than mere remonstrance is needed—such as will show Her Majesty's advisers that the inhabitants of these colonies are determined to use every means in their power to free themselves from the injury inflicted upon them.[61]

And they proposed sanctions:

> legislative action, prohibitive of all intercourse with Western Australia by which means the stigma of being the only convict colony in Australia would be visibly fastened upon her—it will of course be essential that the mail steamer should no longer be allowed to call at any port within the limits of that colony.

With pressure of this kind, coupled with continuing antipathy in England, both from those who thought transportation too harsh and those who were alarmed at an increase in violent crime and saw a solution in heavier punishment in English prisons, the ending of transportation was inevitable. In eastern Australia the reaction was predictable, while in England there was a realization that any perpetuation of transportation was undesirable. Henderson expressed the view that it was a pity, but that it was causing such bad feeling with the rest of Australia that it had to be stopped. Western Australians, also predictably, were extremely angry and began a campaign for redress.

In the first letter, which they wrote in 1864 to the imperial government, they claimed that at the outset it had been understood that 'The numbers annually transported would be considerable, that free emigrants to an equal amount be conveyed to the colony, and above all, that the measure would not be of a temporary character, but that the influx of both classes would be uninterrupted and continuous.'[62] These 'reasonable expectations', they went on, 'have been disappointed in every respect.' The decision, 'in compliance with the demands of the inhabitants of Victoria', to cease transportation had created alarm, and the news that 'the supply of forced labour must soon come to an end', was a disaster. Western Australia 'now labours under the irremediable stigma of having been a penal settlement', with 'not a tithe of the promised public building completed.' Because the convicts had been sent very quickly into the labour market, the only buildings which had been erected had been for penal purposes. They were furious about the easterners' attitude, pointing out that the latter had ensured that they were well established before beginning a protest about transportation. The redress which the settlers wanted was a liberal supply of free labour and assisted passages for small capitalists.

The reply from the minister, Cardwell, written by his private secretary, was contemptuous. It pointed out that Britain sent out as many convicts as the colony had been able to handle. Their petition predicting gloom did not square with the facts set out in a table (Table 2.2) which was enclosed.

It was also pointed out that the settlers had used the word 'temporary', but that fourteen years of transportation was hardly temporary, nor had it yet entirely ceased. Summarizing, Cardwell, through his secretary, indulged in an unequivocal sneer:

> The gentlemen who have addressed Mr. Cardwell remark that not all the power of England could restore Western Australia to her former condition. But on looking to the records of that condition, Mr. Cardwell thinks that the impossibility of restoring it can hardly be a subject of regret.

The settlers did not give in. They replied that they disagreed with his assessment. Without substantial numbers of free settlers the prospect in the colony would be 'fearful beyond description'. The eastern colonies were frightened in case a few Western Australian convicts went there, but how, they asked, should western settlers feel with such a large convict population? They conceded that they had 'undeniably derived' benefits, but they had been drawing attention in their letter to the 'moral disadvantage'.

An especially awkward complication which had arisen was that under the 'Regulations for the disposal of the waste Crown lands in the northern districts of Western Australia' no ex-convict would be allowed to go there. This meant that a free settler who wished to go there could not take his ex-convict workers with him. The alleged reason for this was set out by T. W. C. Murdoch of the

Emigration Board in November 1864.[63] The hope was that free settlers would go to these new districts, but none from the eastern colonies or Britain would do so if convicts were allowed to go. Murdoch pointed out that convicts had adversely affected the movement of free men to Western Australia, and that the only way in which the imperial government had been able to make up the promised numbers of such free men was through the recruitment of enrolled pensioners.

Table 2.2

Cardwell's comparative table

	Population			Colonial revenue [ ]	Grants from parliament, irrespective of money spent on sending out free emigrants [ ]	Imports [ ]	Exports [ ]	Acres in cultivation
	Free	Prisoners and ticket of leave	Total					
1849	4654	Nil	4654	9596	7379	28534	26156	6904
1854	8943	2800	11743	33593	79148	128260	34109	11979
1863	16173	2607	18780	56246	72553	157136	137426	33406

Grants from parliament for expenditure in Western Australia from the year 1851 to 1864, both inclusive.

For convict services and colonial magistrates, and police and gaols	910710
Grants in aid to colony	38801
Total	949511

This however was hardly true, since it was the depressed state of the colony which discouraged migration to it, and this had nothing to do with convicts. It is also arguable that the enrolled pensioner force was primarily a means of saving money on regular troops, and only incidentally an effort to increase population. Nonetheless, nothing could or would alter the imperial government. The *Hougoumont* was the last ship, although convicts and ex-convicts were common in the state for the rest of the century. The last six convicts in Western Australia were pardoned in 1906.[64] It was not until 1910 that the last ex-convict in the Albany district, Nipper Peaks, died.[65]

In eighteen years thirty-seven ships, carrying 9500 men, had been sent to Western Australia.[66] Naturally, there were many different kinds of people amongst them. The supplies had been irregular, even unplanned. There had been, as we have seen, claims and counter-claims about the quality of men sent. In one important respect the imperial government had acceded to the colonists' requests. Although it had been suggested that female convicts should be sent, because of local opposition this was never done.[67] From the point of view of the development of Western Australia, had the experience of transportation been an asset or a liability?

The evidence of the colonists themselves must lead to a bold conclusion that, if it had not been employed, the abandonment of the settlement was a possibility, and much delayed growth a certainty. The convict settlement brought in a considerable amount of imperial money, none of which had to be repaid. The convicts created wealth and markets for the produce of that wealth. When they were angry, the settlers complained that not much public work had been carried out, a claim which it is somewhat difficult to reconcile with the annual reports which were issued by the Convict Department. One for example, that of 1866, records the completion of Fremantle Lunatic Asylum, the building of a light boat and buoy for Albany and the building of York Street in that town, work on police headquarters and the post office in Bunbury, the building of Fremantle Bridge, the metalling of streets in Fremantle and quarrying at Point Resolution.[68] Nor was that all which was listed in the report.

Further, convicts and ex-convicts were employed in a variety of jobs ranging from mining to policing. They settled in large numbers, and some became 'men of large property', a fact which was attested by many contemporary witnesses. They dominated the population in Northam and in Toodyay, where in 1864 there were

570 expirees and conditional-pardon men, and 316 free men. There ex-convicts owned freehold land worth £4000, 795 hectares of crops worth £5500, and other personal property worth £9000.[69] This was 'a formidable proportion of the material wealth of the district'.[70] Anthony Trollope on his visit to Western Australia commented on their contribution as modest but essential, which they rendered as workers, labourers, shopkeepers and even 'convict editors of newspapers'.[71]

As to their behaviour, the evident success which is recorded is indicative of a reasonable standard, although there were exceptions, especially in respect of certain groups such as those from the *Nile*. Governor Kennedy, who had allegedly stated that a lot of crime was committed by ticket-of-leave men, was according to some misunderstood.[72] It is, of course, difficult to be sure of the nature of historical relationships, but there is a fair amount of evidence to support the view that relationships between settlers and convicts were workable at least, and good at best. One Albany newspaper said of convict behaviour that there were 'instances from which our free settlers might take an example'.[73] Henderson was able to report an extraordinary example of sympathy for the ex-convicts in the following exchange:

> And they are under no apprehension of being taunted with their former habits?
> Not at all: they have been received by the colonists just the same as if they were free emigrants.
> They are never taunted with their former position as having been convicts?
> No: I scarcely remember an instance. There was one case of a ticket-of-leave man who assaulted an individual that taunted him in that way; and he was told by the magistrate that he was quite right in having done so; the magistrate told the man that taunted him that he would not listen to his complaint. That was an exceptional case. As a general rule, they have been received by the colonists in the most gratifying way, and they have had every chance afforded to them.[74]

A very warm backward glance at the convict era came during the debates of 1903 on a prisons bill of that year, which will be discussed. C. A. Piesse, in the Legislative Council, recounted his experience of the convict era:

Among them were some really good men. Looking back on it, that period seems like yesterday to me. In my mind's eye I can see those prison parties stationed throughout the country, consisting of decently dressed men, working hard, living in some instances in huts made of blackboys set on end; and when they could not get enough blackboys to make walls in that fashion they used to cut them up in small sections. I vividly remember those camps, and I know that the occupants were well conducted, and did good work for the country. Some of them are still living; and it is pleasing to glance back at those days and to bear tribute to their industry. As an instance, they made a road practically from Albany to Perth; and I am safe in saying that hundreds of miles of that road will stand as a lasting memorial, not only to the physical strength of the labourers, but to the good system on which they worked.[75]

There were, of course, occasions when colonists protested. An example occurred in Albany, when allegedly 107 settlers petitioned to have the convicts removed.[76]

Finally it should be recorded that there were, in association with them and their settlement, the enrolled pensioner force. These were ex-regular soldiers recruited in England and shipped to Australia with their families. They stayed with the prisoners until the next ship arrived, and acted as a military force in the colony. Later they were given land. During the period of transportation 1191 pensioners were enlisted, and they moved to Western Australia with 803 women, 735 boys and 734 girls—a total of 3463 people, which represented a considerable addition to the colonial population.[77]

In spite of all these advantages West Australians, in contemplating the transportation era, seemed to have been depressed about the 'taint' left by the convicts. Battye summed up the feeling when he wrote:

Whatever material advantages accrued from the convicts, they were not, and could not be, sufficient to justify their introduction—they [the settlers] yielded up their principle on the altar of expediency, and all that one can say is that the fact that they were compelled to do so is greatly to be deplored.[78]

Battye's assessment is strongly influenced by Victorian ideas about the nature of crime and the personality of the criminal. The central assumption of the Victorians, validated for them by religious dogma, was that people were either good or bad, and that anyone could be placed in one or other of the categories through an evaluation of their behaviour in respect to the law. There was a lingering hope that the bad could be made good through the infliction of punishment interspersed with periodic doses of religious exhortation. But this was hard and largely unsuccessful work. The disappointment, which was a frequent consequence of the attempt in late Victorian times, met with a new consolation. This was that bad character was inherited. In a world agog with scientific revelation, which seemed indubitable, such a notion was highly acceptable. Especially was this so when a school of 'criminal anthropology' emerged, headed by men such as Lombroso, the Italian criminologist, who tried to set out his case 'scientifically' and began a search for physical and hereditary causes of crime, which has never ceased.

The inevitability of physical transmission of crime, whether through 'sin' or physical make-up, is part of the Victorian ideology. The author of the biography of John Boyle O'Reilly (already discussed) was sorry for his hero because of the convicts with whom he had to live: 'They were the poison flower of civilization's corruption—the overflow of society's cesspool, the irreclaimable victims of sin.' He pondered upon the fate of the 'young generous clean-minded rebel, who had been doomed to herd with this prison scum'.[79] There were not surprisingly Victorian observers who would not have drawn such a clear distinction between this 'scum' and a man who was plotting what they believed to be murder.

Such a simplistic version of crime and its causes, and of concepts of good and bad, have now largely been abandoned. There is today some realization that 'crime' is often no more than an administrative category, and that much socially damaging behaviour is not crime, because those who engage in it do not choose to classify it as such, and they are able to intervene at judicious points to ensure it is not so defined. Not that this awareness has led to clarification of penal policy: quite the reverse. It has inevitably led to confusion and uncertainty, and for the penal practitioner there must sometimes be regret that his job is attended by complications which would have baffled and bored his predecessors. What is now appreciated amongst penal administrators and theorists is that it is the prison experience rather than any criminal taint which distinguishes the ex-prisoner. Trollope showed great insight when he commented, on observing prisoners in Western Australia, that 'the Bill Sykes look of which I have spoken is produced rather by the gaol than by crime.'[80]

The fact is that many of the men who came to Western Australia as convicts had a unique chance to escape the criminal label which had been ascribed to them in Britain. They were often given the opportunity to develop a new image and so begin a new life. The magistrate who refused to punish the ex-convict who had been taunted was willing to concede this, and some settlers certainly had sympathy with the convicts. 'I think', one observed of the wish to start afresh, that 'any man can tell what sort of feeling that is.'[81]

So, although one typical Victorian writer could console her readers with a comment that the deteriorated 'rogues' who were late arrivals in the colony 'rarely married', and that their 'rapid diminution by death promised that this element among the convicts would not leave a large mark on the future population',[82] and although Battye could believe that 'to the absence of the corrupting effect of dissolute women is probably due the fact that so little moral taint remains upon the Western Australia of today',[83] neither need have worried. Western Australians may be entitled to feel a sense of failure because they had to abandon the main principle upon which their colony was founded. But in terms of 'taint' which was so important to the successful Victorian, they may now reflect that as far as most people who arrived in the first fifty years are concerned—whether or not they were 'free' immigrants, convicts or enrolled pensioners—this was in fact almost a matter of chance. Certainly any attempt to correlate worth as a member of society with the outcome of that chance would be very questionable.

3

The Royal Commission into the Penal System
1898-1899

Inquiries into prison system—The 'role of the intruder'—F. C. B. Vosper—The nature of the complaints—The parliamentary discussion—The commissioners—The evidence—The conclusions

On some occasions the reasons why an inquiry is mounted into a prison system are clear. Suddenly the organization finds itself in the midst of a major crisis, and public attention is rivetted upon it. The riot in Attica prison in New York State in 1971, when forty-three people were killed, is an example.[1] So was the crisis leading to the English Mountbatten Report, the central concern of which was the escape of spy George Blake from Wormwood Scrubs in 1965, to which he had been consigned in 1961 to serve a sentence of forty-two years—the longest fixed sentence ever awarded in an English court.[2] Penal history is punctuated by such dramas, which although they may take the organization and community by surprise, are generally the visible expression of deep-rooted organizational stress and conflict.

Some penal investigations are more difficult to analyse. The causes are not so dramatic, and even contemporary observers are uncertain about the dynamics of the situation. Yet these investigations may be very far reaching in their results. There were two in the 1890s in this category. One took place in England and has come to be known as the Gladstone Report. As far as can be judged, there were three factors which contributed to the establishment of the Gladstone Committee. The first was the conduct of the Reverend W. D. Morrison, an assistant chaplain at Wandsworth Prison in London. He wrote several critical articles about prisons and was the author or instigator of the second factor: a serious press attack upon the system, notably in the columns of the *Daily Chronicle*. The third factor was a persistent questioning of the home secretary by A. C. Morton, a member of parliament, about overcrowding in London's prisons. How much influence each of these factors exerted is impossible to know, but it is certain that this report introduced major changes into the English prison system, and into other prison systems which took England as a pattern, and in the early twentieth century turned to it as an exemplar of reform.[3]

In 1898, three years after Gladstone, there was a Royal Commission into the Western Australian prison system, during which there was much discussion of the Gladstone Report and much reference to the personalities associated with it. It is possible that the Gladstone Report itself helped provoke the questioning which led to its Western Australian counterpart.

But as in England, the press played a part, though whether as initiator of or contributor to general uneasiness about the prisons, especially Fremantle, it is difficult to know. In 1892 the *Western Mail* expressed concern about the treatment of debtors,[4] while in the next year the *Inquirer and Commercial News* in a leading article commented:

> The present 'system', if it can be dignified by such a name, is purely punitive and nothing more and must be fraught with evil effect to many. This is unworthy of a progressive and enlightened community and it is to be trusted that reform is near at hand.[5]

Newspapers during the period before the Royal Commission reported prison punishments often with a critical comment. In 1897, for example, the *Inquirer and Commercial News* reported an award of thirty-six lashes and a month's confinement in irons for escaping. The newspaper went on to note that people in the vicinity of the prison when the flogging was being carried out: 'describe the screams which emanated from inside the prison walls as the most fearful and unearthly they ever heard during their lives'.[6] Such press reporting, as in England, was calculated to add to the demands for an investigation.

A further parallel with English agitation lies in parliamentary criticism, although in Western Australia this was less persistent and less voluminous than it had been in England. Nevertheless it demonstrates that in several sections of the community there were degrees of dissatisfaction with the prison system.[7]

A royal commission in Western Australia does not have the status of an English royal commission, in the sense that in Western Australia in the past comparatively minor matters were sometimes judged worthy of a royal commission, whereas in England a departmental inquiry, or some other investigation short of a royal commission might be considered adequate. The Western Australian Royal Commission was probably less effective, certainly in the period immediately after its publication, than its English counterpart, but in many respects it is an important restatement of much that should be basic in a system which displays reformative pretensions. Both the Gladstone Report and the Western Australian Royal Commission arose out of a diffuse concern about prisons rather than a sudden fear, and associated with both are examples of a phenomenon in penal history, which may be called 'the role of the intruder'.

By 'the intruder' is meant a person or persons who, having certain qualifications, by dint of judicious pressure at key points focusses attention on the defects of the prison system and mobilizes enough concern to cause enquiries to be made. Such a process can be gradual but firm, as in the case of the Salvation Army staff who worked for the closing of the French penal colonies in South America. Salvationists lived and worked there during the early part of this century and were largely instrumental in bringing to a close one of the ugliest episodes in world penal history.[8]

Sometimes, as in the case of the Western Australian Royal Commission, and possibly in the case of the Gladstone Committee, an individual persists in his demands for an inquiry, marshalling evidence which sufficiently impresses influential people to gain their support. It is generally not a popular role, and accusations of sensationalism, dishonesty and inaccuracy are rampant. This is where the penal intruder shows that he is no mere penal reformer speculating from the depths of an armchair. His main qualification is close contact with the prison system. Salvationists observed the French penal colonies at first hand for many years. The man who contributed in no small way to the bringing about of the Gladstone investigation was W. D. Morrison, an ex-prison chaplain, whose criticisms were supported by a number of Irish political prisoners who had been in prison for many years. F. C. B. Vosper, who was elected member of the Legislative Assembly for north-east Coolgardie in 1897, had spent only three months in prison in Queensland, but the impact upon him had been considerable. It was he who in Western Australia filled the role of the intruder, and it was his agitation which was to be instrumental in bringing about the Royal Commission.

Frederick Charles Burleigh Vosper was born in St Dominic,

Cornwall, England, on 23 March 1867.[9] He emigrated to Queensland in 1883, where he worked as a newspaper reporter and eventually founded a labour weekly called *The Republican.* While in Queensland he was tried for sedition and imprisoned for fomenting a riot. His prison experience though short, was intense. He was especially upset at the humiliating experience of having his head shaved, and as a result he never cut his hair again. After working as a journalist in Sydney and Melbourne he moved to Western Australia in 1892, and amongst other things was the editor of the *Coolgardie Miner.* He was a central figure in goldfield dissatisfaction with the Perth administration, throwing himself wholeheartedly into miners' affairs. One of his more curious activities was the establishment of an anti-Asiatic league in the goldfields, which mobilized growing resentment over the presence of Afghans.

Such was the background of the young man who brought about the first royal commission into prisons in Western Australia. It is evident from the *Parliamentary Debates* that during the 1890s he had read a lot about prison administration and was acquainted with the main trends, especially with the movement away from repression into more reformative activity, which was characteristic of penal thinking at the end of the nineteenth century.

During the 1890s, as we have seen, there had been occasional expressions of dissatisfaction about prison administration in Western Australia. It seems likely that the appointment of Superintendent George to the key post of Fremantle in 1897 had something to do with this dissatisfaction. In his first Annual Report it is clear that he intended introducing a more repressive regime.[10] He recommended, for example, that all employment outside the prison should cease, ostensibly because there had been passing of contraband. Having brought the prisoners inside the walls he then raised the wall several feet and added armed guards to the remaining outside parties. These moves created an almost impossible situation. Fremantle had been designed merely to house prisoners who worked outside the walls on public works. There simply were no workshops available to employ prisoners within the prison, and, as the Royal Commission discovered, the cells were much too small for men to spend long periods inside them.

Concern about developments, or lack of them, in prisons came to a head in a debate on 6 July 1898, when Vosper proposed the establishment of a royal commission which he hoped would have wide-reaching powers of investigation.[11] He supported his proposal with a long speech in which he set out what seemed to him to be the defects of the system. Most of these defects were dealt with by the Commission and will be discussed later. He began by alleging that prisoners were punished too severely for prison offences. One example he gave was of a prisoner who served twelve months in irons for an attempted escape. In practice this meant that the offender, dressed in black, had to drag a 5.5-kilogram weight of iron which was rivetted onto a leg-iron. Further, amongst other things the sanitation in Fremantle was bad, the food was poor and the system of remission was chaotic. These complaints were in direct contradiction of the claims made by the new superintendent of Fremantle that sanitation and food in the prison were excellent.[12]

As far as the staff were concerned, Vosper claimed that some of the warders had served terms of imprisonment and that the superintendent 'had hardly put his foot outside the prison doors for 35 years'. This piece of hyperbole was designed to illustrate how narrow George's experience was. All of this chaos, Vosper went on, could be put down to the fact that prisons were administered under the Act of 1849 (see Chapter 1), which was grotesque in its obsolescence. He insisted that it was 'not a question of coddling prisoners'—the usual charge made against reformers it may be noted—nor was he launching an attack on staff. This last statement incidentally could hardly be reconciled with what in fact he had said.

In support of his case Vosper drew heavily upon the 'eminent' penal authorities who so impressed the late Victorians. Men such as W. D. Morrison, and German reformer Krohne were quoted, as was evidence to the Gladstone Committee, which Vosper describes wrongly as a 'Royal Commission'. He was eloquent when describing the English system, observing that the English success was due to 'wise and magnificent discipline in the gaols'. This was a view which while it might be acceptable to his somewhat unversed audience, would have been challenged by many English critics, including Morrison himself. He was also guilty of the occasional but important error when he claimed that in England flogging was not inflicted for breaches of prison discipline. In fact prisoners were flogged in England until the 1950s and the punishment was only removed in the Criminal Justice Act of 1967.[13]

He justified the local picture which he presented to the members because of the extensive correspondence he had received from prisoners, and because he had himself had prison experience. The premier, John Forrest, pointed out that that experience was not of Western Australian prisons. 'For that', Vosper retorted in characteristic fashion, 'I am devoutly thankful.' The Legislative Assembly naturally found a lot of this criticism rather difficult to take. As well as accusations of 'coddling', he was accused by G. Y. Hubble, MLA for Gascoyne, a visiting justice to prisons, of inciting trouble amongst prisoners by publishing their letters in the *Sunday Times* and the *Sunday Chronicle*. Some of the examples of excessive punishment meted out to individual prisoners and quoted by Vosper were challenged. Nevertheless Hubble, like other members, concluded by supporting the establishment of the Commission.

The contribution of the premier, John Forrest, was rather odd and somewhat offensive. He alleged that Vosper was being sensational and was deliberately trying to increase newspaper circulation, an allegation which drew a protest from Vosper. Sir John then discussed the period during which he had had oversight of convicts, when, he claimed, prison conditions had been perfect. After admitting that he knew nothing about the present system, he rather unconvincingly concluded that it was probably as good as in his day, for the tenuous reason that 'the present Superintendent was then one of the principal warders.'

Discussing the background of the prison population, he introduced a theme which was developed by the Royal Commission. This was that many, if not the majority of criminals in Western Australia were not native to the state. As an example he pointed out that of 125 prisoners serving sentences of penal servitude on 31 December 1897 only seven were white natives. The premier concluded by proposing that the terms of reference of the Commission should be rather more limited than Vosper suggested. The latter agreed, the motion was carried and the premier, in supporting it, observed that he expected that 'the whole administration of the prisons would come out as clean as the Honourable Members knew it to be.' The enquiry was on; but Vosper was to be very disappointed.

On 28 September 1898 Vosper was on his feet again in parliament, protesting about the composition of the Commission.[14] He complained on two counts: first because there were no members of the Legislative Assembly appointed to it, and secondly because the people invited to join had no experience of, or special interest in penal affairs. 'They had', he observed, 'led lives of mediocre respectability.' Forrest's defence of the selection was based on the fact that members of the Assembly were too busy to serve on the Commission, and that it was hard trying to find anyone that was prepared to do so. Some of Vosper's fellow members also expressed disquiet over membership, and Vosper himself seems to have given up any hope of the thorough-going examination which he had expected. Nevertheless despite this, the Commission began its work.

The composition of the Commission, about which Vosper had complained, was as follows: the chairman was Dr Adam Jameson, a Scottish doctor who had just returned from four years' medical practice in Rome and who was to become a member of the Legislative Council in 1900; the members were Frank Craig, James Gallop, Henry J. Lotz, Edward William Mayhew, Matthew Louis Moss, Horace George Stirling and Harry Page Woodward. They were respectable and solid enough members of the community. Moss for example was a lawyer, the first Mayor of East Fremantle and later Acting Agent-General for Western Australia in London. He was also a member of the Legislative Council and a member of the Legislative Assembly in the course of his political life.[15]

The terms of reference of the Commission were:

> To enquire into the existing condition of the penal system of Western Australia, and to report on the method [sic] now in use for the punishment of criminals, their classification, the remission of sentences, and the sanitary conditions of Fremantle Gaol, as well as to enquire into all contracts for supplies of food and other materials for use in the said gaol.

After eighty sittings, during the course of which they examined 240 witnesses, they produced a three-part report: the first in December 1898, the second in March 1899 and the third and final in June 1899.[16] One of the most honest, and for us one of the most interesting features of the report was the publication of all the evidence which was heard.

The Commission recorded its dissatisfaction with a great deal in the prison system. Stung perhaps by the votes of no-confidence in its ability, and because there was a great deal that *was* wrong, it was very condemnatory, except in the matter of staff behaviour, a matter to which we will return. They took evidence from a wide variety of people, including visiting justices, the sheriff, the police, the superintendent of Fremantle, the chaplain, the medical officer, senior staff, many prisoners and from Vosper himself, who since he gave evidence, had apparently not entirely given up hope.

Two important differences between the Royal Commission, and the Gladstone Committee were, first, that the Commission allowed any prisoner who wished to give evidence to do so. They prefixed their first report with the claim, which seemed to be reasonable, that the Commission wanted 'every latitude for the purpose of enabling them to state their case', adding that 'an unexpectedly large proportion' did so.[17] The Gladstone Committee on the other hand, heard little evidence from people who had undergone imprisonment, and those who did give evidence were ex-prisoners of some stature, such as Michael Davitt, a very distinguished Irish republican. The Royal Commission also heard evidence from warders, which the Gladstone Committee had entirely failed to do. The warders' views provide a rare glimpse into the prison system of the day.

The investigation was wide-ranging. It considered the administration of the prison, the quality of the food, the medical treatment, prison libraries and the unsatisfactory treatment of boy prisoners. More broadly, it considered the absence of an adequate administrative structure, within which staff could function, and chaotic and unjust elements in the broad field of the administration of criminal justice. The members visited Fremantle Gaol, Rottnest Island native prison and Subiaco reformatory.

During the hearing of evidence Western Australia was frequently compared with other states in respect of prison administration. It was constantly claimed by witnesses that they had been better off in prisons in some other Australian states. Thus one prisoner stated that in Pentridge and Darlinghurst prison rules were read aloud to the prisoners.[18] In Fremantle, as we shall see, the very existence of any rules at all was doubtful. Another prisoner related how in Melbourne the deputy governor inspected the meat and how the 'medical inspection of every prisoner [was] most carefully conducted'.[19] Yet another reported how, when he left Pentridge on discharge, he was given 6s.[20] The overall picture which emerged was that prisons in Western Australia in many important respects were inferior to those of some other states.

Another constant theme was one which had been touched upon by the premier in the debate. This was that large numbers of prisoners in Western Australia were not native to the state but came from the eastern states, from Asia, England and other parts of the world.[21] The Royal Commission regarded this matter as being of some importance, since one of the solutions to the problems facing the prison system in Western Australia, they believed, was the return of all 'aliens' to their homes. The relatively low numbers of native-born white Western Australians in the prisons of the state have always been one of the more remarkable features of the prison population. One example which may be quoted is the population of Geraldton prison during the period from October 1903 to December 1927. During those years 952 males were received into the prison, and of that number only 130 were entered as white native-born Western Australians and 79 as Aboriginal Western Australians. Of the twenty-two women received into Geraldton during the same period only three, all Aborigines, had been born in Western Australia.[22]

When the Commission turned its attention to specific complaints, there was concrete evidence of disease and filth in Fremantle and, it may be added, on Rottnest Island, where although the cells were washed out with kerosene, they had not been washed out properly for ten years. One of the Fremantle prisoners reported that he had contracted typhus 'owing to the insanitary condition of the pump yard'. Three or four other prisoners had apparently caught it at the same time.[23] A persistent complaint was that prisoners who had veneral disease shared facilities with each other and with other prisoners.[24] There were many similar serious complaints. One prisoner reported that he had caught crab lice and that he had 'something breaking out on [his] arm now which [was] troublesome'. The witness was examined by Dr Jameson, the chairman, who pronounced that he was suffering from psoriasis.[25] Another prisoner complained that he was suffering from internal fistula, for which he had been operated upon in England. The medical officer in the prison had told him, he complained, that there was no such condition. Once again the chairman examined the man and reported that he was undoubtedly suffering from fistula and that he was not fit for hard work.[26]

The prevalence of disease and illness was hardly a matter for surprise, since prisoners were not given a routine medical examination upon arrival at the prison, and at all times it was incumbent upon them to draw the attention of the doctor to any illness. Not that this was necessarily very effective, since prisoners stated that even if a man was unfit, the doctor would not always excuse him from working. Worse, even if he did, the superintendent might intervene, since he commonly counteracted the doctor's instructions. If this were true, and the evidence seems convincing, then this is a significant indicator of the autocratic way in which the superintendent worked. Normally in prison systems, even at that time, the authority of the medical officer is unquestioned.

Since so many of the complaints were about illness and disease, it was necessary for Dr Hope, the medical officer, to give evidence.[27] 'My duties', he explained, 'are defined rather by tradition than by any specific regulations.' The health of the gaol he described as 'generally good', there having been two deaths in 1898, and the sanitary arrangements were also 'on the whole very good'. As to the question of lack of ventilation in the cells, which was so poor that the Commission proposed to solve it by knocking two cells into one, Dr Hope defended the situation by pointing out that 'many of the prisoners have no liking for fresh air at all.' Asked about punishments, he replied: 'I have never known a case where the dark cells or other forms of punishment administered in the prison had any injurious results upon the prisoners undergoing them.' Lunacy was not 'accelerated by the prison treatment', skin disease had not been communicated by shaving, indecency was unlikely, and in respect to the case of the abuse of a lunatic in the yard, which several witnesses reported to the Commission, he did not believe the prisoners would 'allow such a thing to be done in their presence'.

On the subject of food he expressed the view that the cooking was the source of complaint rather than the ingredients. When prisoners lost weight in prison, he believed the explanation was not that the food was short or unsatisfactory, but because they no longer had access to beer. He did concede the need for some improvement by stating that he now recorded the weights of food regularly and that he separated, on the Commission's suggestion, the 'vencreal' from the syphilitic when bathing, and that their dirty towels were now thrown into a big bucket of carbolic solution. He also agreed that he had ordered the 'battery treatment' (see below), adding that he was not surprised that the prisoners regarded it as a punishment. In spite of, or perhaps because of the presence of medical representation on the Commission, Hope's conduct was not censured, even when from his own evidence it can be seen that his professional performance was devoid of application, to say the least. In its summary the Commission paid scant attention to the incidence of dirt, the presence of disease, the absence of care, and even specific, validated cases of ill-treatment. These were not discussed at all in their summary, and in fact, as we shall see, the doctor was exonerated.

Evidence about food came, as the Commission expected, from 'almost every witness'.[28] One prisoner, who had the unusual distinction of having cooked no fewer than thirty-three Christmas dinners in the prison, described flour which was 'yellowish in colour, rather musty', and how the contractors supplied tobacco to the prisoners 'to induce the men to pass bad potatoes'.[29] Other prisoners gave further examples. The staff in evidence generally disagreed with the prisoners. The acting chief warder stated that: 'The only thing I can say about the food is that it has been good.'[30] Another warder agreed: 'As far as I have seen, I should say the men are on the whole too well fed—prisoners are fed a great deal better than I was when a private and a non-commissioned officer in the Army.'[31]

A universal feature of investigations into complaints from prisoners is that the investigators are always reluctant to entertain grumbling about food. A whole mythology has been developed around the question, the essential feature of which is a certainty, reinforced in recent years by Freudian, and pseudo-Freudian dogma, that expressions of discontent about food are merely symbols or symptoms of some other problem which is generally rooted in a personality defect. The Commission, which in most respects agreed with the witnesses that much was wrong, was in the familiar dilemma of the investigator when it came to food. Although they noted that many long-sentence men had developed dyspepsia 'in various aggravated forms', there was 'at the present time, no ground for complaint'.[32] They did, however, concede that there was a need for a greater variety of food, but stated: 'In our opinion the dietary scale is altogether too generous, both in quantity and quality, for the requirements of any but long sentence prisoners.'[33]

They thereupon set out precisely the amounts of food for each category of prisoner, but such was the emotion generated by the question, that in a report which is in many respects notably humane, they ignored the simple plea of the Asian prisoners for a diet which was consonant with their religious requirements. This was a need which was recognized even by the superintendent and supported by him.[34] The spirit behind their recommendations in this most vital matter illustrates the quandary in which the prison administrator, like the poor-law administrator, finds himself in a society in which there is much poverty.

The quandary arises from the fact that a calculation of how much food a prisoner should have is based on the need to prevent starvation and yet prevent him feeling full. This balance is complicated by the fact that he must have enough food to be able to work. Having made such a calculation and set it out, it then becomes apparent in poor societies that honest men in the community have less to eat. Since prisoners are devoid of virtue, and are in the classic phrase 'undeserving', such a state of affairs cannot be tolerated. So the quantity of food is cut. The same problem faced the English convict service when a board of medical officers in 1863 was called upon to work out 'medically' what the bare minimum of food was, and taking into account complaints such as that of the governor of Leicester Prison about richness of food causing diarrhoea, substantially reduced prison diet. This led to major riots, notably at Portland convict prison. 'Imprisonment', the doctors pointed out, 'should be rendered as deterrent as is consistent with the maintenance of health and strength.'[35] The Royal Commission had evidently read this Report, quoted it and agreed to the concept of a 'penal element' in diet. 'The criminal classes' should not be fed by the taxpayer 'on a higher dietary scale than the honest day labourer can afford to provide for himself and family, but such is at present, undoubtedly the case.'[36]

The Commission examined the fate of boys in prison, and like the Gladstone Committee, recommended special treatment for them. It appeared that there were about a dozen boys, aged from seventeen to twenty-one, in Fremantle. Apart from one hour of schooling a week, the boys spent twenty-one out of twenty-four hours a day in their cells. They were, it appeared, well-behaved, but some faced very long periods of imprisonment: one for example was sentenced to life imprisonment. Several of the adult prisoners expressed concern about the treatment of the boys. One suggested that the only work they had to do was scrubbing the corridors, and that on one occasion a boy who was 'a little off his head' was thrashed by prisoners and that one of the warders approved of this.[37] The recommendations of the Commission in respect of juvenile offenders were elaborate, and were given a boost by the evidence of Commandant Booth of the Salvation Army. The essence of these recommendations was that some reformatory organization ought to be instituted for juveniles, but that in any case boys under the age of sixteen should not be sent to prison, nor should girls under the age of eighteen.[38]

The commissioners evinced great interest in questions about the administration of criminal justice, which went beyond a consideration of prison administration. They were especially concerned at the length of some sentences, and in cases where injustices had been perpetrated, although these were matters which were not strictly within their terms of reference. Indeed, the whole of the second part of the report is devoted to a consideration of individual cases. This section of the report is not entirely relevant to an analysis of the Commission as it affected the prison system, but it may be noted in passing that a great deal was wrong with the sentencing practices of the courts. In many cases the Commission recommended a reduction in the sentence, and sometimes this was accepted by the law officers. On several occasions though, the latter objected to such interference, retorting: 'Unless it is desired to turn loose upon the community a lot of ruffians, I cannot see any reason for reducing this man's sentence' [the Attorney-General].[39]

In another case the reply was: 'I really do not know what process of reasoning the Commission adopts in order to reach this conclusion' [the Crown Solicitor].[40]

It is clear from the report that the Commission's interest in this topic was obviously the cause of some friction. When a prisoner actually began his sentence, he was still not free of legal injustice, outdated legislation and administrative caprice. The Commission revealed three especially crude examples. These were cumulative sentences, remission and extra-judicial punishment.

The first of these was a process whereby a prisoner who committed an offence against prison rules could be given a sentence by a visiting justice, which would be added to the award which had already been made by the court in respect of his original sentence. It followed that a man who was sentenced to, say, two years could serve much longer if he committed such an offence. The Commission deplored this system and noted that it was against imperial law.[41] Nor were they convinced by a magistrate's assurance that Western Australian law allowed it.[42] This provision for cumulative sentences, it will be remembered, was introduced in 1850 (14 Vict. No. 6), when it was part of a law 'to provide for the due custody and discipline of offenders transported to Western Australia'. It had, it seemed, somehow become part of the treatment of colonial offenders. The sheriff, James Roe, who in his role as Inspector of Prisons was responsible for Fremantle, was of little help. He could not recall a case when the term of imprisonment had been increased in this way, nor did he know whether there was any legal authority for doing so.[43] The Commission pointed out that many prison 'offences' would not be regarded as serious at all outside of the institution. They exemplified with reference to escaping, which, remarkably perhaps, they approved of as natural and demonstrative of a desirable amount of energy. The fault for an escape lay with the staff.[44]

When they turned their attention to remission, the adjective they used was 'incredible'.[45] One of the prisoners calculated that he should have been released in the early part of November 1898, despite the fact that the authorities reckoned his release date as 28 November 1898.[46] This, it seemed, was a source of bewilderment to the prisoners, and soon the commissioners were equally perplexed. They were quite unable to arrive at the same dates as the officials. The explanation, once arrived at, was simple if bizarre. It was that the scale of remissions exhibited to the prisoners was not the same as that used by the officials! Further, any prisoner who was *reported* to the visiting justice automatically lost seven days' remission without the direction or even knowledge of the justice. One magistrate expressed surprise on learning about this, but supposed that remission 'is only an act of grace', and if a man 'gives such trouble as to involve his being brought before a magistrate, he must lose some remission'.[47] By the time the Commission reported, the practice had been stopped as a direct result of their intervention.

Other illegal punishments were reported and were generally admitted. One especially alarming example was the custom of making a man undergo a sentence of three days' bread and water in the dark cells. The visiting justices did not know about this practice either. The experience was described by one prisoner as 'very severe'. He had received 450 grams of bread daily and a pannikin of water. Nothing could be seen or heard in the dark cells and the door was opened only three times a day.[48]

The overall picture revealed by the Royal Commission proved that Vosper was right to be concerned, and that the hopes of the premier for a vindication could not possibly be realized. The root of the trouble was not entirely due to laziness or cruelty on the part of staff, and the Commission, as Vosper had done, recognized this. In doing so they hit upon one of the great truths about effective prison administration. Although they were not sophisticated enough to formulate this, the pattern may be set out as follows. In a situation where men are locked up, there must be a strong, intelligible, administrative framework designed to achieve certain ends. The first is to make clear to prisoners what their rights and obligations are. The next is to offer staff of all ranks, in all departments, clear unequivocal direction about their duties, how they are to be carried out, how failure or success is to be judged, and what is to be defined as unacceptable treatment of prisoners. Next, the whole must be subjected to incessant scrutiny by those senior prison administrators who do not work in the prison. And finally, the whole must be inspected by impartial observers representing the community, in whose name the organization is being called into being. Such a model is naturally somewhat Utopian, but it represents a set of goals to which prison systems must aspire; otherwise there is likely to be constant recurrence of a situation as it was in Western Australia at the end of the nineteenth century.

Measured against such a model the system failed abysmally. Members of the legislature, as was revealed in the debate, knew very little. The sheriff, as can be seen from his own evidence, knew only a little more. The position of the superintendent, whatever his personal defects may have been, was clearly impossible 'by reason of the absence of all proper rules and regulations for his guidance'.[49]

It need hardly be said that there were no written rules for warders, and the evidence of the latter showed that directions were passed around in a way which was reminiscent of folklore.

The extant rules, everyone agreed, were 'obsolete, impracticable, and unworkable'.[50] There was an urgent need for a new set of rules. A historic suggestion from the prisoners was that these should be publicly displayed. This simple idea occurs in the autobiographies of prisoners from the sixteenth century to the present day in every country where such autobiographies have been written.

It was perhaps the realization of the impossible situation in which prison staff found themselves as a consequence of the absence of administrative direction, which led the Commission to avoid commenting on the serious allegations made against several of them. They *had* to say something about the doctor however, and they did: the charges against him were 'wholly without foundation'. But there was no comment on the allegations made against the warders, nor indeed, in the course of a summary of complaints made by prisoners, were these complaints even mentioned. It is, of course, extremely difficult to try to sort out facts from fiction when hearing evidence from two groups such as warders and prisoners, who in the Victorian prison were mutually hostile. Nor is this confined as a problem to the nineteenth century. It is the central difficulty facing a modern investigator.

The prisoners recounted a familiar pattern of physical ill-treatment, accentuated at times by dramatic examples, some of which were undoubtedly true. One of the most notable of these concerned the use of a galvanic battery. This was applied to a prisoner described as an imbecile, and the application of it was confirmed by a warder who said that the man 'would not move until the doctor gave orders for a galvanic battery to be applied to him'.[51] The doctor, as we have seen, admitted doing so.

The problem here was not one of cruelty alone, but reflected the unsatisfactory nature of the organization itself. The basic difficulty was that people who were mentally ill and mentally defective were confined in the prison. One warder reported that one-fifth of the gang under his command were lunatics.[52] In more modern times this problem has been partially solved with the removal of those people who are demonstrably suffering from mental illness or who are mentally defective. But even in modern systems this is a familiar enough problem. It is a common experience of prison staff that they have to deal with people who they are convinced belong in a mental hospital of some description. The problem nowadays tends to be that mental hospitals feel that the same individuals belong in prisons. And so these people oscillate between prison and mental hospital, with the staff of both being convinced that they belong somewhere else.

Another example of unsatisfactory behaviour on the part of staff occurred when a prisoner, who was a professional accountant, set out in some considerable detail allegations of dishonesty by certain warders in respect of contracts.[53] Not all the prisoners, however, complained about ill-treatment or corruption on the part of staff. On the contrary, some said that they had been well treated by warders. One, who was very critical of some, said of the warder in charge of the hospital that he was 'the most humane man [he had] seen about the gaol'.[54] Others noted wryly that there had been an improvement in behaviour since the appointment of the Commission which 'has struck terror into the hearts of the officials'.[55] There had, it may be noted, also been improvement in the quality of the food since the appointment of the Commission.

Vosper in his evidence, like his hero Tallack, who was the secretary of the Howard Association in England,[56] stated his disgust at the uniformed staff.[57] 'The warders', he said 'are usually people of inferior standing. Men who could get a better class of work will not take it.' In respect of remission his view was that 'in no case should the warders have any discretion in the matter.' This was a familiar enough view amongst penal reformers at the end of the century, and in some circles this spirit is by no means dead.

The root of the problem as far as the staff were concerned was the absence of classification and the 'association' of prisoners, whereby they were allowed to mix with comparative freedom. Fremantle, like all Victorian prisons, based as they were directly or indirectly on the Pentonville 'model', was designed for the 'separate system'. In terms of the development of penal administration the separate system was the most important and the most controversial step in the nineteenth century. It was the outcome of concern in the eighteenth century about the evils of 'contamination', a theme which, as we have seen in respect of the boys in Fremantle, occupied the attention of the Royal Commission.

The real advantage, however, of the separate system was that it ensured control within the prison. It is evident that isolation of individual prisoners in individual cells ensures inability on their part to collude, with the consequences that escape or riot become almost impossible. During the last century the separate system became one of the main planks of the reformers' case, since they recognized in it a solution to the horrors of mass association, described by people like John Howard in the previous century.[58] The most significant problem in modern prison administration has arisen because prisons which were designed to ensure separation are now called upon to allow association. In the very first sentences of the first report the Commission showed that they recognized this. They observed that: 'The general plan of the prison is such as to needlessly increase the work of supervision and maintaining discipline among the inmates.'

It was to a restoration of the separate system that the Commission looked as a crucial key to reforming the prison. Not only would this eliminate the classic problems of contamination and brutality amongst prisoners, a factor which incidentally is often ignored by those who disapprove of the separate system, but it would enable staff once again to control activities within the prison. The warders approved of what they called classification, but by which they meant separation,[59] and the superintendent too approved of it. He went further and asked that prisoners should be masked,[60] which had been abandoned as a practice in England some years before, and which is an example of the nightmares which can emanate from the theorizing of some reformers, in this case Jeremy Bentham, who had first suggested masking prisoners at the end of the eighteenth century. Until the 1860s prisoners in Pentonville did in fact wear masks.[61]

The Commission recommended that the first six months of a sentence should be 'strictly on the separate system', but on 'maturer consideration' the period proposed was reduced to three months.[62] At the end of this period of separate confinement the prisoners should be transferred to another establishment. They supported their recommendation by quoting Tallack and Du Cane. Tallack was well known internationally as a penal reformer. He had been a prominent witness at all the investigations into the British penal system in the last quarter of the nineteenth century. Du Cane, who had important associations with Western Australia, had achieved an administrative task of enormous proportion in his centralization of the English prison system. By the 1890s however, he was under attack from reformers. Both these international figures had been in favour of separation, and their views were dutifully reported by the Commission. Du Cane was also justifiably proud of the considerable amount of public work done by convicts in England, especially at Portland in Dorset, where an elaborate defence system had been built. The Royal Commission envisaged the employment of prisoners on similar schemes in Western Australia.[63]

The policy of separation had given rise to considerable controversy. Despite the obvious advantages to the weaker prisoner and to the staff of prisons, occupied as they were in problems of control, reformers believed that it was unnecessarily cruel. Indeed, in England the period of separation had been progressively reduced. And at the very time when the Royal Commission was recommending its reintroduction, the system was losing credibility in England. One of the reasons for the establishment of the Gladstone Committee was dissatisfaction with the separate system, expressed in allegations that it led amongst other things to insanity. One of the most significant recommendations of the Gladstone Report was a modification conducive ultimately to abolition of the separate system. This, as it turned out, was to lead to the inevitable problems which were being faced at that very time by prison staff in Western Australia.[64] Nevertheless, it was at the time discredited. Tallack, one of its strongest advocates, was a voice from the past.

Historically the most effective investigations into prison administration have done more than simply recommend minor improvements. The best of these theorize and speculate, causing people to reflect upon and re-examine penal problems from first principles. The Royal Commission was valuable apart from anything else because it initiated discussion about the causes of crime, and brought to the attention of the community and of lawyers and prison professionals names of people who were shaping the development of thought about crime and punishment. They discussed people such as Lombroso and Ferri, who were tracing relationships between physique and crime, and who were trying to establish a 'science' of criminology. They discussed penal systems in other states and in other countries, drawing to the attention of people in Western Australia, for example, the famous Elmira system in New York State, which had such a high reputation at the end of the last century. Above all they suggested the elimination of much that was vicious and cruel in the existing system. They recommended the abolition of flogging for all prison offences, the abolition of the dark cells, 'a relic of barbarism', the use of irons and the use of the crank.[65]

In respect of the administration of criminal justice they not only recommended the establishment of a court of appeal, but they questioned the ability of a judge to sentence a man wisely, considering how little contact he had with him. In this they were on their own admission following Beccaria, pioneer of reform, who had in 1770 observed that the office of the judge was only to pronounce whether the action of the prisoner was lawful or not: 'The judge, whose office is only to examine, if a man have, or have not committed an action contrary to the laws.'[66] The Commission, extending and applying this notion, proposed that a sentence should be awarded by a board of medical jurists. The prisoner would be given an indeterminate sentence, and this board would decide when release was appropriate.

This idea which owes a great deal to the theorizing of criminologists such as Lombroso, led to a conclusion that the punishment should fit the criminal, rather than that the punishment should fit the crime. The effect of this theorizing can be seen at the present time in the operation of indeterminate sentences (a matter to which much attention will be paid in this account of imprisonment in Western Australia), and in that element of flexibility which is generally found in the treatment of young offenders in, for example, the English borstal, and in the operation of parole systems. And, of course, the Commission recommended reform of some situations which seem hopeless in almost every prison system. They wished for fruitful employment—as every investigation into prisons always does—with such little effect.

Although parallels have been drawn between the Gladstone Report and the Royal Commission, their investigations reveal crucial differences between the English system and the system in Western Australia at the end of the century. In England the ramshackle prison organization had been pulled together by Du Cane in 1877, and while reformers complained about the treatment of prisoners, they did not generally complain about the ill-treatment of prisoners. What Du Cane had succeeded in doing was destroying once and for all the violence and the capricious cruelty of the English system, which had characterized it for a thousand years. He had introduced an intelligible administrative structure, where staff knew clearly what was expected of them and where there were definite limits put on their behaviour.

Western Australia had begun penal administration with the same kind of potential, since Henderson had set up a system which was very reminiscent of that of England. However, prison administrators in the last part of the nineteenth century in Western Australia failed to consolidate the Henderson initiative. Nor did they have the heritage which the English had of many years of prison experience, which served as a constant reminder of the possible damage which could be inflicted upon prisoners. Western Australia had not even had the experience of the horrors of early transportation, and so there was little in the penal history of the state to remind and to warn. The question which the Royal Commission left with the Western Australian prison system was: how much of other peoples' experience was relevant to Western Australia, and how far could the changes and improvements, large and small, recommended by the Royal Commission be carried into effect?

4

1900-1920: 'There is undoubtedly great need for reform in our State prisons' [1]

Aftermath of the Royal Commission—The first open prison—A new Prisons Act—Staff dissatisfaction—Another Royal Commission—Changes at the top—Hann and Fremantle reforms—Two major changes in the law—Indeterminacy and sentencing policy in Western Australia

The publication of the report of the Royal Commission attracted no comment at all in Parliament, and apart from verbatim reporting, little in the press. During the following years the newspapers very occasionally paid attention to prison affairs. The *Morning Herald* in 1901, for example, complained in a leader that the recommendations of the Royal Commission had been ignored, and went on to claim: 'There can be no doubt that the tendency of our present penal system is to manufacture criminals.' [2] This lack of sustained interest is understandable, since in these years there took place some of the great debates in Australian history, notably over the proposed Australian Federation. Interest in the fate of prisons anyway customarily declines when dramatic events in prison end, and macro-political debate begins, and the turn of the century in Western Australia was no exception.

Another factor contributing to the absence of discussion of the report in parliament were Vosper's wide-ranging and expanding interests, which included the discussion about Federation. Any possible resurrection of his interest in prison affairs was in any case precluded by his early death at the age of thirty-three of appendicitis in January 1900. Although he had been an atheist, he received a Roman Catholic burial, at which the priest delivered a somewhat exaggerated but basically true assessment of the man. Drawing attention to Vosper's mental qualities, the priest observed that 'that intellect had been used in defence of the poor and helpless.' [3] Vosper might have been pleased to know that so far as prisons in Western Australia went, his agitation was certainly to make some difference.

The most notable change immediately after the publication of the Commission's report was an improvement in the quality of annual reports on prisons. In the years prior to the Royal Commission, reports had been made, but they tended to be brief and rather trivial. Sheriff James Roe's report for 1899 shows that even if parliament was interested in more grandiose affairs, some people were still concerned about prisons.[4] The reports in the ensuing years set out in some detail a description of the population of the prisons of the state. Included are the daily average number in each of the thirteen state prisons, their ages, their sentences, their racial background, their countries of origin and a host of other details. From the tables it can be seen that in 1899, the year in which the Royal Commission reported, 2150 people were sent to prison, of whom 197 were females, and 6 were juveniles; that 1433 of the committals were to Fremantle, the largest prison, and 8 to Busselton, the smallest; and that the average annual cost of keeping a prisoner was £42 2s ½d.

One of the most interesting features of the prison population during the next twenty years is how it became a reflection of the expansion and contraction of areas of the state. Thus when the eastern goldfields were active, prisons were opened and filled at places such as Kalgoorlie, Coolgardie, Cue and Southern Cross. As areas declined, so did the prison population, which led eventually to the closing of a particular prison. In the same way in the north, the population in prisons reflected activities in the community at large. In Broome for example the prison population rose from 80 in 1915 to 128 in 1916. This was due to a peculiar local situation. It was

the contention of pearlers that the coloured crews of pearling vessels, knowing that their masters are liable for their maintenance in prison, deliberately commit acts of insubordination with the object of embarrassing the employers and eventually securing deportation to their home countries.[5]

It is clear too from these earlier reports that at least some of the recommendations of the Royal Commission were to be implemented. The superintendent of Fremantle, still George, reported that the prison had been divided into four wards as a preliminary to a system of classification, which had been one of the most insistent recommendations of the report.[6] The aim, it will be remembered, was to eliminate 'contamination'. As well as this, 'nearly 100' cells had been enlarged, another recommendation of the Commission, which had improved the health of the prisoners. Also 'some of the prisoners on discharge' had been given money. This last, however, was a sporadic activity which had taken place before the Royal Commission. These were the only improvements which had been carried out as a consequence of the report, and both George and Roe pressed the claim for more, drawing upon the Royal Commission as authority. Above all they wished to see new prison statutes and new gaol regulations, the draft of which had been sent to the Crown Lawyers several months before, the introduction of teachers for the younger and more illiterate prisoners, and separation of the roles of Inspector of Prisons and Sheriff, since both were still vested in the same person.

The Annual Report for 1900 contains the same background information about the prisoner population, and cataglogues a few more improvements, at the same time setting out the same list of desiderata.[7] One of the most noteworthy of the former is progress in the building of workshops in Fremantle to enable prisoners to be kept inside during the day, and of the latter the continuing absence of rules because of parliament's pre-occupation with other matters. This meant, as before, that the prison administrator still had to try to operate within the framework of legislation and rules devised for a system and prisoner population which no longer existed. A further note of *déja vu* was struck when the officials asked that those ageing relics of the convict era, the imperial invalid paupers, be moved from a block within the prison in which they lived to the old-men's home in the town. The building could then revert to its use as a prison hospital. This situation had arisen because of that remarkably casual attitude to the law which characterized much West Australian prison administration at the time, since the detention of free men within a prison was of dubious legality. The authorities were more aware of correct procedures in respect of one of the most remarkable prisoners in Western Australian history. He was 'a Chinaman of weak intellect' who died in 1920, having served thirty-five years in Fremantle Prison and who had never learned to speak English. The Crown Lawyers ruled that he could remain in the invalid depot in the prison, as a pauper, after he had been classified as such.[8]

Continued steady progress is reported for 1901. The paupers had gone, new workshops had been opened for bootmaking and tailoring, and the prisoners could now earn gratuities. Separate confinement, the major recommendation of the Commission, was now enforced in Fremantle, but only for those doing more than six months—'a wholesome deterrent' it was hoped. Superintendent George had visited prisons in the eastern states and noted that he had gained much information of importance in connection with the employment of prisoners and teaching them various trades. As usually happens when practitioners travel to observe other systems, he returned convinced of the need for a new prison, 'arranged and equipped according to the latest modern ideas'. He was, he wrote, 'glad to learn that steps are now about to be taken for the selection of a site for a new prison'. In the light of developments in later years this turned out to be a very optimistic hope. At last in April 1902 a new set of prison rules and regulations came into force, although there was still a plea for a new Prison Act. The *Morning Herald*, which was generally critical of the prisons, welcomed the rules as 'a very distinct advance in our penal system', and pointed to 'abundant cause for congratulation in the reforms for which they provide'. The newspaper supposed that the influence of Jameson had caused something to be done after the lapse of time.[9]

One very significant development was reported in the year. This was the opening of Hamel (Drakesbrook) Penal Outstation in the southwest of the state. The report for 1901 records that the buildings were being erected by prison labour, and that the men sent there would be employed in clearing and draining land.[10] The historical antecedents which led to the opening of Hamel, and the general penological experience of the opening of this outstation, are of some general interest and significance.

In most situations prisoners are only sent to work outside the prisons during the day, and have to return to the security of the prison at night. Until very recent years, when prisoners were on outside work, they were chained, and if considered dangerous, were supervised by a gun guard. This was, for example, the system employed in England in the last quarter of the nineteenth century and was universal in the southern United States of America until comparatively recently. In the early part of the twentieth century many societies began to express concern about the indignity and oppression of such a system. Prison systems then, typically, chose one or the other. As we shall see, Aboriginal prisoners in Western Australia were chained until the 1940s, chaining of prisoners was carried out in parts of British colonial Africa until British colonial Africa existed no more, and even English prisoners at Dartmoor were under gun control until 1954. Some prisoners were more unfortunate than others: those for example in the southern United States and in the northwest of Western Australia were chained during the day, and because their base buildings were insecure, were chained at night as well. Hamel, many years before such developments occurred to reformers in Europe, seemed likely to do away with both chains and guns. The reason, however, is especially interesting, and derived from traditions of imprisonment which were already becoming established in the state.

Open conditions are a victory for the powers of reform. They herald the reduction, or even elimination of the manifest oppression of the closed prison. There were, however, in Western Australia additional pressures which encouraged the venture. The convict era had established the tradition that prisoners should labour on public works. To engage in such constructive work for the community means clearly that prisoners have to work outside the prison. Hamel represented the perpetuation of this tradition, and although it was short-lived (it was closed in 1907), it was chronologically a link between the public-work tradition and a most unusual feature of imprisonment in Western Australia at the present time. This is the use of prison labour for community work in the area in which the prison is located. This acceptance of the notion that prisoners can be usefully employed in the community is strengthened by the Australian tradition evidenced by the host of voluntary clubs of community self-help, especially in small towns some distance from the metropolis. This is an example of the fact that the pattern of prison administration is shaped substantially by the history and traditions of the society in which prisons are set. This latter fact accounts generally for the failure of attempts to transplant penal ideas from one country to another.

The next Annual Report, for 1902, was equally buoyant.[11] There was comment on the progress of the workshops, including the expectation that a printing shop would be set up, and a note that a qualified teacher had been appointed to teach the juveniles. There was also that same 'hope' that the 'long promised bill' to update prison law would soon be passed; but difficulties were arising.

The principal constraint on development and change in prisons is, crudely, finance, a truism which soon became apparent to the policy makers. Money problems now began to feature in the annual reports. Hamel for example, the Annual Report for 1902 noted, 'has proved an expensive undertaking', and at Fremantle the 'efficient classification of the prisoners' simply could not be carried out 'without considerable alterations and additions'. Further, the employment of a trade instructor and school master caused an increase in expenditure. And most significant, in the light of the growth of staff discontent during the decade, the hours of night staff were 'unduly long'. Superintendent George, as a solution to this last problem, proposed the appointment of an additional three warders.

At long last the promised Bill to update prison legislation was introduced. The first and last major Act to range over the whole business of administration had been that of 1849. After that, such legislation as had been enacted was concerned with patching up defects and with the removal of unworkable anachronisms.

The colonial secretary, Kingsmill, moved the second reading of the Bill in the Legislative Council in July 1903.[12] He pointed out that there was 'a great necessity for effecting improvements in the laws relating to our prisons.' It seemed that there were three main reasons for introducing the Bill. First, there was the need for a proper system of classification, which would end the ancient complaint of the reformers: 'contamination'. Next, there was a need for work for prisoners, which would contribute to the cost of their maintenance. Penal outstations would be set up to that end; indeed Hamel by that time already existed, albeit strictly illegally. Throughout the debate it was pointed out that the legal status of Hamel was in need of regularizing. The third aim of the Bill was to enable detailed regulations to be made. To assure those—and in any political debate about prisons there are plenty—who were likely to see the existence of properly-constituted authority for prison administration as 'coddling' he stated: 'We do not wish to make them like the prisons which I believe exist in some parts of the world—places of pleasant retreat from the rigours of winter or the heat of summer.'

In the resumed debate next day Sir E. H. Wittenoom was one who welcomed this assurance that it was not 'the intention of the Government to make the prisons too attractive'.[13] Wittenoom went on to parade the familiar objections to prisoners being better off than free men, without asking basic questions about just how prosperous these free men really were. It rarely occurs to such critics that social jutice might demand the raising of the standard of living of free men, rather than the depressing of that of prisoners. Wittenoom's point about relative eligibility has a place in every debate about penal treatment, and has now become an almost inevitable ritual ingredient in such discussion. Wittenoom was, of course, supported in what he said by several other members of the Legislative Council.

The discussion in the Legislative Assembly was altogether different and much more sophisticated. In his introduction to the second reading the minister for works reiterated the objects of the Bill, and additionally expressed the hope that since visitors could be appointed under the Act, it might be possible to arrange a system whereby female visitors could visit female prisoners.[14] After this the debate began in earnest, with the emergence of a vocal cadre of liberal opinion.

The members expressing this opinion were: Illingworth, who was English and a noted temperance worker; Moran; Pigott, who distinguished himself on account of his pearling activities in Broome; Bath, who was perhaps the most distinguished of the group, and was *inter alia* a member of the 1910 Royal Commission into the establishment of the University of Western Australia; and Taylor, who like Vosper had been to prison.[15] He had been imprisoned in 1891 for activities in connection with a shearers' strike in eastern Australia. This very mixed group of men took some of their criticism outside the narrow confines of the Bill itself. The informed nature of their comments was impressive to such a degree that it is difficult to believe that a discussion about the same subject, imprisonment, had been held in that chamber only some six years before, when Vosper had battled alone to interest people in prisons. This new group was sufficiently interested to challenge many of the assumptions underlying the clauses in the Bill, courageous enough to take a stand for the reasonable treatment of prisoners, and informed enough to draw the attention of the Assembly to situations elsewhere.

Illingworth began by broadening the issue to include a consideration of the problems facing prisoners on release.[16] In the course of his remarks he drew attention to the phenomenon of police harassment of ex-prisoners, which amongst other things took the form of pointing out to employers the fact that an individual had been to prison. Moran, for his part, had visited New Zealand, and described an open experiment which he had seen there, observing that prison treatment was 'an expert science'. This statement reflects the emerging faith in social science, which for the next sixty years was to lead penal theorists and practitioners to hope that it would be possible to prescribe and evaluate penal treatment. Bath contributed an account of the reformatory at Elmira, in New York State, which at that time was still attracting the attention of many people who were baffled and concerned about the inadequacies of their own systems, and who saw some hope in the commitment to training, which was the basis of the Elmira programme.

In the last speech of the debate Bath introduced an inevitable but for the reformer confused topic: staff behaviour. It was proposed in the Bill that 'pretending illness' should be treated very harshly as an 'aggravated offence', which could be punished by solitary confinement or corporal punishment. This Bath thought too severe, and in fact succeeded in removing it from the list of 'aggravated offences'. In the course of his objection he recounted:

> Instances have been brought under my notice of prisoners really ill having been deemed by brutal warders to be only shamming illness and punished . . .
> And there have been cases of warders actually kicking a prisoner and brutally assaulting him because he was really ill.

He then launched a progressive attack on corporal punishment, stating that provision for it 'should be struck out of any Bill dealing with prisons'. On this spirited note the debate ended.

The lengthiest and most radical discussion took place at the committee stage of the Bill on 1 October. The clauses of the Bill were commented upon in some detail, the need to legalize Hamel and other possible outstations was again mentioned, and the Royal Commission was referred to as an authority to set up a constructive work programme. Then the liberal attack on the system, hinted at by Bath in the earlier debate, began in earnest.

Taylor catalogued a number of first-hand experiences, such as that where a prisoner had had his jaw broken because of defective machinery, and where another was put in a punishment cell even though the doctor had agreed that his knee needed treatment. Taylor expressed his concern, as he had done before, that the regulations which could be made under the Bill must be controlled. In fact, he claimed, compared with the regulations the Bill 'was absolutely harmless'. In a comment on northern prisons another member, Connor, pointed out that alterations in the law should affect black as well as white. 'The binding of prisoners to gum stumps should not be allowed.' This point was not taken up.

Prison staff did, however, have their defenders. One stated 'that those who had managed the prisons in the past had, as far as they knew, done their best to make the prisoners work at work that would be of advantage to them outside.' 'People', he went on, 'who lived in glass houses should not throw stones.' This provoked another familiar argument. Were the critics attacking *all* staff or just individuals? They tried to impress upon the members that they meant individuals, but the tendency was to see the remarks as a general indictment of the staff. Jacoby was another staff supporter attacking 'Sunday school speeches'. One of his more astute observations was that 'No matter what the Act might be, the practical success of carrying it out, depended upon the administration and efficiency of the warders.' He appealed for more support for them, and for a recognition that there were bound to be individual cases of injustice.

The most extensive discussion was about the meaning of 'solitary' and 'separate', and whether or not dark cells were to be used. The use of dark cells had been roundly condemned by the Royal Commission, and there is no doubt that the extraction of an assurance from the minister during the debate that there was no provision for their use led to their ultimate abandonment. Bath began by asking for clarification of the clause authorizing separate confinement.

It was explained that this could only be awarded by a visiting justice, and that cells must be lighted and ventilated, so that the health of the inmates would not suffer. Bath returned later to the question of solitary confinement and initiated the most sophisticated discussion in the whole series of debates. He stated that solitary confinement as a punishment 'should be absolutely abolished in connection with prisons'. The minister for works, assured him that dark cells would not be used. But Taylor was not satisfied. He now mounted an attack on the notion of separate 'treatment', saying that 'it had been proved beyond doubt' that only men very strong mentally would remain unaffected. Further,

in a return to his concern about 'regulations', he was confident
that when these were drawn up, they would include the provision
of dark-cell punishment. To assuage him the minister offered to
change 'solitary' to 'separate', since Taylor had claimed that the
distinction in the eastern states was that separate punishment
meant light cells and solitary punishment meant dark cells.

Some members now expressed impatience with the whole
discussion. One had been in Fremantle recently, where 'the dark
cell . . . was so little used that it was almost forgotten.' An
appropriate comment at this point could well have been about the
shortness of memory. The minister in desperation commented that:
'one could not have imagined that this admittedly good measure
would arouse so much discussion.' He again promised to change
the word solitary to separate. Jacoby thought it 'not altogether
wise' to abolish dark cells. But the liberals had gained the concession they sought and the debate ended.

When the Legislative Council discussed the Assembly's amendments in November, the word 'solitary' was in fact changed to
'punishment'.[17] Most of the amendments were accepted, except
one. The Assembly had tried to establish the right of members of
the legislature to visit prisons, because such visitors could act in
some kind of inspectorial role. This was firmly opposed by the
Council, in spite of the colonial secretary's recommendation that
it should be agreed to. If it were, one claimed, 'it would give an
opportunity to a meddlesome Member of Parliament to put the
State to a considerable amount of expense.' 'Lately', another observed, 'we have seen in various directions the mischievous effect
of the constant meddling, finding fault, and holding up to ridicule
and contempt' of public figures. The clause would, another said,
'be inadvisable, as it would do away with prison discipline by
bringing political influence into prison management.' So that
clause was rejected, much to the fury of Taylor who saw in the
rejection a lesson to be drawn about the arrogance of the Council.
He wanted to make an issue of the matter, but, he complained:
'look at this thin House, an evidence of the apathy and neglect of
those sent here to do the country's business.'[18]

The last stages of debate on the Bill, in November, found Bath
and Taylor making a last, unsuccessful stand against corporal
punishment.[19] This they pointed out was deplored by 'all the
acknowledged authorities on criminology and penology'. 'One

grew tired', Taylor said, 'of listening to the argument of "deterrent influence".' Once a man was flogged, he was ruined. Moreover, he would have expected capital punishment to have ended by that time. The enthusiasm of this group did not diminish. They continued their commentary on what they believed to be unsatisfactory in the Bill, such as 'malingering'.

So the first major Prisons Act for fifty-four years was passed. It was a direct consequence of Vosper's agitation which had led to the Royal Commission, and some of whose recommendations had in turn been refined by the radical cadre in the Assembly. This Act remains important, since it is still the basis of prison administration in Western Australia. As we shall go on to see, there have been amendments to it, but there has not been since 1903 a major Act affecting prison administration.

The provisions of the Act touched upon every aspect of prison administration. The previous sixteen statutes concerned with prisons were repealed, including the Act of 1841, which, as we shall see, established Rottnest Island as a prison for Aborigines. Hamel, the legality of which had been a matter of such concern in the debates, was 'declared' in the second Schedule of the Act to be an outstation. Rottnest, because of the repeal of the Act of 1841, which established it as a prison, no longer had the status of one. It was, however, declared a gaol again in January 1904,[20] a declaration which was varied later in a clarification of which areas of the island were to be the 'prison'.[21] Strictly, this meant that the prisoners who were there between the passing of the Act and the new declaration were not lawfully detained.

There was in the Act a great deal of reiteration of what emerged in the nineteenth century as the irreducible basis of a humane prison system. Thus for example, female prisoners had to be kept separate, and limits were set on punishments, all of which had to be the consequence of a proper hearing, and all of which had to be recorded in a punishment book. Restrictions were placed upon the keeping of prisoners in irons, a provision which, as we shall see, made no difference to the native prisoners in the North-West, who were kept in chains for many years after this Act was passed.

Not all of the recommendations of the Royal Commission were implemented. Indeed, while the Act was being debated, the *Morning Herald* on 3 September 1903 complained that the Bill was only a 'feeble' reflection of the scheme proposed by the Commission in its report 'that is in itself a liberal education to the student of criminology'.

There was notably still a provision for the infliction of corporal punishment, but it would have been a truly remarkable fact if an Act at this time had not included it. Contemporary attempts to abolish corporal punishment in England were equally unsuccessful. However, many of the provisions recommended by the Royal Commission were incorporated in the Act and in the subsequent regulations. These achieved notably the primary aim set up by the Royal Commission, which was that staff and prisoners should understand clearly what their rights and duties were. There were three especially important changes which arose from the world-wide general body of reformative experience and policy, and which were especially effective as attempts to remedy specific defects in the Western Australian situation.

The first of these was the question of who should be in charge of the prison system. It has been pointed out that Western Australia had adopted the historic English tradition that the Sheriff should be responsible for the prisons. But also as in England, the Quarter Sessions had authority too, which historically had led to considerable problems in respect of demarcation of responsibility. There is no doubt that much of the confusion in prisons in Western Australia at the beginning of the twentieth century was due to there being no permanent paid official at the head of the prison service.

It was to remedy this defect that the Royal Commission had recommended the appointment of a Comptroller-General. The idea of creating such a post, however, met with opposition in the parliamentary debates, especially from the reforming Taylor, on the grounds of costs. The Act as a result enabled an appointment of Comptroller-General of Prisons to be made, but went on to provide that 'the office of Comptroller-General of Prisons and the office of Sheriff may for such time as the Governor thinks fit, be held by the same person'. In the years immediately after the passing of the Act, precisely this was done, but at least the legal constitution of the post was a considerable move forward, and began a move away from the historical disastrous amateurism of the Sheriff's control.

The second major change was concerned with the cumulative sentence. In the sections on punishment, prison offences were

divided into minor and aggravated, with specific punishments prescribed for each. There was no mention of the cumulative sentence
either in the Act, or in the discussion leading to it. One of the
interesting facts about the history of prison punishment in Western
Australia is that this abolition did not last. Cumulative sentences,
as we shall see, were reintroduced, and are now part of the penal
code once again.

The third important recommendation has already been discussed:
the separation of prisoners with a view to the elimination of contamination, and the 'proper classification of prisoners'. There was
no time limit, the new law being that a prisoner could be confined
'during the whole or any part of his imprisonment' in separate
conditions. In fact, prison practice had already preceded this provision, such haste being due probably to the function of separation
as a means of regaining control of the activities of the prisoner
population. It had, however, already run into difficulties and was
to prove unworkable. Not only does separate confinement involve
large numbers of staff—to issue food for example—but it requires
a purpose-built prison, the central feature of which is the provision
of work in each cell. Unlike some English prisons, such as Pentonville, Fremantle, with its tradition of public work, had simply not
been designed to operate in this way. But above all, separation
was old-fashioned, discredited as an effective treatment and
deplored by reformers as inhuman. It had no chance whatever of
being implemented in the state prisons outside Fremantle, which
grew up with entirely different buildings and methods of operation.
It could not survive anywhere in the state, nor did it.

After the passing of the 1903 Act the system settled down to a
period of consolidation of the new rules, but in 1905 there was the
first hint of a new kind of trouble for the prison administrators.
This time it did not involve prisoners and their treatment. It was
rather the first hint that staff were becoming militant about their
unsatisfactory situation. In August in the Legislative Assembly it
was proposed that: 'In the opinion of this House the time has
arrived when the hours of the warders employed in Fremantle
Gaol be reduced to 8 per day.'[22] The motion was outvoted, but in
July 1907 questions were asked again about warders' hours.[23] It
was stated that the staff at Fremantle worked 12 hours a day; that
they worked 94½ hours in one week and 84 hours in the next; that
there was a recommendation that the government should fix an

8-hour day; and that the practice of broken shifts should be stopped. The premier in his reply denied the accuracy of the figures and claimed that broken shifts were inevitable. Later in the year Taylor, who had figured prominently in the debates on the Act of 1903,[24] asked the premier if he had done anything about representations made about warders' hours. He replied that claims about excessive work would have to be proved.

In December 1908 a spokesman for the staff brought forward new aspects of staff unrest.[25] He wanted to know how many officers had been 'dispensed with' at Fremantle in the previous twelve months, how many had been taken on, the total staff strength and their hours of duty. The replies were unremarkable, except for the persistence of the claim that staff in fact only worked eight hours a day. In the next month, yet again, questions were asked about officer's hours, and as before, the premier gave a placatory answer.[26] By now these questions and answers had begun to develop a pattern. This was that the warders arranged the questions to be asked, drawing attention to their long hours of work. However, they apparently overstated their case, and when the premier answered, the questioner was not sufficiently well-informed to challenge his reply. There was, however, obvious dissatisfaction amongst the staff.

In October 1909 a lengthy motion proposed that employees in the prison and lunacy departments should be given the right of an appeal to a board.[27] It was pointed out that employees in those departments were the only public servants who did not have the right of appeal. This was why for a long time ministers had been 'pestered' by questions about hours of duty, and such trivial matters. The motion was unsuccessful and questions continued to be asked. By November 1911 another member was asking about night duty,[28] and it was clear that there was still no proper channel for the communication of grievances. Indeed the situation seems to have been more blocked than ever, since staff felt constrained to ask the premier parochial questions such as the reason why the prison baker was exempt from certain duties. just how difficult it was for prison staff to persuade authority to listen to them can be gauged from the odd fact that none of their manifest dissatisfaction, or any attempt to put matters right, is even mentioned, not to say commented upon in the annual reports of the department during these years.

Prison staff have never, since the development of modern communications, existed in isolation. They are susceptible, like other members of the community, to change, and are aware of what is happening in other places. The dissatisfaction expressed by staff in Western Australia at the time should therefore be viewed against the background of events elsewhere. Thus this attempt by prison staff in Western Australia to register protest about their conditions was parallelled by similar movements in other prison systems at the time, notably in England. There the period after 1900 is substantially dominated by prison staff trying to gain the right to form a staff union, which would be recognized by the government—a right which was withheld until 1939. This was some twenty years after prison staff struck, were dismissed and never reinstated. The small group who did strike however, has never earned a place in trade-union martyrology.

The recipe for staff antagonism to policy makers in England is found in other parts of the world. As freedom increased for the prisoners, the restrictions and strain on staff increased proportionately. In such a situation any attempt to liberalize, or even change a prison system is doomed, especially if, as happened in England, policy makers ignore the evidence which is thrust at them in the form of underground magazines, illegal meetings and questions in democratic assemblies. The end of the nineteenth century, as we have seen, was a period when prison policies were being reviewed generally, and in these reviews prison staff tended to be the object of a great deal of criticism. Whilst on any staff some people deserve and get censure, the impression given to staff, which hardened into certainty, was that they were regarded as less worthwhile than the prisoners they held.

This is a feeling which was given added strength because of the deep-rooted class assumptions which the reformer of that time brought to his analysis of what was happening in prison. The term 'superior' staff and the now defunct 'inferior' denoted not simply a professional relationship, but a social relationship as well. In the first decade of this century, prison officers in Western Australia, like their peers in England and elsewhere, were becoming increasingly frustrated about the constant implication that inferiority in the one respect meant inferiority in the other.

This was also, of course, the period of the growth of working-class militant politics. The arguments that the public service was analogous with the armed services, that 'combination' was the same as mutiny, and no protest should be made, were becoming increasingly unacceptable. Civil servants in England shocked the English-speaking world in 1891 by going on strike—'the first recorded strike of civil servants'.[29] In Western Australia the police strike of 1912 was an indication that men in government service, in uniform or not, were capable of industrial action. The dissatisfaction of Western Australian subordinate prison staff had two sources: one was the general questioning by working men of the apparently inexorable social and political system which grew out of the nineteenth century, and the other was the especial injustices which accrued to their position as prison officers, deserted, as they believed, by the powerful vocal middle-class liberal people who ought to have been their supporters, but in fact threw in their lot with the prisoners. Herein was the root of the modern paradox, that prison officers who collectively tend to support left-wing parties for economic and other reasons, rarely ally themselves with the penal reform bodies such as the several Howard organizations in which left-wing people are often prominent.

The situation could no longer be ignored, and it was announced in the Legislative Assembly on October 20, 1910 that the warders at Fremantle had made a number of requests to the comptroller-general with the support of W. A. Murphy, the Member for Fremantle, and that an independent board was to be set up. The original intention was that the Public Service Commissioner would sit on the board, but in the event a Royal Commission was established and Captain C. E. D. F. Pennefather, the Comptroller-General of Prisons in Queensland, was appointed.

He was to report 'Into the administration and conduct of the Fremantle Prison and matters incidental thereto'. Although his report was tabled both in the Council and in the Assembly, it was not published, and unfortunately no copy has survived. The Council's copy was probably eaten by ants, and the Assembly copy has disappeared.[30] It is possible, however, to deduce from such commentary as was made at the time what the contents of the report was. This commentary, which fortunately is profuse, is to be found in newspapers, in the Annual Reports and in J. M. Drew's *Penological Reform in Western Australia,* published in 1916. Apart from a motion that the report should be tabled, there was no discussion about the report in either the Legislative Assembly or in the Council.

This is perhaps not surprising, in view of the change in the interests of parliamentarians since 1903. It was reported that an invitation to appear before the Commission was extended to the public, and in response three members of the Legislative Assembly, including Murphy, and three ex-officials of Fremantle Prison appeared before Pennefather. Apparently a deputation representing the Women's Service Guild also gave evidence, especially in regard to the female prison. But although a direct invitation was extended to six particular members of the Legislative Assembly, who had 'in Parliamentary discussion evinced an interest in matters relating to prison administration', none accepted the invitation or even acknowledged it.[31]

In spite of such lack of interest the Commission worked hard. It sat on sixteen occasions, ten at Fremantle, five at Perth and one at Rottnest. Seventy-nine witnesses were examined, which included 55 prison officials, 4 official visitors, 3 members of parliament, who have already been mentioned, 3 ex-officials and, significantly, 14 prisoners. In addition to which it was reported that Pennefather had had interviews with the auditor-general and his officers, as well as with the stores manager in regard to the prison stores and account system, and he further made a careful inspection of the gaol and other buildings, in company with the medical officer and the acting superintendent.

The report expressed views on matters affecting both staff and prisoners. One important issue affecting both was the physical state of Fremantle Prison, which was condemned by Pennefather, as it has been condemned by others before and would be again. 'The construction of the old gaol building', he wrote, 'does not appeal to one as being adapted to the application of modern prison principles.'[32] He considered further that the attempt to ameliorate the position by the building of a new division has been a mistake. There remained a need for 'one entirely new penal establishment'.[33]

He especially disapproved of the female prison. It was wrong to have it within the male prison, and it was 'badly constructed and badly ventilated'. He noted:

> The surroundings are dull and hard, and the unpleasant conditions are accentuated by the nature of the employment, and the unbecoming and slatternly dress of the prisoners. Instead of being employed to wash the heavy moleskin clothes of male prisoners,

which work seems unnecessarily arduous and degrading, the women
should be given clean work, such as laundering and similar light
work, and should also be taught to use sewing machines in connection with dressmaking, shirtmaking, etc. I feel sure that a very
beneficial effect would follow the introduction of a neater and
tidier dress, including white caps.[34]

A consideration of the plight of female prisoners led him to a
discussion of the question of inebriates. He submitted for consideration a suggestion that as in New South Wales, a state reformatory should be established, especially for female inebriates
and vagrants. There was indeed a need for special inebriate treatment for both sexes. In 1914 a home for inebriates was opened at
Whitby, but it did not last.[35]

He went on to make some general comments about the prison,
reviewing favourably the work carried out in the workshops, although he expressed concern about the system of accounting. He
added a recommendation that discharged prisoners should always
be given a rail ticket at the end of their sentence. Pennefather
went on to deal with some major, by now familiar defects. Like
the commissioners of 1899 he was not happy with the power that
magistrates wielded, especially their ability to lengthen sentences.
There was by now no provision for cumulative awards, but
prisoners could still be penalized through loss of remission. Instead
of this he advocated the use of a 'marks system'. If a prisoner was
guilty of misconduct, then he would lose marks and consequently
remission. The separate system, of which Pennefather approved
for deterrent purposes, was not, he observed, universal at Fremantle, especially in respect of that very class which, in his view,
needed it most: 'youthful first offenders'. Pennefather's report
went on to make one major recommendation, which was to have
considerable impact on the future of the Western Australian prison
system. This was the suggestion that indeterminate sentences
should be introduced for habitual criminals.

He was not the first to advocate this; it had for example been
suggested by the Comptroller-General of Western Australian
Prisons in 1908.[36] Pennefather quotes extensively from experience
in other countries, and most especially from statements made in
the then prestigious International Prison Congress.[37] A new
scheme, which had been introduced in New South Wales and
Victoria, he believed, 'had already been attempted with success

especially in regard to its deterrent effects'.

The question of the indeterminate sentence was very much to the fore in penal discussion at the time. It had its roots in the development of the search for a science of crime and punishment, and in the growing conviction that the punishment should not in the Gilbertian phrase, fit the crime, but should rather, after the Lombrosian school, fit the criminal. The feeling was growing that if there is to be a scientific study of the individual criminal, then the courtroom is not the place to carry it out for two main reasons. First, in the bustle of the courtroom there is not time to spend on such a study, and secondly, the awarding of a sentence which is 'fixed' is likely to fail in allowing for the factors of human growth and change in a prisoner. As 'scientific penology' came into vogue, bringing its Lombrosian undertones with it, its advocates felt sure that the transfer of the decision about how long a prisoner would serve from the courtroom to officials would be more just and more effective. It was a hope, like many in the heyday of penal reform, which has not been realized.

Indeterminacy has to some degree been present in many sentences: borstals, preventative detention, approved schools and life sentences. It finds its most universal expression in the parole system, where a prisoner can be released after a certain time has been served, often with a substantial proportion of his sentence remitted and put on parole. The advantages, as has been stated, are obvious. The disadvantages, however, are more subtle, but have become increasingly obvious. There are considerable dangers in removing decisions about length of sentence from the public arena of a court to an administrative body, which is inaccessible and, typically, as in England, gives no account of how it arrives at its decision to the person affected by it. The real reason for this is that the criteria for release centre around such generalities as 'attitude', 'co-operation', 'stability' and the rest. Only very arrogant people would claim skill at evaluating such features of human behaviour, and only extremely persuasive people would find it possible to convince others, especially customers, of the accuracy of their analysis or the certainty of their predictions. It is for these reasons that at the present time indeterminacy in sentencing is being questioned, and in many cases—such as preventive detention and borstal—has been abandoned as a *modus operandi*. Pennefather, of course, had not had this experience. The idea

seemed sound to him, and as we shall see, was introduced into the
Western Australian prison system, where it has remained a central
feature of penal policy.

The prison staff must, on the whole, have been rather disappointed by his commentary on their situation. He reported that
'a good deal of discontent was shown by some of the married
officers in regard to the condition of and accommodation afforded
in the quarters provided.' He inspected these and found 'nothing
to complain of' in three, but added that the others were 'to put it
mildly, far from what they should be in regard to accommodation,
cleanliness, sanitation and decency'. Because the houses were so
small and the families were so large:

> it is hardly necessary for me to add that an officer coming off duty
> to such a home, where he cannot get much rest or peace, is hardly
> fitted for his next duty at the prison, and this naturally causes irrita-
> tion and discontent. The fact that some of the buildings are infested
> with vermin adds to the discomfort.[38]

Although he conceded, in an examination of gun duty which
went into some detail, that ten hours a day duty was too long 'to
keep constantly on the alert', in other matters his report must have
been of little consolation. The staff of sixty, which included female
officers, 'seems abnormally large', although the design of Fremantle Prison did not help. The staff could supervise double or
treble the present numbers in his view. The hours of work, compared with other states in Australia, were not excessive, and the
suggested eight-hour day could only be introduced if staff were
increased.

Above all his report gives the impression that he felt that the
staff needed stricter discipline. He stated that 'drill and fire-arms
training should be introduced, so that the officers may present a
smart appearance and be encouraged to take a greater interest in
their work, and to show respect for themselves as well as those
superior officers.' Opportunities should also be afforded officers
for rifle and revolver practice. Since the next part of his report is
so important, and since it is not easily accessible, it is appropriate
to record it in detail. Pennefather recommended that

> approved candidates, after passing an education examination,
> should be appointed in the first instance for 12 months only as pro-
> bationary warders, and should be gazetted as such so that they may

exercise the powers of warder under the Prisons Act. If found unsuitable at any time within that period their services should immediately be dispensed with. At the end of 12 months, having shown
themselves proficient in their drill, possessed of a knowledge of the
Prisons Act and Regulations, and found to be in all other respects
suitable, their appointment would be confirmed. They would then
rank as classified officers in, say, the fourth class, and receive a
fixed annual salary for a term of four years. After serving these
five years and having been found diligent, of good conduct, and
their general proficiency confirmed, the officers would be automatically promoted to the third class at an increased fixed salary.
After a further term of five years they would under the same conditions pass to the second class, and at the expiration of another
period of five years would pass into the first class, with an auto-
matic increase of salary . . . It should, however, be clearly laid
down that promotions from rank to rank would not follow as a
matter of course, but would depend upon officers proving themselves fitted for it. An officer found guilty of misconduct, or proving
inefficient, would be liable to reduction in rank for a certain time.[39]

Pennefather went on to suggest a system of punishments and
appeals for officers which were subsequently, as will be shown,
accepted by the system. He added a recommendation, as investigators have always done in contemplating the Western Australian
prison system, for the closure of Fremantle Prison. He noted that
the most urgent need was for a new prison, since 'regulations and
ideals are of little use without the means and facilities to do so.'[40]

The promulgation of the report of the Royal Commission did
not end parliamentary complaints. Questions about the length of
officers' hours continued, and even after some changes had been
instituted, there was an unsuccessful motion to have papers about
the dismissal of warders from Fremantle laid on the table of the
Assembly.[41] Change, and quite major change, was however
imminent.

As often seems to happen, almost coincident with the publication of a report which reflects dissatisfaction, there was a change
of administration. Octavius Burt, who had been sheriff from 1901,
retired in 1912. W. A. George, who had been superintendent at
Fremantle for many years, retired in 1911 and died soon afterwards. Dr J. W. Hope, the medical officer at Fremantle and
Rottnest, who seems to have led, professionally, a charmed life,
also resigned in 1911—'after discharging the onerous and respon-

sible duties of his Fremantle appointment with the utmost tact, skill, and conscientious recognition of their difficulties for a lengthy priod'.[42] He went on to become Commissioner of Public Health for Western Australia.

The next change was very important. This was the long awaited separation of the jobs of Sheriff and Comptroller-General. It was in 1912 that the first professional head of the prison system in Western Australia was appointed: F. D. North. Although he had other responsibilities as under-secretary, and permanent head of the Colonial Secretary's Department, he was at least a professional administrator. To the vacancy left by W. A. George was appointed Hugh Hann in 1911. He was an Englishman, who had worked in the clerical departments of three English prisons—Wormwood Scrubs, Manchester and Ruthin. In 1900 he was appointed head of prisons in Sierra Leone, and in 1906 became Superintendent of Prisons in Ceylon.[43] The importance of Hann's role in the development of prison policy in Western Australia springs from this background. Although the English prison system had only just begun a programme of reform and change after the Gladstone Report of 1895, it had firmly turned its back on much of the Victorian policy. Hann would have had some experience of the new policy and the debates and controversies preceding it, and it was this experience which made his contribution so vital in the changing situation in Fremantle.

Hann was to be an energetic, imaginative, and so inevitably controversial figure. The old guard had presumably performed as well as they could, but forty years in one prison was not likely to encourage a superintendent to innovate. Times had changed a great deal. Attitudes amongst prisoners, amongst staff and in the community at large were different, but nothing could be done until the pillars of the old system went and outsiders were brought in. The most important factor in the development of an imaginative prison system, conscious of constraint but sympathetic to possible development, is the infusion of outsiders into key positions. Hann was a very good example of this. To support them Hann and North had, for the first time in the history of the system, a political power with a real interest in the subject: the colonial secretary, J. M. Drew, who was appointed to his position in the second Labour ministry of 1911. Drew wrote two pamphlets advocating reform and chronicling what had been done.[44]

With regard to staff, there were some important changes. The first of these would appear to have been the recognition of their union in 1912, but this is little discussed, and since another was recognized later, it would appear that the 1912 union did not survive.[45] The next development was the issue in 1913 of a new set of 'Regultions relating to the management and control of the prisons of Western Australia'. These new rules, in respect of the treatment of prisoners and the specification of work and responsibility of individual staff grades, were largely identical to those of 1902.[46] But there were some important differences.

Under the new rules warders had now to undergo a twelve months' probationary period and had to pass examinations in 'duties', handwriting, spelling and arithmetic. This had been recommended by Pennefather. Staff were reminded too, rather sharply, that the prison system did not just mean Fremantle, but was a state-wide service, and transfer to any part of which was a condition of service. The main concession gained by the staff was that although they could still be guilty of committing the same prison offences as had been laid down in 1903, and for which they could be fined, reduced in pay or rank or dismissed, none of this could now happen without a 'proper enquiry being held'. This too was based on suggestions in Pennefather's Report. There was no fixed scale of fines under the new rules, as there had been under the old, but officers could be fined up to £1 by the superintendent, and up to £5 by the comptroller-general. An officer had to be charged in writing and had to plead. If he pleaded not guilty, witnesses were to be called, whose statements were recorded, and who could be cross-examined by the accused. Most important was the provision that if he was dissatisfied with the superintendent's decision, he could appeal to the comptroller-general. If the comptroller-general had heard his case in the first place and the officer was dissatisfied with *his* decision, then he could appeal to a board consisting of one person nominated by the government, one by the comptroller-general and one member of staff elected by ballot. He could not employ a solicitor, but could be assisted by an employee of the department or a secretary of a trade union. Such concessions were a big step towards some kind of proper representation for uniformed officers.

Up to the time of the Royal Commission and the appointment of Hann the treatment of prisoners throughout the state had remained fairly constant. In the prisons of the North-West, Broome, Wyndham, Roebourne and Carnarvon, as we shall see, Aboriginal prisoners continued to be chained while working on roads, on the reclaiming of marshes and other public tasks. At the end of 1904 out of 720 prisoners in the state 245 (34 per cent) were Aboriginal prisoners, 16 of whom were with the 35 white prisoners on Rottnest.[47] One of the features of the period was the enthusiasm of Aboriginal prisoners for escaping. In 1904 fifteen escaped, twelve from Wyndham alone. One of this latter group was shot dead. These attempts to escape are a subject of most Annual Reports, 1914 being especially remarkable. Four who tried to escape from Wyndham in that year were fired upon and one was killed. A road party of twenty-eight, also at Wyndham, suddenly fled. Two of them attacked a warder and took his rifle, but one of the prisoners was shot in the head with a revolver. He died, as did another who was shot in the thigh.[48]

In the south, prison management was more peaceful, if not especially exciting. By 1908 a schoolmaster had been appointed at Fremantle,[49] and in 1906 the Salvation Army opened a hostel in North Fremantle.[50] Superintendent George visited England in the same year, and afterwards recommended the establishment of evening classes and of a home for inebriates. The experiment at Hamel had not been a success because, it was suggested, of shortage of work and the shortage of suitable prisoners, and it was closed in 1907. But for the first ten years of the twentieth century the Annual Reports recorded very little that was unusual. They observed, as reports on prisons everywhere do, that most of the inmates were serving short sentences for trivial offences such as breaches of the laws in respect of fisheries and railways.

The attempt to introduce useful work ran into another classical and, so far in most prison experience, insuperable problem. Often the absence of useful work for prisoners is due to the lack of imagination and lack of industrial experience of decision makers in a prison system. In Western Australia an additional complication was the desire of Superintendent George to eliminate work outside the walls of Fremantle, which reduced the modest, useful community work which had, as has been pointed out, always been an important constituent of the Western Australian heritage.[51] Above all, attempts to initiate useful work programmes for prisoners are often blocked by a familiar argument (to which reference has been made), which is that prisoners should not be better off than free men, nor should they compete for work.

In 1906 the first protest was raised about the printing of government material in Fremantle Prison, which had recommenced some two years earlier.[52] The connection between Fremantle and the Government Printer was quite old. The *Government Gazette* was printed in Fremantle until 1870. But by 1906 organized labour was beginning to make an impact. Why, it was asked, should this printing have been carried out there, rather than in the Government Printing Office? This matter was raised again in 1908, when it was complained that 'a large amount of printing had been done in Fremantle Gaol.'[53] Does the treasurer, it was asked, 'regard it as desirable to discharge old employees of good character and long service in order that the work may be done by prisoners?' The treasurer replied that the reduction had been caused by reorganization.

On 5 August a much more extended discussion took place.[54] An interesting and typical paradox was that the discussion was initiated by Bath, who had been a leader of reformative design in the debate conducive to the 1902 Act. He objected to the 'very considerable amount' of printing done at Fremantle. He conceded that such action should be 'commended', 'but the position was that the livelihood of printers outside was involved, and if it were not for the fact that a great many were unemployed, there would be no objection.' The solution, he believed, was an extension of more institutions like Hamel, which, incidentally, was by now closed. In January 1909 he resumed his attack: 'more men employed at the book-binding trade within Fremantle Prison than are employed at the trade outside the prison.'[55] Later in the year more objections were raised.[56] This kind of *volte-face*, understandable as it may be, is calculated to leave prisoners without work, and to make prison officers extremely cynical about the sincerity of reformers.

Hann then inherited a fairly traditional system which had just been examined by a royal commissioner, and it seemed to him that the system could be improved. He emerged as a committed reformer who, to judge from his comments in Annual Reports, was not much given to restraint. In his report for 1911 he discussed the treatment of delinquent women—about whom he was always concerned—in what were for the time in a government report somewhat colourful terms:

it is a disgrace to our boasted chivalry to women, and the women of the State should see whether something could not be done, instead of rubbing delicately gloved hands together when they meet, as they must, one of their fallen sisters rolling about the streets drunk, and saying dreadful creatures![57]

It was up to Hann and the new comptroller-general to see which of the recommendations of the Royal Commission should be accepted. Their views on the report are not recorded, but Drew, the colonial secretary, regarded the report as 'the finding of a disciplinarian rather than a prison reformer'.[58] In spite of Drew's reservations, in the Annual Report for 1912, the deputy comptroller-general recounted that sixty-one recommendations of the Commission had been effected, that four had been 'partially completed', and that ten were structural and legislative suggestions, which were therefore more complicated.[59] It also happened that some important changes were made, about which Pennefather had expressed reservations himself. The most important of these, from the staff viewpoint, was the introduction of an eight-hour day, the first in an Australian prison service. The deputy comptroller-general reported, with obvious pleasure, the inaccuracy of Pennefather's prediction that additional staff would have to be appointed. In fact, at the time, staff were reduced. There were several other hopeful developments. These included improvement in staff quarters, a better scale of uniform, the abolition of white uniforms, an annual leave roster and the establishment of a departmental board which would examine the question of pay.

In respect of the treatment of prisoners the Royal Commission made a considerable difference. The most important action was the reintroduction of the marks system, which, having been introduced in 1857 into Fremantle, had been abolished in 1865 because the staff were not using it properly.[60] Prior to its reintroduction any remissions granted were on a standard scale, with provision for extra for certain acts, such as saving life, or, of all things, being a chorister! Under the new system, marks would be awarded, and if a prisoner did not earn full marks, then he would be reported. Prisoners earning full marks could buy fruit, eggs and other luxuries, and earn one quarter maximum remission. Separate 'treatment', which previously had not included those serving less than six months' hard labour, or first offenders, now included everyone except inebriates. Once again, however, this attempt to reintroduce and re-enforce separate confinement was doomed to failure. There was also some attempt to improve the female prison, and association for meals and games was now permissible.

North described other developments in this 1912 Annual Report, including regular inspections of prisons throughout the state, the establishment of a preventive detention committee, to consider cases under this new sentence which was aimed at habitual offenders, and a strong 'Prison Gate Committee'.[61] This latter meant 'that the latest and most up to date matters in this important branch of prison reform [would] be brought into operation in this State'. A prison newspaper from New South Wales, the *Compendium*, was being obtained and it was hoped to start up a newspaper in Fremantle.

Hann's report, also in the Annual Report for 1912, shows the direction in which he intended that Fremantle should go. He examined statistics in detail and pondered on their implications. He discussed the problem of women in prison at some length, and then added to the comptroller-general's list of improvements. He announced that games had been introduced, all clothing was now treated in a disinfecting room, a vegetable garden was established, which combined therapy with profit, educational classes were going well and the government had approved the introduction of international correspondence school courses. He had very definite views about such ordinary matters as prison clothing. He suggested 'the total abolition of any outward and visible sign of prison marking on clothes', and instructed that collars should be put on the shirts, that ties should be issued, together with a looking glass, a hairbrush and razors and brushes. He wanted a smarter jacket, and he wanted the whole uniform linked to the stage system. 'All our efforts at reform', he concluded, 'are thrown away unless we can make them feel that they are not mere brutes and get them to hold their heads up again like men.' It is worth noting that these simple but effective reforms were not introduced into England until some ten years after Hann had insisted upon them in Fremantle.

During his period as superintendent, Hann never lost his impetus, nor did North fail to support him. 'Fremantle Prison', the new comptroller-general noted in 1913, 'is our criminological centre and it is here the main activities of prison reform find vent.'[62] The catalogue of changes, described by Hann for 1913, is long. There was the continuing effort to enlarge the cells—a residual task from the 1899 Royal Commission—systematic extermination of vermin by injecting acid into crevices and scrubbing of hammocks. The garden had produced 9837 kilograms of vegetables, and another garden had been created, where prisoners could sit, and talk and read. Hann justified this by observing that 'their lives are black enough in all conscience'.

The female prison was improved by the addition of a visiting room, a matron's office, a reception room and a bath. The government had approved the issue of railway passes and money to selected discharged prisoners. Hann organized the forty-five white prisoners on Rottnest Island into squads on a military pattern, headed by corporals and sergeants elected by the prisoners themselves. All the Rottnest prisoners were paid, they had a canteen, and they could play games, and fish and swim. Drew, describing Rottnest, pointed out that the system there was introduced into Fremantle later, where a committee of ten was elected by the prisoners 'to assist in the maintenance of discipline, and to elevate the moral tone of the institution by the force of good example. The use of bad language within the gaol has sensibly diminished, the 52 male prisoners have taken the pledge of total abstinence.'[63]

This modified form of democracy in prisons was again many years ahead of parallel developments in other parts of the world. It heralded, though probably did not inspire the work of Thomas Mott Osborne, one of the more remarkable of the American pioneers of the attempt to involve prisoners in the running of their own affairs.[64] Perhaps the most important change was that, despite the recommendations in the reports of two Royal Commissions, Hann abolished the separate system, which he believed obsolete and damaging.

The outbreak of the First World War in 1914 did not lessen his enthusiasm. Throughout the war years there was a steady drop in the numbers in prison, which he attributed to his new methods. The response of prisoners to appeals for help in the war was also attributed to the raising of morale. It was reported in 1914, for example, that a group of prisoners had offered to go on a bread and water diet so that the money saved could be given to the Red Cross.[65] The daily average number of prisoners in Fremantle dropped steadily from 363.59 in 1912 to 317.76 in 1914, to 309.63 in 1915.[66]

It is a bold claim that a reduction in the numbers in prison is due to treatment methods, although when there is controversy, people make it. Clearly, it may be due to changes in the law, sentencing policy and a host of other variables, notably at this time the war itself. Hann, though, was a classic, convinced reformer, and had no doubts that the decrease was due to his new policies. In 1915 he decided to brighten up Christmas and issued ham, eggs, cigarettes, hung up decorations, and thereafter, because of the experience on that day, replaced eating tins with plates, basins, knives and forks. The staff benefited too from this reformative spirit. In 1915 his proposal was accepted that 'black marks' against warders for discipline offences should be expunged after a suitable period of time.[67]

One of the greatest difficulties facing the enthusiastic prison reformer lies in convincing the wider public—who have little interest in prisons, but have very decided views on how they should be administered—that new schemes are working. An attempt to do so often founders on the familiar confusion about the aims and objectives of imprisonment. Hann was convinced that the object was to reform, and was certain that the repression of earlier times had gone for good. Many people in society, especially Anglo-Saxon society, are not so sure that the elimination of deterrence is a good idea. They usually demand that prisoners be punished, or at least that they should not be manifestly better off than free men. So the reformer has to cope with a great deal of antagonism, and he can only survive it if a body, however small, of powerful articulate people are as enthusiastic about the reforms as he is himself. Hann did indeed have some strong supporters in Drew, North, the Salvation Army and others. They could help him face criticism about prison being made too easy. But from one complaint they could not save him: protest over escapes.

A policy of deterrence, because of its coercive repressive nature ensures safe custody. The change to a policy of reform involves not only a change from deterrence to reform, but an inevitable weakening of security. As important as the numbers that escape is the nature of individuals that do so, and it became apparently a matter of some concern that an undesirable feature of the much vaunted 'new penology' was more escapes. Matters came to a head in 1918, when it was reported in the press that the 'radical changes' of this 'new penology' had been the 'subject of considerable controversy', especially because of the frequency and apparent ease with which prisoners escaped.[68] A Board of Enquiry was 'highly critical of the manner in which the prison [was] conducted' at the time, several warders had been suspended, and the whole matter had been referred to the Public Service Commission.

The next day, April 5, the press announced that Hann had been suspended.[69] This incredible action was compounded by an announcement that he was being charged under the Public Service Act of being negligent or careless in the discharge of his duties, and of being inefficient or incompetent, 'such inefficiency or incompetency appearing to arise from causes within his own control'. This took place when Drew was no longer colonial secretary and North was away on sick leave. The upshot was that an enquiry was held by the Public Service Commissioner, the result of which was reported by North. 'I am glad to say', North wrote, 'that Hann had been exonerated in respect of all charges.'[70]

Very soon afterwards Hann had to retire because of ill-health. It is ironical and indeed sad that his ill-health arose 'from injuries received whilst pluckily assisting in preventing an escape from the prison'. The reformer must expect little gratitude from his contemporaries, but the historian can adjudge that Hann was probably the most important figure in the history of Western Australian prisons since the convict period.

The demise of Hann coincided with the enactment of two major pieces of prison legislation. Both were concerned with another recommendation of Pennefather, which was the introduction of an element of indeterminacy into the process of criminal justice. The first was an extensive Criminal Code Amendment which contained two clauses which introduced indeterminacy.[71] Since they were to be of considerable importance for the next forty years, it is worth quoting them in full:

> 661   When any person apparently of the age of 18 years or upwards is convicted of any indictable offence, not punishable by death, and has been previously so convicted on at least two occasions, the court before whom such person is convicted may declare that he is an habitual criminal, and direct that on the expiration of the term of imprisonment then imposed upon him, he be detained during the Governor's pleasure in a reformatory prison.
>
> 662   When any person apparently of the age of 18 years or upwards is convicted of any indictable offence, not punishable by death whether such person has been previously convicted of any indictable

2 Fremantle Prison from the clock-tower. Note the V.R. 1855 sign and Wray's gate.

3 Female accommodation in Broome Prison, 1975

4 Geraldton. One of the new converted open prisons

5 Wyndham open prison. A new converted prison in the North-
West

offence or not, the court before which such person is convicted, may, if it thinks fit, having regard to the antecedents, character, age, health, or mental condition of the person convicted, the nature of the offence or any special circumstances of the case—

(a) direct that on the expiration of the term of imprisonment then imposed upon him, be detained during the Governor's pleasure in a reformatory prison; or

(b) without imposing any term of imprisonment upon him sentence him to be forthwith committed to a reformatory prison, and to be detained there during the Governor's pleasure.

As was stated in the ensuing debates, this legislation was lifted almost entirely from the Criminal Code of the State of Victoria. There was considerable discussion in parliament about these amendments, especially sections which do not concern us here, i.e. on the subject of sexual offenders. T. Walker, the Member for Kanowna, a widely-travelled man and a staunch advocate of reform,[72] complained bitterly about the untidiness of the Bill and its intention that punishment should be increased.[73] In a later debate he said: 'I would abolish all punishment, and would adopt preventative and curative methods for all offences against society.'[74] He was supported later by Collier, who objected especially to the power given to the courts in respect of first offenders.[75] Such objections were common. Angwin, who was one of the few members who had taken the trouble to give evidence to Pennefather, wanted clause 662 entirely removed.[76]

The debates on the second piece of legislation, an amendment to the Prisons Act, was much more concerned with the specific question of the *treatment* of prisoners undergoing sentences with an indeterminate component. It was introduced into the Assembly on 5 February 1918.[77] In a brief exposition later in the month the attorney-general described how it was designed to vary the provision for preventive detention to 'an indeterminate sentence to be served in a reformatory prison'.[78] It was therefore necessary to legislate for both, and also to establish an Indeterminate Sentences Board to consider transfers from the ordinary gaol to the reformatory prison, to advise on the release of reformatory prisoners on probation and generally to superivse the system. This was necessary because the basis of the amendment was that any prisoner could be transferred to or from the reformatory institution. There was also provision for useful work. The Bill was, however, delayed, and was reintroduced in the next session of parliament in September 1918.[79]

The attorney-general now went into more detail. It was made clear that *anyone* could be given an indeterminate sentence, whereas preventive detention had been reserved for a small group of habitual offenders. Further, a reformatory prisoner could be 'released temporarily with the object of testing the reform of such person'. This was an early example of what has come to be known in several penal systems as 'home leave'. A prisoner could also be released temporarily for causes such as hospital treatment. On 1 October a lengthy, though somewhat repetitive, debate was initiated by Walker.[80] He was still complaining that the attorney-general had not gone into enough detail about the intention of all this legislation. He wanted to hear 'reference to the experiments made in other parts of the world'. His main complaint, which was repeated by him and others, was that the passing of a Bill was an empty exercise unless money was allocated to achieve the aims set out in it: 'Artificial divisions in Fremantle gaol can, in no sense, render Fremantle a reformatory institution.'

Walker wanted much more consideration given to the nature of crimial behaviour and the methods used to cope with it, which should be reformative rather than punitive. Further, it was useless expecting any initiative from people in the prison system, because all they understood was the ringing of bells, the opening of doors and 'trotting the prisoners to prayers'. For this new proposed board, men were required 'who do not start upon the assumption that all men are born with equal free-will to do as they like, and that if people do wrong it is because they want to do wrong'. He certainly did not want 'those fanatics who are to be found in every community here and there, killing time by heading charitable movements'. After a great deal of bickering, which provoked an announcement that Rottnest was a probable place for the first reformatory, the debate ended.

The committee stage was held two days later.[81] The attorney-general now mentioned Coolgardie and Albany as possible sites for a reformatory prison. This was because of continued pressure from Walker and S. M. Rocke, who before his election in October 1917 as Member for South Fremantle had spent seven years as an assistant storekeeper in Fremantle gaol.[82] Walker pointed out that he saw an ominous precedent in the situation where the government had avoided building a home for inebriates by simply setting aside part of the existing asylum as a 'home'. Walker also spent some time telling members how grateful they should be that they had been lucky enough to be where they were, and not in prison.

An amendment which proposed that no part of Fremantle gaol should be used under the Act, and which was enthusiastically supported by several members, was defeated by one vote. This narrow defeat is perhaps the most significant single event in the prison history of Western Australia. We shall go on to see how in fact a part of Fremantle gaol *was* set aside, as Walker suspected it would be. Finally there was discussion about the status of an ordinary prisoner, and how and why he could be transferred to a reformatory prison. This discussion was unsatisfactory and inconclusive because the attorney-general did not know the answers to the questions.

The discussion in the Legislative Council on 17 October was less heated.[83] It emerged that Fremantle was to be used as a classification centre for the proposed reformatories on Rottnest Island and in Coolgardie, and it was made clear that any ordinary prisoner transferred to a reformatory would not be held beyond his normal release date. The notion of 'parole', now mentioned for the first time, was expanded upon, with an assurance being given that an offender could be recalled if his behaviour on parole was unsatisfactory.

At the committee stage there was a protest about using Fremantle for reformatory purposes, and discussion about whether a period on probation in the reformatory should count if the man was returned to prison.[84] The Assembly had recommended that it should count, but a compromise was reached with the provision that it would count unless it was stated otherwise in the Order in Council which arranged the transfer.

Sir E. H. Wittenoom made his familiar contribution by observing that: 'those who go to prison nowadays do not get much punishment but that prison life is made comfortable.' He wanted the profit from the prisoners' work, which in the Bill was intended for their families and themselves on discharge, to be 'devoted to paying the cost of such person's imprisonment'. This suggestion was defeated. Another member, Holmes, in the same spirit claimed that: 'it will be necessary to commit some offence in order to learn a trade in this country.' In spite of all the objections both amendments became law, and Western Australia has ever since been committed to a policy of indeterminacy which has permeated the entire administration of criminal justice in the state.

5

1920-1960: The Regressive Years

The work of the Indeterminate Sentences Board—The 'Reformatory Prison'—Establishment of Pardelup—The open prison—The effect of the Second World War—A revival of parliamentary interest—The contribution of the Indeterminate Sentences Board—Towards indeterminacy

The end of the first decade of the century had seen the juxtaposition of a crisis in prison affairs and a change in the two key positions, those of Comptroller-General and Superintendent of Fremantle. Now at the close of the second decade this pattern was repeated, as was an announcement that the retirements had been provoked because of ill-health. Hann and North both retired in 1919. The new comptroller-general was H. C. Trethowan, but it would appear that the authorities were not going to repeat what probably seemed to them on reflection to have been a mistake, which was the recruitment of an outsider to Fremantle. The new superintendent, A. T. Badger, had worked in prisons in Western Australia since 1895 and had had experience at prisons in the North-West of the state.

From a governmental standpoint these appointments were shrewd, since neither man created any trouble. The next thirty years were to be the most placid in the history of the system. The exercise of a caution which obviates any embarrassment for governments has obviously certain other effects which may be regarded as disadvantageous. The most inevitable of these is the stagnation which is partner to stability. There is inherent in the situation an even greater danger which is that regression may take place. A notable tendency in prison systems is that failure to develop, results in a movement backwards. Stability and, Pardelup apart, stagnation were to be the key-notes of prison administration in Western Australia for almost the whole of the next forty years.

There were no dramatic changes, nor even new patterns, in the make-up of the prison population during the period under review. The daily average in 1919 was typical enough: 266.93, of whom 101.36 were Aborigines. The total number of individual prisoners who received sentences in the year was 970. Out of the 1581 offences committed by this group, 514 were for drunkenness, 96 for disorderly conduct, 50 for being idle and disorderly, 40 for using obscene language, 32 for cattle killing, 52 for common assault and 3 for murder.[1]

Such a pattern is typical of most prison systems. Contrary to popular belief most prisoners are convicted of minor offences. One has to look hard in a prison to find examples of the villain whose physical appearance would confirm the naive Lombrosian theory which has been encapsulated in the prison genre of the Hollywood film. Further, most prisoners serve only very short sentences. In 1920, for example, only fifty-one prisoners had been awarded sentences of over one year.[2]

The Badger regime in Fremantle did, however, achieve one important aim: the number of escapes dropped. For a few years after he took over, there were no escapes, although in 1923 there was doubtless some excitement because of the fact that the only escapee in that year was a woman! In the other prisons escaping occurred sporadically, notably at the troublesome Wyndham, where seventeen prisoners disappeared in 1919.[3]

Another general administrative characteristic exemplified by the Western Australian prison system at the time was a tendency for indifferent administrators to make a virtue of measures of economy. There was, of course, a need for economy in the inter-war years, but the attempt to reduce expenditure in the Western Australian prison system was very subtle. Two examples may be given. In 1919 it was reported that 'the tabulated statements are not attached to the printed report, but such are available for reference.'[4] Henceforth the Annual Reports became short and repetitive, but this was not solely due to the need for economy. The sheer absence of developments to report was certainly a factor. Had it not been for the reports of the Indeterminate Sentences Board, which from 1920 onwards were appended to them, and the opening of Pardelup, which became a great solace to people trying to compile a report about a moribund situation, the reports would certainly have been devoid of interest.

In 1929 this particular economy was complete. From then until 1961, thirty-two years later, Annual Reports continued to be laid on the table of the parliament, but were not, generally, printed. For two years, 1945 and 1946, there appear to have been no reports at all. For many years in the 1930s the wording of the Annual Reports is identical year after year. Another 'saving' was effected by a progressive conversion of common gaols to police gaols, which because of the reduction in staffing facilities were less expensive to run. By 1928 it was reported that of the twenty-one institutions that the Department of Prisons administered, only three were common gaols. The bulk of the department, therefore, consisted of lock-ups, where nothing was done at all except to detain prisoners.

There were a few developments during these years. There was the opening of Pardelup in 1927, to which we will return. But the rest were minor, even trivial. Although there was no cohesive system of after-care, assistance to released prisoners continued its extraordinarily erratic course. In 1922, going on one of its periodic upturns, it was announced that after-care was 'of a more generous character than hitherto'. The Prison Gate Committee did its modest work, a feature of which became the giving of lectures and concerts in Fremantle. The provision of adequate work continued to be difficult, a situation which was not helped by an announcement that the Government Printer had restricted the amount of printing carried out in Fremantle.[5] Undoubtedly this was the consequence of the ceaseless agitation which has already been discussed.

Other 'reformatory' highlights are remarkable only because of their rarity. In 1924 a prisoner newspaper was started at Fremantle and in the same year:

> A delegate representing all the prisoners in the gaol now attends the cook and bakehouse daily in order to see that the food received is according to regulations, and that each prisoner received his proper proportion of food according to the class of diet he is entitled to.

Just why this practice, which is still continued, was instituted was not explained. There are two possibilities: one is that there was trouble or incipient trouble over food, and this was a managerial device to offset it; the other is that it was a concession to democracy. The latter is the less likely, but in any case if it was, it was a very pale imitation of Hann's efforts to introduce an element of self-government into prisons.

Altogether it is clear that most of the training described was really only a veneer. In 1925 for example, it was claimed that in

Fremantle 'special attention' was being given to educationally-backward prisoners. The amount can be gauged from the example quoted: one youth had been taught to read by a fellow prisoner.[6] Gradually, the professional teacher, who had been albeit erratically part of the scene since the 1850s, disappeared altogether. For many years it was reported that the duties of a schoolmaster were performed by an inmate.[7] One incident, which was not elaborated upon, was a riot in Fremantle in 1929. The causes, course and outcome of this was not described in the Annual Report. All that is noted in the report for 1930 is that in March 1929 there was a riot and that 111 prisoners were involved.

In respect of staff in Fremantle, each year Badger reported 'cordial relations' between the gaol officers' association and himself, and indeed there is no evidence, in these years, of dissatisfaction amongst the staff. In several respects their conditions improved, as in 1922, when the establishment of telephone links between the prison and the warders' quarters meant the ending of reserve duty, which had necessitated sleeping in and which had always been greatly disliked.[8] Again, in 1927 the staff were given a forty-eight-hour week, with a day off on an average in each week.[9]

Much later in the period under review there were two significant changes in the organization of the staff. In 1949 the most senior officers, that is to say chief officers and superintendents, were brought under the Public Services Act. This allegedly was prompted by a strike of staff at the Claremont Mental Hospital in 1947, and the raising of the status of senior staff was intended to remove them from the officers' union, to which, hitherto, everyone in the prison service had belonged. As in many other prison systems, including England, this elevation of senior staff resulted in their joining a very large civil service union, or association, in which they have very little influence. The move does however ensure that the whole prison staff cannot easily unite against the government.

This was to lead to dissatisfaction on the part of senior ranks, both because they increasingly became weak in bargaining terms, and because the staff structure was fragmented. The consequence was that any benefits gained by union members were not now applicable to senior ranks. In recent years the hope of some senior ranks has been that the recently formed Federation of Prison Officers Union of Australia would have some chance of realigning all ranks in the prison services into a cohesive unit.[10]

The only other major development in terms of staff structure occurred in the next year. Another dusty recommendation of the 1899 Royal Commission was finally accepted. Since the appointment of F. D. North in 1911, the under-secretary in the Chief Secretary's Department had been the Comptroller-General of Prisons. In 1950 these two ranks were finally split and a full-time Comptroller-General was appointed.

These events were some way ahead. The moratorium of the 1920s, 30s and 40s in prison development was reflected in the slight parliamentary interest in prison affairs. There were occasional isolated questions, such as one about the conditions under which solicitors could visit prisoners,[11] or another about the cost of keeping prisoners in Fremantle.[12] Of more significance was the first of a number of questions about the establishment of a prison farm.[13] There was only one long discussion on the subject of prisoners, and which was only incidental to the matter of imprisonment itself. This was about the transporting of prisoners, especially between Perth and Fremantle. There was considerable objection to their exposure to public view, and the debate was quite lengthy, in spite of the Minister of Justice's opinion that: 'While there is perhaps some need for improvement, the matter is not so vital that the business of the State should be stopped while the House gives attention to it.'[14] The outcome was a resolution that the system should be changed, since it was, as one member said, the case that 'every time a prisoner comes down it is a perfect zoo.'[15] It was to be some twelve years before prisons were even mentioned again.

The main task of the prison system after 1918 was, of course, the implementation of the new provision for indeterminate sentences. It will be remembered that the Prisons Act Amendment (31 of 1918) ordered the establishment of reformatory prisons, and the Criminal Code Amendment (32 of 1918) allowed for new kinds of sentences to be awarded. Now if a person was over eighteen and was convicted of an indictable offence and had two previous convictions, he could be declared a habitual criminal. This meant that after completion of a fixed sentence awarded by the court he could be detained in a reformatory prison during the governor's pleasure. Another clause allowed the court to hand down the same sentence, even if the previous convictions were not present. The court could also simply award a person a sentence that he be detained during the governor's pleasure without a preliminary fixed term. Finally, an ordinary prisoner could be transferred to a reformatory prison, the advantage of this procedure to him being that he then became eligible for parole or probation in the same way as those confined during the governor's pleasure. The whole of the post-sentence period was to be administered by the Indeterminate Sentences Board.

With regard to the operation of the system in the early days, the gloomy predictions of parliamentary critics were fully realized. Despite their hope that prison officials would not be on the Board, Badger was appointed as one of the members. As time went on his position must have become stronger, since other members resigned and retired. He was in the classic position of accruing information and therefore power, because he was the constant factor in a fluid situation. In respect of the 'reformatory prison' their expectations were similarly fulfilled. As they had forecast, a part of Fremantle was designated a reformatory prison. The reformatory prisoners consigned there were allegedly kept apart, but it is evident from a cursory glance at the Annual Reports that at least at work they associated with the ordinary prisoners.

There was some discussion in the Annual Reports of the early 1920s on the subject of building a reformatory prison, and at first the intention was that it would be built on Rottnest Island. There, experience was showing that far from the growth of tourism expediting the evacuation of prisoners, quite the reverse was happening. The authorities were relying more and more on free prison labour to develop and maintain the facilities. Then in 1922 it was announced that a site had been picked at Whitby Falls for a farm colony. In that year the Indeterminate Sentences Board was responsible for fifteen prisoners, ten of whom were at Fremantle and five of whom were at Rottnest.[16]

The new Board had a disastrous beginning. There were three resignations and three appointments in less than two years, because apparently it was difficult to find 'members who took that interest in the work which is so essential to make it a success'.[17] But at last there was a modicum of stability, and the Board settled to its task. By 1923 seventy-four prisoners had been dealt with, fifty-eight of whom had been transferred, on their recommendation, from ordinary imprisonment to reformatory imprisonment. The Board allowed 'temporary release' to six men in 1923, which the members felt was a better process than 'probationary release'.[18] The difference was that the former meant that the prisoner was obliged to maintain contact with the Board itself, which could be done discreetly, making it possible for his background to remain unknown to members of the community in which he lived. Probation, which legally was a mandatory sequel to the 'temporary release' process, later called parole, required that he had to report to the police 'or some society', the most likely outcome of which would be that his status would soon be common knowledge. This observation is an interesting comment on the claims of police harrassment which had been discussed years before.

The Board quickly learned something else about governments and prison systems. This was that the fiction of declaring parts of Fremantle as reformatory, combined with a constant government plea that money was short was certain, as time went on, to put off, perhaps forever, the establishment of a special, genuinely-reformatory institution. Already by 1923 they were conscious of this, and in their report for that year took a firm stand. Pointing out that a prison farm had been asked for in every report since the Board was founded they added: 'Unless soemthing is done soon in the direction indicated the Board feel that their sphere of usefulness being so limited, they must consider the question of resigning their position as members of the Board.'[19]

Far from this threat leading to any improvement, the situation deteriorated and the fiction that Fremantle was a reformatory continued. In the same year in which the Board threatened to resign, Rottnest 'reformatory' was closed and the inmates were transferred to Fremantle. The move necessitated the declaration of a part of Number 3 Division in Fremantle as a reformatory prison. The attempt to leave Rottnest was, like all previous efforts, abortive since the island could still not survive without prison labour. In 1924 the 'salt house' prison on the island was fully operational and had a daily average of 30.75 'ordinary' prisoners.[20]

The situation now verged on the farcical. The knocking together of two cells to make one, which had been carried on spasmodically since the 1899 Royal Commission, was continued. Now though, the implication was that this operation was in some way associated with the development of reformatory facilities, and its genesis in a twenty-five-year old report seems to have been forgotten.[21] On several occasions the Board observed that reformatory inmates 'are well cared for, and seem to be contented in their roomy, well ventilated, and comfortable cells'.[22] The superintendent for his part reported that he was trying:

> to make the best possible use of that portion of the prison gazetted as a reformatory prison by making the environment as bright as circumstances will permit, with the hope that the inmates will believe the authorities are endeavouring to reform them, and that they in turn will reform and lead better and straightforward lives on their release.[23]

The same year in which this was reported, 1926, the superintendent of Fremantle had to deal with an unusual change in the prison population. In that year there was an increase of 100 per cent in the committals of prisoners born in Great Britain, due to their refusal to perform their duty under maritime law. A quarter of the prison population for that year consisted of British seamen.

The situation became Kafkaesque when the Board began to declare solemnly that 'During the year one inmate in the reformatory, owing to his bad conduct, was transferred back to Fremantle prison as an ordinary prisoner.'[24] In 1925 two of the Board members did resign. The ostensible reasons were not because of dissatisfaction, but in the case of one because of business pressure, and in the case of the other transfer to another state. The new members were probably consoled by the distinct possibility that a farm would be bought and would become the reformatory prison. The idea of a prison farm was one which appealed to many people in the community. A typical view was given in the periodical *Women's Co-operation* which, in commenting on prisons, supported the idea: 'Prison farms where nature can take a hand in her usual miraculous fashion in the healing of sick minds, will do infinitely more to effect a real reformation than can ever be done by prison walls.'[25] After a series of rather evasive replies in parliament on the subject, such as that which pointed out that 'although considerable attention' had been given to the matter, 'no definite statement' could be made,[26] in 1927 Pardelup was proclaimed a prison farm.

Pardelup is 29 kilometres west of Mt Barker in the south-west of the state. It is an old established property which was settled early in the colony's development. This fact Drew, chief secretary at the time, believed to be an asset because the prisoners sent there were 'continually confronted with examples of conquest over the very great difficulties and hardships'.[27] It was bought for £7000 for the double purpose of setting up a pine plantation and a prison farm. For the latter 1337 hectares, 606 of which were first class, were set aside. The land was suitable for fruit-growing, live-stock and crops. The existing buildings had to be adapted to their new purpose, and a start was made when the first four prisoners were transferred from Fremantle in mid-July 1927. A year later there were nineteen prisoners and three officers there, and the intention was that eventually there would be forty prisoners and four officers. The new arrivals earned 4*s* a week, 2*s* of which could be spent on extras such as eggs, tobacco and newspapers. There was naturally a great deal of freedom, since the estate is entirely unfenced (except for the control of animals), and according to Drew the prisoners responded to this trust by working voluntarily at those critical periods which inevitably occur in the farming seasons.[28]

The potential in the site, both for agriculture and reform, seemed to the initiators to be considerable. It quickly became the show-piece of the prison system, and was constantly pointed to as proof that 'both in legislation and in practice, Western Australia is well in the forefront of the most modern ideas in penology and crimin-ology'.[29] This belief is frequently expressed in the brief comments made in the official visitors' book at Pardelup. The theme of all these remarks is of satisfaction. 'The staff', one typical entry in 1950 reads, 'has the prisoner's welfare at heart and one feels that every effort is made to assist the inmates to rehabilitate them-selves.' 'Contentment', wrote one visitor, 'is reflected in the face of everyone in the area including staff and their families as well as inmates.'[30]

More of the satisfaction was due to the success of the agricul-tural enterprise than it was to less-easily-measured success in re-forming prisoners. Nevertheless it must be conceded that the opening of Pardelup was showing great enterprise and was well in advance of what was happening in many other countries. England, for instance, which at the time was leading the world in prison reform, did not open its first open prison for adults, New Hall, Yorkshire, until 1936, nine years after Pardelup. The latter re-mained a beacon in an increasingly-drab penal landscape. Un-fortunately the enthusiasm generated by its inception, as had happened before in Western Australia, was not sustained. There was nothing quite like it again until the expansion of open establishments in very recent years.

It is now half a century since the notion of truly-open, reformative institutions was introduced into the administration of prisons. Before that there had, of course, been chain-gangs in remote districts of several countries, but these cannot be classed as 'open', since they had no reformative aim at all. The establishment of open prisons was an important turning point in prison history, and after many years of experience it is possible to generalize about some universal features of their origins and methods of operation, features which Pardelup has exemplified very well.

There is first the question as to why an open prison is established at all. The obvious answer is that given by the reformer, which is that it provided a welcome and wholesome contrast to the heavy oppression of the classic Victorian fortress. The fact that prisoners can buy eggs, play football and wash when they want to, seems to reformers to be justification enough for an open regime. The latter has another, less controversial advantage. This is simply economic. A constant complaint about prisons is their cost, so little of which is offset by prisoners' work. This constantly recurrs in parliamentary debates in Western Australia and is usually accompanied by demands that prisoners should be given useful work, which would be good both for them and for the community. This argument is unanswerable and leads to the unusual spectacle of reformers and the punitive opposition joining forces to encourage the development of open prisons. In fact, the economic argument is the only one which encourages modification of those reactionary attitudes which constantly confront the reformer. Drew in his early remarks about the success of Pardelup was quick and wise to point out that already a ton of jam had been made and sold by the Department of Prisons to the Aborigines Department.[31] In addition to these general pressures, there was in Western Australia a special factor. This was the expressed resentment of the Indeterminate Sentences Board, and presumably prison officials, over the hypocracy in which they had been forced to indulge because of governmental failure to implement the 1918 legislation properly. The situation was increasingly intolerable, since Fremantle, it seemed to critics, was rapidly degenerating into one of the worst prisons in Australia.

The next feature of open prisons is that they tend to distort the reality of a prison system. They are given great prominence in accounts of the system—Pardelup again being a very good case in point—and it is easy to lose sight of the fact that the numbers who go to open prisons are so small that they make very little real impact on the total numbers incarcerated. At the most, in the 1930s, there was a daily average of forty to fifty prisoners there. The bulk of the prisoners in the state continued to live under traditional conditions, notably at Fremantle. An analysis of the distribution of the prison population of any country will reveal the same phenomenon. Nevertheless, in spite of this caveat it should be pointed out that a mere head count of numbers is an inadequate method of assessing the impact and success of the open prison.

Perhaps the most important contribution it makes overall is to introduce into a traditional system a commitment to training or treatment which can, and usually does, permeate the rest of the system. The establishment of a manifestly more liberal regime will tend to attract more liberal staff, who see in the new developments an opportunity to engage in constructive remedial work. Promotions and transfers mean that such people will move from one institution to another, which can stimulate an inquiry into alternative ways of operating in the more traditional establishment. The clearest example of this fact is the English borstal system, which has always been part of the prison complex, and which is designed for those under twenty-one. The development of the English borstal in the 1920s and 30s under the direction of Alexander Paterson remains one of the most spectacular events in penal history. To make the system work Paterson relied on the recruitment of senior staff from *outside* the service, often of a high educational standard, most of whom later worked in traditional closed prisons. Often, they took their training experience in borstal with them. So the open institution, however small, has this important role as an agent of change.[32] This role is recognized and, of course, deplored by those who do not subscribe to the desirability of introducing reformative policies into prisons.

Although the whole business at first looks simple enough, the open prison soon presents administrators with a dilemma. This is that the persistent offenders who need those very opportunities and resources it allegedly offers, tend to be the very people who, because they *are* persistent, are the least likely to be sent. The people who are sent tend to be those with the lighter record. Thus the paradoxical situation occurs that those with the greatest need for some kind of help get least, and those who need the least get most. The operation of the reformatory sentence in Western Australia shows this. This was aimed at habituals, who were poor prospects. But the legislation allowed, as we have seen, for the conversion of an ordinary sentence to a reformatory sentence in those cases where the prospects were good. The 1918 legislation, and Pardelup therefore, had to try to do two mutually exclusive jobs: to help those for whom there was hope, and detain those for whom there was none. The ultimate reality of the selection process for the open prison is that almost the sole criterion becomes the likelihood of escape, and because of the offence, or behaviour when on the run, the degree of embarrassment likely to arise.

The style of management of an open prison is a compound of reward and threat of punishment. Much to the disappointment of reformers the excitement of the new venture wears off and new generations of prisoners are no longer grateful for the opportunity they are being given. The open prison becomes a normal variant of the system, and appeals for good behaviour so as not to jeopardize the establishment begin to fail. An early claim of the builders of open prisons is that there are no escapes. This soon changes, and the beginning and the increase of escapes is a sure sign that that prison is entering a new phase in its career. As the situation deteriorates, community reaction is prompt, and when prison was discussed, as it was only rarely in parliament during the 1930s and 40s, it was Pardelup which was usually the topic. The subject matter was, of course, escaping. Such a situation arose in 1945, when four men absconded from Pardelup, and when recaptured broke out of the Mt Barker lock-up.[34] It was pointed out that one was convicted of violence and one of incest. Later 'grave concern among residents living on the farms in the district' was reported over the number of escapes.[35] During the next few days the question of compensation for thefts committed by escaping prisoners was raised, and a further question was asked as to the truth of the allegation that Pardelup prisoners had stolen three cans of cream from a farm, a motor vehicle and some goods, but had nevertheless made a prompt appearance on parade in the prison the next day. This was admitted to be true.[36] In another debate Pardelup was described by its implacable enemy, Watts, Member for Katanning, as 'a menace to the surrounding territory'.

6 & 7   Two of the drawings in the elaborate cell in Fremantle

8 Moondyne Joe's cell,
Fremantle Prison

9 Aboriginal prisoner's paintir
Fremantle Prison

The nine escapes which had taken place in 1942 were 'not viewed favourably by the people in that district'. When Watts was asked if the Pardelup prisoners were in his constituency, he replied: 'Unfortunately; by reason of this infernal prison system, they are; but as they have no electoral rights I am not very much concerned about them.'[37]

The main reward which can be offered to prisoners to counter the temptation to escape is of course being allowed to stay in the prison. This privilege is of such value that it soon becomes easy for the burden of maintaining stability in the institution to be shifted from the staff to the prisoners. In the case of work, for example, the prisoners are expected to perform satisfactorily. If they do not, they know that they will be returned to the closed institution. So a group ethos develops which expresses itself in intolerance to those members who do not work sufficiently hard. This is the way in which Russian prison camps are managed, where failure to achieve a work target results in sanctions against the whole group. In the same way the Pardelup prisoners soon found it necessary to set up what they called a 'Fairway Club' which was approved of by the authorities since it was designed to ensure that no one shirked: 'The Fairway Club is functioning well, has been of material assistance to the officers, and has by "moral suasion" [*sic*] induced the inmates to "play the game" by honouring their word to the Superintendent.'[38]

Quite how this 'club' operated was not explained, but generalizing from other experience, it was probably extremely harsh in its treatment of those incurring its censure. In this balance of reward and punishment lies the skill of the good open-prison administrator. Skilful management is essential, since there is always determined if small opposition to open prisons, and indeed Watts might well have caused Pardelup to be closed if a new prison had been built.

While such episodes were annoying to local residents, and causing a mild embarrassment to the prison authorities when they were raised in parliament, they were trivial affairs. After the opening of Pardelup the only major administrative landmark was the issue of a revised set of prison regulations in 1940.[39] They were the most extensive so far, and while much in the earlier regulations was retained, some rules were expanded and others introduced. In the section dealing with staff there were the usual, by now slightly anachronistic relics of Victorianism such as those which ordained that officers had to live in quarters and could not have guests, except with the permission of the officer in charge of the prison . They were forbidden to canvass for appointments or promotions and they had to guard against 'familiarity' with prisoners—a certain indication that the officer's role was still custodial. An offence which was peculiar to Western Australia was once again reiterated: this was 'wrangling' between officers. Slight modification of one rule occurs in the statement that no officer could discuss the prison with any outsider, but an exception was made of the union, to whom he could communicate 'such information as is necessary'.

From the rules affecting prisoners it is clear that irons had not been abolished, since authority is given to the officer in charge to use them if necessary. 'Chinese and other foreign prisoners' were to be acquainted with regulations—a job assigned to the chief warder. There were no fewer than nine complicated diets for different categories of prisoners, besides different regimes. Thus a prisoner under sentence of imprisonment only, as opposed to hard labour, could provide his own food and clothing, while debtors retained their historic privileges such as letters and the right to maintain themselves. There is in the rules a quaint reminder of how quickly times change. This is the instruction that the tails of hair worn by the Chinese could not be cut off 'except when convicted of a crime after having previously undergone a sentence for some criminal offence in the State, or when especially recommended by the medical officer'.

The Second World War, which broke out in 1939, brought major problems. The most difficult of these was the decision to evacuate Fremantle because of the possibility of bombing. In March 1942 the women were sent to the police gaol at York. Unfortunately, because of the enthusiastic operations of the Special Police Squad the York prison population rose and the women had to be returned to Fremantle.

The difficulty involved in finding accommodation for approximately 200 men may be imagined, especially since the military authorities took over Broome Prison. Added to the fact that there simply was not another closed prison of a comparable size in the state, was the demand of the armed services for public buildings. Eventually it was decided that a new prison would have to be opened, and the site chosen was Barton's Mill, just outside Perth. A barbed-wire fence was soon erected, tents were put up, and in

April 1942 the prisoners moved in. On the first night thirteen escaped. The situation was, of course, difficult. In spite of this the staff came in for their share of criticism, since 'not all were able to live up to the strain imposed by the difficult and novel conditions, and in some cases disciplinary action was necessary.' The perimeter of the prison was forthwith strengthened.

Despite these troubles the Barton's Mill experience, with all its difficulties, evidently brought new life to the prison service. The first account of the operation at the prison was positively enthusiastic.[40] The move out of Fremantle benefitted both staff and prisoners, although there were casualties in both groups. It was reported that the experience enabled the staff 'to visualise a gaol, which [would] not only hold offenders against society, but [would] restore some of them to society'. One prisoner, it was noted, within forty-eight hours of arrival had installed a complete hot-water system for the improvised hospital. There is little doubt that the amount of work which had to be done, which was considerable, was of great advantage. This included permanent accommodation, workshops and cookhouses.

The problem of escapers was, naturally, difficult. Eventually an agreement was reached with the military, who had taken over Fremantle, that one division in the prison should be set aside so that recalcitrant prisoners could be sent there from Barton's Mill. The total experience of the establishment and organization of Barton's Mill seems to have rejuvenated prison administration in the state: 'Nor will the lessons of Barton's Mill be lost when plans for a complete and up-to-date gaol are being made.' Barton's Mill was, however, closed in 1975 before any 'up-to-date gaol' had been built.

In October 1945 the chief secretary initiated a debate which always interests people—the need for a new prison and its possible site, especially since he named Claremont, a residential area of metropolitan Perth, as a possibility.[41] Along with several other speakers, he felt very strongly when he said: 'Fremantle Gaol is a relic of the past, and should be replaced with a new institution based on modern conceptions of prison administration and control.'

It is one thing to agree on the need for a new prison, but it is quite another to decide where it should be built. Even before the Claremont proposal had been announced, the chief secretary had

encountered organized opposition from people who objected to
the establishment of a prison anywhere in the metropolitan area.
It was decided after a great deal of discussion, mainly about who
should serve on it, to set up a committee to look at the problem.
This committee would be 'an education to some of our members'
and would assist the prisons department 'to solve what has been a
very embarrassing problem for some considerable time past'.

In the Legislative Assembly on the same day, 3 October, Hill,
the Member for Albany, proposed the establishment of a royal
commission and moved:

> That in the opinion of this House the Government should immedi-
> ately appoint a Royal Commission, including at least one person
> from outside Western Australia with a wide knowledge of modern
> methods of penology, to inquire into and report upon—(a) better
> methods of management and administration for this State; (b) the
> site for the necessary new gaol or gaols, and the best types of build-
> ings to suit modern ideas and ensure safe custody; (c) desirable
> amendments to our prison laws; (d) any other matters calculated to
> improve gaol conditions and to assist in the reform of prisoners
> who are capable of reformation without exposing prison staff or
> any other citizens to undue risks of loss or injury.

During the course of a long speech he discussed crime in the
state and its treatment, but ultimately his motion was unsuccessful. This was regrettable, since a major overhaul of the system
was indeed due, and the wide-ranging areas of investigation suggested by Hill would have gone some way to remedying major
defects that had persisted and worsened. Two of the most notable
of these were the absence of a properly organized system of after-
care for prisoners and of special treatment for serious offenders
under the age of twenty-one. In both these respects other countries, notably England, had made considerable progress in the
previous forty years. The failure to pass his motion resulted in the
prison system having no stimulus for many years.

A committee did sit to look into the question of the site for the
new prison, but very little came out of their work. In 1949 it was
announced that a site in the Melville and Canning districts was
being considered,[42] and in the next year that Bulls Creek in Canning had been chosen.[43] Work would start 'in the indefinite future'.
But four years later it was stated that no site had yet been selected.[44]

The situation in the years after 1945 really became rather critical.

As forecast by the chief secretary in his speech, and as is usual after wars, the prison population started to rise. By 1949 there was a daily average of 364.76 in the prisons of the state. On 30 June 1949 there were 303 white males, 30 Aboriginal males, 11 white females, and 5 Aboriginal females in prison.[45] The situation was made more difficult because of the neglect suffered by buildings which had been used by the military during the war. Just how bad the situation was is a little difficult to judge, since for 1945, 1946, 1948 and 1951 no reports were made by the Department of Prisons—which in itself may be of considerable significance. The one noticeable development was the appointment by the Department of Education in 1950 of a full-time teacher to Fremantle to take classes for illiterate prisoners. By 1954 education had expanded to the extent that thirty prisoners a day in Fremantle were attending school, and thirty-six were taking correspondence courses.[46] In addition there were programmes of educational films.

The end of the 1950s saw the winding up of the Indeterminate Sentences Board because of the passing of legislation—which will be described later. Their last report was made for the years 1963-64, and a summary of the work of the Board since its foundation recounted that since its inception in 1919 the Board had dealt with 1077 inmates, an average of about thirty a year.[47] During the last years of its existence the Board had been a valuable agent for reform, and there is no doubt that its agitation about the conditions of the prisons stopped the prison system in Western Australia from disappearing entirely from public scrutiny. It was in the early 1950s that the Board began to take a much broader interest in what was going on in the prison system, and discussed matters which were strictly, not their concern. In 1953 for example, it drew attention to a sinister problem which had been produced by the introduction of indeterminacy.

In previous years the government, through the Department of Native Affairs, had control of several institutions to which Aborigines could be sent when they were released on probation or parole. These places were in the 1950s being handed over to religious organizations, and the Board suggested that the prison department should reserve the right to place ex-prisoners in these institutions. The Aborigines 'are deserving of something better than permanent imprisonment'. Because of this changed situation the position was arising when the only reason why a prisoner continued to be locked up was that there was nowhere for him to go.[48] In one case an elderly Aborigine was held from 1953 until 1960 when he died, with the Board reporting each year that he could and should be released. Such a situation easily arises where prisoners are docile, sentences are indeterminate and after-care arrangements haphazard. If the policy is to be one of indeterminacy, then a properly constructed set of after-care arrangements is a priority.

In 1957, by which time a prison welfare officer had been appointed,[49] the Board recommended the appointment of a probation officer, the extension of Pardelup and its division into three units: one for alcoholics, one for young offenders and one for first offenders. The Board were the first people to express concern about the rise in the numbers of Aboriginal prisoners, suggesting the need for a special prison. They also registered a protest at the practice of sending old people to serve indeterminate sentences, since they would probably never be released. In 1960 they developed the case for an alcoholic unit.[50] During that year, they pointed out, 3 alcoholics had been sent to prison a total of 77 times, and in the same period 462 individuals had been gaoled for drunkenness in Fremantle and Perth alone, between them accumulating 1351 committals. Had the Board not been abolished, it would probably have been of great help to the prison department, since at the beginning of the 1960s it needed all the support it could muster. The prison population continued to rise to what were for Western Australia formidable proportions. In 1954 and 1955 the daily average was 490.77,[51] in 1957-58 it was 628.02,[52] in 1961-62 it had risen to 714.89,[53] and the effects of this pressure were now beginning to be felt.

Not only had the numbers risen, but there was detectable a change in the composition of the prison population for the first time in many years. The people being sent at the beginning of the 1960s were, it was claimed, noticeably younger, a claim which cannot easily be investigated because of the curiosity that statistics in the Annual Reports do not include the ages of prisoners. Not only was it claimed that the prisoners were getting younger, but they were proving more difficult to handle. Prison punishments increased steadily: there was a rise from 283 to 353 between 1957 and 1959,[54] and in 1962, for the first time in many years, a prisoner was birched in Fremantle.[55] The juveniles, described in one year as 'completely lawless', were causing additional problems,[56] since because of their bad behaviour many of them were not suitable for open conditions.[57]

The other important change in the composition of the prison population was an increase in the number of Aborigines in prison, especially young men and women. In June 1949 out of 333 men in prison 30 were Aboriginal (9.009 per cent), and out of 35 women 5 were Aboriginal (15.6 per cent).[58] In 1961-62 out of a daily average of 679.38, 106.44 were Aborigines (15.7 per cent), and out of 35.51 women 19.57 (55.1 per cent) were Aboriginal.[59] Another set of figures demonstrates the same change. In 1963-64, the year in which the Indeterminate Sentences Board was abolished, the backgrounds of the major groups being sent to prison in Western Australia were:

Born in Western Australia (Aboriginal): 1053 males, 384 females, total 1437.

Born in Western Australia (white): 1667 males, 63 females, total 1730.[60]

Some years before this, in 1953, J. B. Sleeman, MLA for Fremantle, who had succeeded in changing the degrading system of transferring prisoners some twenty-eight years before, rose to his feet in the Assembly and initiated a far-reaching proposal: 'That in the opinion of this House, the Minister for Justice should bring down a Bill providing for the parole of prisoners similar to the Canadian Act.'[61]

In the course of a long speech Sleeman was critical of the present system and wished there to be more flexibility, as was the case in a number of countries and as had been proposed in Victoria. He gave a detailed exposition of the system in Canada, which was his model. Everyone who spoke, including the Minister of Justice, supported him, but were seemingly unable to understand his main point. This was that the opportunity for the shortening of a sentence in Western Australia was confined to those undergoing 're-formatory' training. He wished the *entire* prison population, apart from a few dangerous offenders, to be given a chance of getting parole. He found it difficult to conceal his frustration when Members on the one hand expressed support for his motion, but on the other hand claimed that the Western Australian system was superior to that which he proposed. Of one Member he said: 'he cannot agree with me and yet vote against my motion.'[62]

The Minister of Justice reported to the Assembly that he had discussed the matter with the prison authorities and with other law officers. He then delivered a summary of the situation as it seemed to him, and his colleagues: 'It is the opinion of the Comptroller-General that the Western Australian system is as good as anywhere in the world.' He then went on to compare it with the Canadian system and concluded that the Western Australian system 'achieves the same aim of the Canadian system but by a better method'.[63]

Sleeman—who incidentally went on to a very distinguished political career—was no doubt baffled at the confused views expressed in the Assembly. The situation became even more confused because his motion was successful, although nothing was done at once. He had, however, planted the seed which was to germinate ten years later, when parole was to be introduced into the Western Australian penal system and was to dominate, as it continues to dominate, the administration of criminal justice.

6

The Imprisonment of Aborigines

Attitudes and policy—Rottnest Island—Superintendent Vincent—
Allegations of cruelty—The legislature and Aboriginal imprison-
ment—Further ¯allegations—Enquiries—Closure of Rottnest—
Aboriginal prisoners in the twentieth century

So far in this account of imprisonment in Western Australia we have
made passing reference to the imprisonment of Aborigines. Because
of the importance of this question and because of its increasing
importance in recent years, this will now be discussed in more depth.

An analysis of the history of the imprisonment of Aborigines in
Western Australia reveals that this part of the penal experience
may be divided into three periods. These periods are demarcated
by what may be loosely described as varying 'policies', which, as
always in penal administration, are a microcosm of what is happening in the wider society. There was first, the period from the
founding of the colony until the end of the nineteenth century.
During these years a liberal tone was expressed in the attitude of
some pioneers, which was encouraged, and even insisted upon by
the imperial government and those pressure groups which during
the life of the British Empire interested themselves in the treatment of natives. It was this liberal tradition which was such an
embarrassment to people like Superintendents Vincent and Jackson in Rottnest Island prison. The dominant white attitude though,
was a dislike of the native population, which in the early years
was generated by fear.

There is for present purposes little point in trying to adjudicate
on degrees of justification for mutual killing. It is enough to note
that when the Aborigines were a physical force to be reckoned
with, it appeared to the Victorian that severe punishment would
be certain to deter. So natives were murdered in retaliation. But
again, in typical Victorian fashion, this retributive policy was
elevated and formalized into a legal practice. Aborigines were
condemned to death, and to heighten the terror, when they were
executed on Rottnest in the prison, the executions sometimes took
place in the presence of the other prisoners. In 1883 three were so
despatched for the 'murder of Europeans in the northern parts'.[1]

In 1888 a new refinement was reported. As well as being publicly executed, the prisoner was made to watch his gallows being erected, since: 'the erection of the gallows in the prison yard, within view of the condemned man, must of necessity add to the horrors of his impending fate.'[2]

By the beginning of the twentieth century attitudes to the Aboriginal population had radically altered. They were no longer a considerable physical threat to the lives of white settlers, but had become an irritant, especially because of their persistent killing of livestock. For this offence many were sent to prison for very long periods. So capricious was the sentencing policy in respect of cattle killing that even the Comptroller-General of Prisons was on several occasions moved to protest about the number of native prisoners who had been convicted on their own admission for killing cattle. He was of the opinion that a plea of guilty should not be accepted from 'an untutored savage'.[3]

As white settlers gained the ascendancy, physical fear of the Aborigines turned to contempt. Because of the absence of resistance from native people, who by this time were well advanced in the process of demoralization, imprisonment became a very squalid affair. After the closing of Rottnest as a prison for Aborigines, the latter were dispersed all over the state, although they were kept apart from white prisoners.[4] In the northern districts chain-gangs were a common sight, since both prison officials and police officers used chains. The 1904 Royal Commission on the condition of the natives revealed that the police generally brought witnesses in from rural districts on a chain. All of this upset very few white people. It is interesting to observe that many of the statesmen who have an honoured place in the history of Western Australia were agreed about the need to crush the native population. Remarks by politicians of the stature of Alexander Forrest and Sir E. H. Wittenoom are typical and are only occasionally tempered by an appeal for moderation. Very rarely in the history of the legislature is there a categorical denunciation of the conditions under which Aborigines were imprisoned. Apart from the abolition of chaining, which appears to have been achieved in the late 1930s, there was little change in those conditions. A significant though isolated development occurred in the mid-1950s, when the first Aboriginal prisoners were sent to Pardelup, an experiment which an official visitor recorded as a success.[5]

The 'problem' of the Aboriginal prisoner is far from being just a part of penal history. We have seen that in the 1960s the number of Aborigines being sent to prison in Western Australia rose sharply and that many of these were young. In the early 1970s the formal separation of black and white in the prisons of Western Australia was abolished in accordance with the broad political decision to move towards a new examination of the status and future of the Aboriginal population. This new political attitude marks the beginning of the third period. This long overdue re-examination does not, of course, in itself solve any problems. Indeed, although segregation has officially been abolished, in some prisons there continues to be segregation, which prison staff claim is a consequence of the perpetuation of group relationships outside prison.

The Western Australian prisons, especially outside of Fremantle, still hold substantial proportions of black prisoners. There is in addition some evidence, as in other parts of Australia, of the development of that political awareness and radicalism amongst blacks, which originated in the United States of America and which is increasingly a feature of plural societies.

Immediately and inevitably there was a clash of interests in the early days of settlement between the newly-arrived settlers and the native population. As is usual in such situations, there was a gradual deterioration in relationships between the groups, which was characterized by considerable violence. Hasluck has shown how in the early days of contact between the races there was a certain amount of optimism about resolving the conflict. He describes how it is possible to detect a certain degree of tolerance towards, and understanding of the anger of the natives because of a realization that the settlers, because they *were* settlers, were responsible for the situation which had arisen. Towards the end of the century, however, such tolerance had markedly abated.[6] During the first seventy years of settlement the Aborigines moved towards the lamentable position, consolidated in this century, of being disproportionately represented in the prisons of Western Australia.

In the years immediately after white settlement, because of the strife between the races, it was considered necessary to establish some kind of special prison for native offenders, and the government, casting about for ideas, decided upon Rottnest Island. Rottnest lies some 19 kilometres off Fremantle. It is about 11 kilometres long, and is 4.8 kilometres across at its broadest point. It has a total area of 1914 hectares. The island was discovered and named by a Dutch sailor, Willem de Vlaming, in 1696. Apart from subsequent casual visitors the island was unoccupied until the early years of the Swan River settlement, when for a brief period an attempt was made to settle it.

Islands are always attractive to a society wishing to remove people, since they have a number of obvious advantages. First, there is the actual physical removal of offenders, which is a great consolation to people who cannot bear even to look at deviants. Secondly, because the prisoners are out of sight, no one is called upon to worry unduly about how they may be treated. Those few who are interested in the question of treatment, generally find it difficult, if not impossible to obtain accurate information about life on a penal island. Added to the fact of geographical isolation, there is a customary reluctance to accept prisoners' evidence as being reliable, and in the case of Rottnest this universal phenomenon was complicated by the fact that the prisoners were Aborigines. Again, escape, the perennial fear of gaoler and community, is extremely difficult and sometimes impossible. So the island constantly occurs to the maker of penal policy as a solution to his problem.

Australia itself is the best known example of this particular penal policy, but there are much smaller islands which have accrued a great deal of ill-repute. The French, when they were in a fury over Captain Dreyfus's alleged treason in 1894 opened the most notorious penal island of all, Devil's Island, off the north coast of South America, and despatched him there. The gangster Al 'Scarface' Capone was amongst the first to be sent to Alcatraz, the famous federal prison island in San Francisco Bay. Alcatraz also received Robert Stroud the 'birdman'—so called because of his astounding success with the breeding of cage birds—who was consigned to solitary confinement by the American government for over fifty years.[7]

England at the present time has three prisons on the Isle of Wight, off the south coast of England, and was tempted to build a fourth, as recommended in the Mountbatten Report of 1966. This report, although recent, once again reflected on the question of island prisons and considered the possibility of establishing institutions on some of the more deserted Scottish islands.

Rottnest Island did not hold a Dreyfus or a Capone; it merely contained generations of unhappy and anonymous Aborigines. As a penal island it does have one distinction: it lasted longer than most. Devil's Island lasted some sixty years (it was closed in the 1950s), Alcatraz only some forty. Rottnest held prisoners from 1838 until 1932, black prisoners being replaced on the whole by white at the beginning of the twentieth century.

The reasons for the establishment of Rottnest are set out in the preamble to the Act of 1841 which constituted it a prison,[8] and in correspondence on the subject addressed to the imperial government. Governor Hutt wrote to Lord John Russell, posing the question as to how: 'The Criminal Code of England can be best applied to meet the circumstances of a race so totally opposed to ourselves in every one of their customs, ideas and opinions, as are the Aborigines of Australia'.[9]

In the preamble to the Act it is noted that 'close confinement is prejudicial to their health, as being so uncongenial with their ordinary habits.' This statement not only underlined the fact that imprisonment was especially unpleasant for Aborigines, but also recognized that any means of holding them without close confinement was doomed to failure. This was because of the ease of escape and the difficulty of recapture if any attempt were made to imprison them on the mainland. On Rottnest the difficulty of escape was happily combined with 'a greater degree of personal liberty'. There they could be 'instructed in useful knowledge, and gradually trained in the habits of civilised life'. The instructions to the first superintendent made this quite clear. He was told: 'Improvements and instruction—more than their punishment, is the object.'[10]

In fact the island was already functioning as a penal establishment before the passing of the Act. In August 1838 a soldier called Welch went over to the island with ten prisoners to establish the colony. There was delay in the passing of the necessary legislation because of what appeared to the imperial government to be an important, but for our purpose irrelevant, constitutional argument. The Act set up Rottnest as a native prison, but there was also a clause that if necessary, white prisoners could be confined there too. For most of its life as a prison this happened. White prisoners were commonly sent in small numbers, usually as tradesmen of various sorts.

The Act is typical of much prison legislation in that, assuming that imprisonment is inevitable, it sets out an ideal with which it is difficult to quarrel. The problem is that such good intentions are very difficult to translate into practice. From the beginning there were difficulties, the most significant being the presence on the island of settlers, a fact which seems to have been ignored by the legislators, but which threatened to cripple the implementation of the primary aim of allowing the prisoners that freedom which was the very kernel of the scheme. Ironically the most prominent of the settlers, Robert Thompson, had moved to Rottnest precisely to escape what he regarded as 'the barbarity of the Aborigines'. Now he had ten native prisoners under Corporal Welch confronting him, a number of whom promptly sailed off in his whale-boat and left it wrecked on the mainland.[11] Hutt solved the problem by causing the surrender of all grants of land on the island.[12] The embryonic white community moved away, legislation was passed forbidding access to the island except on prison business, and Rottnest settled down to implement its lofty ideals.

In 1839 the first superintendent, Henry Vincent, was appointed to Rottnest. He was to rule Rottnest for twenty-seven years with, it may be fairly said, a rod of iron, the weight of which was to be the subject of some very serious complaints against him. He was forty-two years of age when he took up his appointment, had been a soldier in the Napoleonic Wars, had been wounded and had lost an eye. He has left a memorial to his prison regime in the shape of several buildings, which because of their architectural oddness have become the most distinguishing feature of the island. Before appointment he had been a gaoler at the Round House in Fremantle.[13]

Vincent presents all the classic problems of evaluation of a controversial figure in penal history. The principal difficulty is that such evidence that there is about his behaviour comes from himself, from officials who had appointed him and from government spokesmen who were in sympathy with the severity with which he administered the island. As is commonly the case, the most valuable evidence, that of the Aboriginal prisoners, is very sparse, consisting as it does of a few brief remarks during inquiries of various kinds. It should be stressed too that Vincent was in a familiar penal dilemma, which is that he was faced with conflicting opinions about how the natives should be treated. Some people wanted less severity, other more. Vincent and the superintendents

who succeeded him were expected to make the island prison pay
for itself, but at the same time were accused of working the
prisoners too hard. Even taking such concessionary factors into
account, the verdict on Vincent must be that he was an ignorant,
autocratic, cruel man who must surely have been responsible for
creating more unhappiness amongst Aborigines than most other
individual white men in the history of the state. He must also rank
as one of the harshest penal overseers in recorded history.

It can be seen from his correspondence, which is ill-spelt, that
he was a poorly-educated man. It is evident too that an attempt
to stray into what he believed to be his territory would be firmly
dealt with. Hasluck has pointed out that one of the major aims of
colonial policy towards the Aborigines was to convert them to
Christianity.[14] One expression of this policy was the appointment
to Rottnest in 1847 of a man called Armstrong who was a 'moral
agent'. This man's brief was to improve the 'habits and morals'
of the prisoners and to acquaint them with the 'great truths of
revelation and the fundamental rules of Christianity'.[15]

It was not long before Vincent had taken a dislike to him, and
in a letter Armstrong complained that Vincent had said to him: 'I
will see your neck as long as my arm and the Government in the
middle of the sea before you shall send a report.'[16] On another
occasion two Chinese basket makers were sent to the island to
teach the prisoners to make baskets. Vincent at once registered
dissatisfaction with them, claiming that they were not willing to
teach, and so they were promptly sent away.[17] But he was not only
autocratic; he was cruel, and his cruelty will be a recurring theme
in this account of Aboriginal imprisonment. Nor can he be exonerated because he was acting in the alleged spirit of the times. The
fact that he was constantly the subject of investigations is indication enough that his behaviour, at least as a public servant, was
aberrant even in his own day.

Charles Symmons, appointed in 1840 to be one of the first two
Protectors of Aborigines, in his annual report for 1842 confesses
disappointment that the Aborigines were not becoming 'civilised'.
In the next year's report he notes that Rottnest is dreaded by the
natives, and although they did not become 'civilised', they at least
abstained from 'acts of aggression'.[18] In the same year, events
were to give some indication of the reasons why the settlement
was dreaded.

In March 1842 there were twenty-three prisoners, most of whom were serving sentences of between six months and six years. They were allowed to 'roam in freedom', but this did not prevent 'a charge of undue severity on the part of the Superintendent towards the prisoners' being made.[19] Symmons reported in December 1842: '[this charge] has been promptly and thoroughly investigated by the Chairman of the Quarter Sessions and a Bench of Magistrates, and I have great pleasure in stating that his full and honourable acquittal, even on the testimony of some of the former prisoners, was the result.'[20]

These complaints were brought by a Mr W. N. Clarke, who wrote to the secretary of the Aborigines Protection Society in London in December 1842, elaborating on the charges against Vincent. Clarke complained that several people had died on Rottnest and that there was much speculation about the causes of their deaths. He added that the natives were forced to work harder than they could bear, that Vincent lashed them unmercifully, that he cut their hair close and pulled out their beards with pincers. In January 1843 he observed that the 'investigation ended, as was anticipated, in an acquittal'. This was because witnesses who could have sworn to the circumstances of the deaths of natives were not called.[21]

In February 1844 Hutt wrote to Lord Stanley denying Clarke's allegations. He insisted that Vincent did not punish prisoners harshly, and that a native who had been singled out for special mention had died of a bowel condition in 1840, which was some two years before any suggestion had been made that Vincent's cruelty had caused his death. It was true, he agreed, that the hair of the natives was kept short, but this was to ensure that their heads were clean, and to offset this they were given Scotch caps to wear as protection against the sun. As for the alleged pulling out of beards, this was nonsense. But he went on to say that conversations with natives who had been to Rottnest revealed that 'some of their fellow prisoners were considered by them to have been treated very harshly'. Hutt then marshalled the classic defence of the penal administrator under investigation when he said that 'statements of these people must be treated with caution'. After all, he pointed out, he had sent several people to enquire into affairs on the island, including an army officer who had asked the soldiers stationed there as a military guard their opinion of what was happening. The result was a complete failure to substantiate the allegations against Vincent.[22] Lord Stanley replied in a short letter that he was entirely satisfied with Hutt's explanation,[23] a conclusion which may have been facilitated because Clarke, as he admitted in his letters, had applied for a Protector's job and had been turned down.[24]

In 1846 there were between forty-six and fifty-two prisoners on the island. In September of that year the *Government Gazette* published an account of an investigation in the prison.[25] A letter from Symmons, included in the account, in a very spirited fashion once again defended Vincent against the charges. He reported that he had gone on the instruction of the governor to the island to investigate amongst other things an allegation that the superintendent had killed and buried one or more of the prisoners under his charge. This particular charge he described as impossible and absurd. Standard documentation, he believed, would make such an act impossible, since lists were regularly sent naming prisoners, and any discrepancy would at once become apparent. 'All parties in any way acquainted with the native character will', Symmons went on, 'agree with me that the superintending or overseeing of a convict establishment such as Rottnest, must be a peculiar difficulty, alike trying to the temper and irksome in its duties.' Many of the natives on the island were:

> Noted desperadoes—all eager for liberty—constantly armed with such offensive weapons as grubbing hoes, spades, etc.—many of them capable of shedding the blood of a fellow man with as little compunction as that of a sheep or kangaroo—and watched solely by an unarmed overseer and a miliary sentinel.

The superintendent, he believed, was 'highly efficient and humane', and he drew attention to his honourable acquittal on similar charges some years since.

Symmons seems to have based his conclusions on the sworn depositions which are also printed in the *Government Gazette*. These are from a number of soldiers of the military guard on the island, from Vincent himself and from the 'moral agent' Armstrong. The issue in these depositions is not whether he had hit the prisoners, but how hard he hit them. Even those witnesses who were obviously on his side stated that he had in fact struck prisoners, but as one stated, only 'a light stroke or tap on the shoulder to one of the men who was rather awkward.'

Another said that he had seen Vincent occasionally 'give a native a blow with a stick for inattention', but, the witness said, such firmness was necessary. The evidence of one Private John Williams was rather more serious. He described how fellow soldiers had struck natives with their fists, hit them with sticks, and on one occasion broken a pitchfork across a native. He had seen Vincent pull a native by the beard, and, most bizarre of all, he said that he had seen a part of a native's ear lying on the ground, and that Vincent had pulled it off.

The mention of the ear caused Symmons to recall some witnesses, the first one of whom agreed that he had seen Vincent grab the ear of a native who had disobeyed him. He merely pulled the ear lightly. Another native had picked up 'a small piece of something that looked like dry skin about the size of a pea, or a little larger'. When Vincent was asked to give some account of the ear incident, he admitted that he had given a native: 'A slight pull of the ear', but 'he had a small scab on his ear which I suppose was rubbed off by me, as I saw a sore place afterwards. I have often given natives slight pulls of the ear, or pulls of the beard, sometimes half in joke, but never to hurt them or in a passion.'

The truthfulness of prisoners' complaints in any age may to some degree be measured by the persistence with which they are made. When over the course of a number of years different prisoners keep making the same allegations about an individual member of staff, they are likely to be true. It had been four years since the allegations that Vincent pulled beards was categorized as 'nonsense'. Now in 1846 Vincent admitted that he did so as a regular practice.

The entire population of prisoners were asked if they had any complaints of ill-usage. Their reply was categorized as negative. However, it appeared that Vincent had occasionally pulled their beard or their ears, 'but not violently'. Several remembered the incident of the pulling of the ear, and said that 'the ear was sore previously, and the outer skin was pulled off.' They also confirmed that Vincent had in fact pulled hair out of their beards.

Armstrong, the 'moral agent', who was the interpreter, expressed the view that since certain charges had been investigated some four years before, there had been fewer complaints from the natives. He believed, like most people in authority, that the natives exaggerated greatly and that they would certainly overstate any harsh treatment received on Rottnest. Another soldier who was an eye witness to the ear incident said that he saw the native in question with part of his ear missing. For his part he introduced a new charge, which was that on one occasion, when some natives ran into the bush, Vincent went out with his gun in the dark and fired towards them. They had been wounded. The conclusion which must be drawn from the evidence is that Symmons was much too easily satisfied. He ought to have been much more concerned about some of the evidence he heard than in fact he was.

At the same time as these investigations were taking place, it appeared as though the penal island would be closed. This was not because of concern for the prisoners, but because they were needed for employment on public works around Perth. To this end the majority of the prisoners were transferred to the mainland in 1848. In November prison authorities found themselves in the most embarrassing situation imaginable. The whole group of twenty-six prisoners dug under the wall of the Perth gaol and escaped. For a short time after 1849 the system of assigning Aboriginal prisoners to employers was introduced.[26] This system was welcomed by the settlers who realized that they had much more control over an assigned prisoner than they would have over a free man. They also acted as mail carriers. Once the imperial convicts began to arrive in the early 1850s, there was little need for the natives to remain on the mainland, and in 1855 the Rottnest establishment was reopened. Apart from the arrival of the convicts, the same arguments were used for the reopening of Rottnest as had been used for its original opening: close confinement was a wretched experience for Aboriginal prisoners, and the necessity for preventing their escape if they were not so confined involved the use of chains and manacles. Vincent was again appointed to be superintendent.

From the time of the re-establishment of Rottnest as a native prison the situation deteriorated. The idealism of the founders such as it was, and although it had been worth very little in practical terms, seemed now to have been completely forgotten. Vincent's son William, who was appointed deputy to his father, following what looked suspiciously like a family tradition, was dismissed for cruelty in 1865. At an inquest on a native prisoner it was stated that he had been guilty of 'violent and brutal ill-usage of a sick native prisoner'.

In January 1866 he was charged with aggravated assault on a native called Dehan. This prisoner was between sixty and seventy years old and physically frail. It appears that Dehan was being moved against his will and that he was crying. Vincent shouted 'Damn you, I'll soon make you quiet.' He then hit him on the head with his keys, punched him in the stomach and kicked him. Dehan died the next day and was swiftly buried, joining the hundreds of native prisoners buried in unrecorded graves on Rottnest. The government ordered that his body be exhumed, but it had deteriorated so much that no conclusion could be drawn as to the cause of death. From circumstantial evidence however, Vincent was found guilty and sentenced to three months' hard labour.[27]

Vincent senior continued to be in charge of the establishment until 1867, when he was compulsorily retired through 'old age and general infirmity'. He apparently finished as he had probably begun, by excessive use of cruelty, which was not helped by 'increasing age and instability of temper'.[28] He was succeeded by W. D. Jackson.

From this time until the end of the century, with the growth of representative government, the elected representatives showed only occasional interest in what was happening on Rottnest. For the next twenty-five years very few had anything good to say about the establishment. Initially the complaints centred especially around the cost of maintaining the prison. In 1876 it was noted that Rottnest was increasing in cost every year.[29] The cost at that time was £2087 10s 0d. The Member for Swan, Padbury, who showed some interest in the affairs of native prisoners, suggested that they could be better used on the roads. The reply to this was to be reiterated many times. It was that if natives were to work on the road, then they would have to be in chains, but that this was barbarous and unacceptable. Padbury also expressed a humane view when he complained that it was cruel to discharge prisoners from Rottnest and then expect them to travel home over long distances and often through hostile tribes. The government, he believed, should offer protection to them on these journeys. But the best solution of all was that the government should assign the native prisoners to settlers. How far these complaints about the cruelty of forcing natives to go through hostile areas on their way home were genuine, and how far it was a plausible argument to persuade the government to introduce assignment is difficult to know.

It was in the early 1870s that Anthony Trollope toured Australia and New Zealand, including in his itinerary a visit to Rottnest. He expressed considerable sympathy for the prisoners, but did not believe that they were harshly treated. He especially disapproved of the corroboree which was ordered on his behalf: 'When the order was given, I could not but think of other captives who were desired to sing and make merry in their captivity.'[30] He was conscious too of the cultural abyss between the races, and how the Aborigines were baffled by the white man's laws. The prisoners, he observed ironically, were 'not alive even to the Christian's privilege of lying in their own defence'.[31]

In 1878 a Committee was appointed to enquire into the work of certain departments in the Public Service.[32] Included amongst these were gaols and the native prison on Rottnest. The members of the Committee were Messrs Fraser, Leake, Shenton, Marmion and Knight. The party visited Rottnest without warning and expressed themselves surprised and pleased with what they saw. They thought that the food was good and that the 'cells were as clean as could be expected when occupied by native prisoners.' They expressed the growing interest in making the establishment pay for itself. To this end they suggested the planting of large numbers of olive trees, for example, and expressed concern that there was no intelligible system of storekeeping. They suggested that a storekeeper could be appointed, who might also run the proposed reformatory for white delinquents on the island. A memorandum from a colonial surgeon was very much more critical. He expressed the view that the dietary scale was insufficient and that its balance was entirely unsatisfactory for native prisoners. He believed that much of the illness which occurred on the island was due to this factor and also to the absence of amusements and exercise. He suggested a number of improvements, such as the introduction of quoits. He thought too that the natives would respond to a system of rewards such as the distinction of 'an old hat with a feather in it', which he believed 'would be greatly esteemed by these adult children'.

This report attracted no comment in the legislature. The only reference to it was in response to another complaint: that Rottnest was costing too much. It was pointed out in answer to this complaint that the 1878 Committee had noted that administration was conducted as economically as possible.[33] During the next few years objections to the maintenance of Rottnest continued. In

1881 it was observed that £100 was being spent on religious ministration to the natives and the questioner wondered if this was proving effective.[34] The establishment of warders on the island, which seemed to some members in these years to be unnecessarily expensive, was justified because 'there were some notoriously bad characters among the native prisoners who had been causing a great deal of trouble.'[35]

Meanwhile rules for the management of the prison continued to be written and re-written. In 1879 a set of rules was promulgated, which were probably, as previous rules had been, generally ignored on the island. In the rules it was pointed out that the superintendent should impress upon the subordinate staff that firmness, tempered with kindness, in the treatment of the prisoners would best ensure the discipline of the gaol and the maintenance of good order. The authorized punishments included bread and water, solitary confinement and irons, but no corporal punishment.[36]

In 1883 there began the most important series of investigations of conditions on Rottnest.[37] In the years immediately before, there had been a considerable increase in the population of the prison, due in part to the opening up of the northern areas of the state and the appointment of magistrates in those areas. This contributed to an increase in the prison population, which rose to 149 in the first nine months of 1883. On 2 January 1883 two justices reported an investigation which was a consequence of critical articles in the *Daily News* on 23 November of the previous year.[38] They visited Rottnest by surprise, not using a government boat, and in their own words 'ransacked the prison'.

As was by now traditional in reports on Rottnest, several of the facts reported by them ought to have given cause for great concern. Nevertheless their conclusion was, apart from a few necessary adjustments, that the prison was working satisfactorily. They reported that the cells were clean, the accommodation satisfactory and the food was good. On the other hand they reported that the superintendent chained refractory prisoners without legal authority: that the meat served to the prisoners was not weighed but guessed at; and that vegetables should be introduced as a change from rice, since vegetables were never served. They found no evidence of brutality, but came up with the highly significant recommendation that 'a proper register of deaths' should be kept. Seeking refuge in one of the eternal consolations of the penal investigator, they recommended that there should be another warder on the island, owing to the increase in the number of prisoners. The supposition behind this recommendation is that additional staff members will, in some way, make things better.

In spite of these assurances the middle of 1883 saw the appointment of another inquiry, which was held by the colonial surgeon, Dr Waylen. There had been an epidemic of influenza on the island, which was not helped by the cold weather and the overcrowding. He reported that the prison could hold 106 prisoners at the most, but at the time of the outbreak there were 170, and in May there were 179. The total of deaths from the epidemic, it later emerged, was sixty, which was over a third of the total population of the prison. After laying the doctor's report on the table,[39] the colonial secretary reported that the governor was to appoint a commission to investigate the state of Rottnest prison and the whole question of native imprisonment. The attitude of interested people in parliament at that time displays a subtle change of attitude towards Aborigines. The physical fear which characterized the early days seems to have been replaced by a mixture of sympathy and sorrow at the predicament in which the Aborigines were. But there was also a blatant vein of contempt.

This can be seen from the debate on Waylen's report. One member clearly felt sympathy, when on 10 August 1883 he suggested that twenty-seven Aboriginal prisoners, who were due to be moved from Geraldton to Rottnest, should not be sent because of the epidemic.[40] In the previous month the colonial secretary was asked if he had seen articles in the *Inquirer* of 27 June and 4 July about the treatment of Rottnest prisoners. The colonial secretary replied that the superintendent had denied these allegations, and that the visiting magistrates had been told to make a surprise visit, which, however, they had not yet managed to do.[41]

In the next month dissatisfaction was expressed yet again with the administration of Rottnest, and the observation was made, shrewdly enough, that the superintendent had denied the allegations, but that was only to be expected. This sympathy for the natives led to a retort from Lee Steere that Rottnest was not a deterrent, that the natives came out 'looking much better than when they went in', that the allegations about the superintendent's behaviour were untrue and that the natives ought to be made to work on public works.[42]

In September 1883 there was the longest debate about Rottnest in the whole of its period as a prison.[43] Carey, the Member of the Legislative Council for Vasse, who constantly complained about the conditions on Rottnest, said that the present management was not at all satisfactory, 'unless the establishment was intended to serve as a graveyard'. He had heard very disturbing accusations about what went on on the island and about the corruption of the superintendent. For example, the superintendent managed to pay himself a fee for the use of his own boat on government business.

The superintendent, Jackson, had his defenders. Marmion claimed that the charges had proved to be groundless. The superintendent was a 'most careful painstaking, and trustworthy officer'. He had had a certain amount of money when he assumed the post and he had prospered. This prosperity had naturally made people jealous. It was perfectly proper, in Marmion's view, for the superintendent to hire out his own boat if he had tendered for the work and if his tender was the lowest.

John Forrest replied that far too much had been made of the epidemic, and that it was impossible to put prisoners on public works because of the necessity for chaining. Wittenoom failed to see any severity in the use of chains at all. It had been perfectly alright some fifteen years before and 'it was absurd to give way to sentiment when dealing with the blacks.' This view was typical of those expressed by Wittenoom on any occasion when the affairs of the poor or the imprisoned were discussed in the legislature. Another Member noted that Padbury, who had spoken on the subject of Rottnest on previous occasions, had offered to take any number of native prisoners on his stations, treat them well and return them to their homes when their sentences expired. Forrest replied that that would be no better than the prison.

The members of a subsequent Commission were Forrest as chairman, Shenton, Maitland-Brown, Marmion—a significant choice in view of his firm support of the superintendent—Stone, who was the superintendent of convicts, and Dr Waylen, the colonial surgeon. The report is an important source of information about Rottnest at the time, but it is also significant because of the tone of its discussion of the Aboriginal population.

The report begins with what is to modern ears a somewhat hollow statement: 'It is a melancholy fact that throughout Australia the aboriginal race is fast disappearing.'[44] It goes on to note: 'we have no hope that the aboriginal native will ever be more than a servant of the white man.' Turning its attention to the prison, as in previous reports, the conclusion was that on the whole, treatment was 'kind and humane'—this in spite of the many criticisms which they list about the establishment. When they visited Rottnest, there were in addition to Jackson himself one chief warder‾ and six assistant warders, together with eight soldiers. There were a total of thirty-seven adult Europeans on the island, of whom ten were women and twenty-seven were children. There were 148 prisoners, nearly all of whom were suffering from measles. Their discussion of diseases introduces a new theme in assessments of Rottnest. This is that the native was incorrigible, probably because of congenital defect, and that he was responsible for the predicament in which he found himself. For example, the Commission blamed the spread of disease, especially that of measles, on the Aboriginal custom of exchanging clothes. The fault therefore did not lie in the existence or condition of the prison but in their adherence to the custom.

The Commission noted too, in this connection, that when food was handed out in the prison, it took several minutes for the eating to begin because the prisoners exchanged food with each other, a long and significant process. This business of exchanging had a rather more serious aspect, because the Aborigines also exchanged the metal identity discs which they wore, and the consequence of this was that many of them were serving sentences which they had not been awarded. It also led to great confusion when it came to identifying individuals in the process of sentencing and punishing.

With regard to the conduct of the superintendent it appeared, as far as can be judged, that he was either uninterested or incapable. The clothes of the prisoners were never washed, their blankets were scarcely aired, their hair was never cut and they never washed. The cells were much too small, being 4 cubic metres, and it was recommended that they should be doubled in size. Furthermore, the cells were damp, and some of them held five prisoners in a space of 1.8 x 3 metres. When the prisoners were wet, there was no way in which their clothes could be dried. And they still had no vegetables, only the inevitable rice. This was in spite of the fact that there was a substantial garden, which, however, the superintendent regarded as his own. The Commission recommended that this should become a prison garden, noting that it produced nothing for the prison and little for the government except carrots, which were 'sometimes given to the Superintendent's horses'. In spite of the abundance of fish around Rottnest the prisoners were not given hooks and lines so that they could fish, although they sometimes borrowed these from the Europeans. If they were given fishing tackle, the Commission noted, they could supply fish for the whole prison. The overall position had deteriorated to the extent that the superintendent apparently now did not bother to send in an annual report.

The superintendent's evidence was really rather remarkable, even for a Rottnest Inquiry. He reported that when a magistrate had ordered it, prisoners worked in irons, although this was illegal. The longest sentence, in his experience on Rottnest, had been eleven years. He went on to say that the 'uncivilised' natives had no idea of how long their sentences were or when they could expect to be released. It was hardly surprising that the Commission noted that the natives hated the place, and to allay the suspicions of their colleagues, stressed that it was 'not a pleasant retreat for a holiday'. In spite of these criticisms the Commission felt unable to recommend the abolition of the establishment, because the alternative was still to use chains on the mainland. Finally, if anybody had ever believed otherwise, they confirmed that the 'system pursued is not calculated to have any great civilising effect.' Waylen, the colonial surgeon, was frankly disgusted by the place. In his memorandum he noted that 'natives were brought from a warm climate, in overcrowded steamers during cold and wet weather, and placed in an overcrowded prison with total change of diet, surroundings, and occupations,' He commented that it was not surprising that they died in large numbers. No major action took place as a consequence of the investigation.

From the time when this report was published, until the end of the century, life in the prison became increasingly depressing. Jackson retired, possibly as a consequence of the report, and was succeeded as superintendent by W. H. Timperley. The latter's son wrote an account of life in the prison, which gives an insight into the routine there.[45] He describes how native prisoners arrived weekly, and how they were chained together during the crossing from Fremantle:

the natives who were usually thoroughly uncivilised and clad in the
scantiest of filthy rags—highly nervous and apprehensive as to
what would happen next—and with long hair and matted beards
together with lime charcoal and grease, presented an awesome sight
on landing at the small jetty.

The diet which they were to enjoy seemed to Timperley to be
good. Breakfast and tea consisted of bread and tea, and the midday meal comprised thick vegetable soup, stew and bread. 'On
this diet they grew sleek and contented.' He goes on to draw a
jolly picture of the corroborees which the prisoners enjoyed.

The crude brutality of earlier years was apparently by now replaced with a kind of classic colonial paternalism. There were still
regular outbreaks of influenza, which accounted for 95 per cent of
the deaths among the prisoners, but Timperley records how his
father was gifted with hypnotic powers and was able to lull raving
patients to sleep for hours on end. Prisoners still continued to die
however. In 1897 it was reported that at the beginning of the year
there were eighty-one prisoners on the island. During the year
fifty more were received and thirty-three discharged. Also during
the year there were twenty-six deaths from influenza. This represented approximately one-third of the entire prison population.[46]
This colonial milieu was completed by the presence on the island
of the governor and his party, who used the prisoners as beaters
when they wished to shoot birds and wallabies. The demoralization of Aboriginal prisoners, and more generally of the Aboriginal
population in the state appears by this time to have been nearing
completion.

The Commission of 1884 was entirely ineffective. Demands grew
for the abolition of the establishment and for the employment of
Aboriginal prisoners on public works on the mainland. Forrest
continued to defend Rottnest on the grounds that it was better
than chaining prisoners, and also that it did discourage crime.
Many members of the legislature did not agree. One noted that
natives were 'more cunning, more lazy, and greater rogues than
when they went in'.[47] Expenditure on the prison continued to be a
subject of constant complaint. In 1887, for example, the superintendent asked for a larger hospital in case there were further
serious outbreaks of illness. In spite of the revelations about the
horrors of epidemics this was turned down.[48] In December of the
same year, it was observed that 'they did nothing at Rottnest,

apparently, but eat and drink—the majority of them.'[49] By 1890 then, the two-pronged attack on Rottnest consisted of complaints, on the one hand that it was ineffective as a deterrent, and on the other that it was unnecessarily expensive.

These objections were voiced in sustained criticism until the prison as an establishment for Aborigines, was finally closed. In 1892 it was claimed that it was 'monstrous' that forty natives cost £1262 10s 0d in salaries alone.[50] In the same year it was pointed out that Rottnest 'had been a perfect failure'.[51] This was partly because the superintendent of the day, one member had stated, 'knew nothing about natives'.[52] But the main theme of parliamentary comment on Rottnest centred around a belief that the prisoners were having too good a time. This attitude was consonant both with the puritan social illiberalism which was one of the salient features of the late Victorian world, and with a deterioration in relationships between the races. In a debate which was designed to authorize the punishment of Aborigines by whipping, in 1892, the attorney-general made the observation:

> I have come to the conclusion myself, and I have done so for years, that the only way of effectually dealing with all these coloured races, whether black fellows or Indians, or Chinamen, is to treat them like children. I have proved it, in my own small experience.[53]

A similar popular, increasingly public, sentiment was expressed by Alexander Forrest in 1895:

> Natives who were taken to Rottnest were pampered too much, and, when liberated, were as bad as when they were first imprisoned; but when they had to do a hard-days work, chained to a wheelbarrow, and occasionally flogged for bad conduct, they generally recognised that it was not desirable to spear cattle or break the law in any way.[54]

During the 1890s a new objection to Rottnest was voiced. This was that the existence of the prison meant that the public were barred from the island. It occurred to people that the island should be opened to the public, since it was 'a place of much value as a residential retreat'.[55] Eventually Rottnest did become a holiday island.

The Royal Commission of 1899 included the native prison on Rottnest in its report.[56] The Commission were both sympathetic to

the plight of native prisoners and condemnatory of Rottnest itself.
They were aware of what has come to be known as 'culture conflict', a situation where an act which is regarded as acceptable or
even mandatory in one part of a society, is often deemed illegal by
another part of it. A liberal, if somewhat paternalistic attitude is
evident in the statement that it was unjust for a man to be punished
for an offence against tribal law by tribal authorities and possibly
a second time by the 'laws of the race which has dispossessed him
of his hunting grounds and taught him the vices of civilisation'.
The Commission believed that there was no point in imprisoning
natives, especially since such imprisonment did not deter others.
All the natives knew was that 'a man had disappeared.' Rottnest,
which they visited and which at that time held fifty-one Aboriginal
and European prisoners, they opined had 'none of the conditions
essential to the proper treatment of Aboriginal offenders'. Finally,
as had already been stated, Rottnest was closed as a native prison in
1903.

The closure of Rottnest prison did not improve conditions for
native prisoners. Despite the persistent, formal, rejection of chains,
native prisoners in the north of the state were usually kept in
chains.[57] This practice was to continue until the beginning of
the Second World War. From time to time questions were raised
about the desirability of such treatment, but the conclusion for
many years was that it was more humane than secure imprisonment.

In the course of a Royal Commission on the condition of the
natives in 1904,[58] visits were made to the prisons at Carnarvon,
Broome, Roebourne and Wyndham, which between them held 300
prisoners. A tradition, first established in the Forrest Report of
1884, was strongly in evidence again. This was that while the situation was entirely unsatisfactory, no-one could be held accountable,
since because of their behaviour the Aborigines had brought it on
themselves. The usual 'humane supervision and considerate treatment' was reported.[59] But in a situation where prisoners wore
neck-chains all day and night, some for two to three years, it is
difficult to reconcile such a comment with the reality of the situation. At Roebourne prisoners were in addition chained to the
wall at night.[60] There was incidentally no legal authority for chains,
except an instruction (illegal) from the Comptroller-General of
Prisons that they could be used on Aborigines.[61] The consequence

was that, since legally chains did not exist, there were no regulations about weight and size.[62]

The royal commissioner agreed with the gaolers who gave evidence that neck chains should be replaced by wrist or ankle chains on outside work. He recommended that inside the prison there should be no chains at all, but that some kind of perimeter fence should be built.[63] Of the several northern prisons only Roebourne had a wall. Apart from the question of chains, there was much in the treatment of Aboriginal prisoners with which the royal commissioner expressed dissatisfaction. There was first, irregularity in respect of employment. Prisoners commonly worked for local authorities without pay, although some received gifts. At Carnarvon the mayor gave the prisoners a little tobacco out of his own pocket. The commissioner recommended that local bodies who 'employed' prisoners should pay for prisoners' rations and for clothes on release. This latter was especially necessary, he observed, because a departmental regulation precluded the giving of gratuities to Aboriginal prisoners on release, although whites were entitled to them.[64] The commissioner went on to recommend that resident magistrates should not issue instructions to gaols in their area, but the gaols should be firmly under the control of the comptroller-general. He further recommended that because of the heat in the north of the state six hours' work should be the absolute maximum.[65]

The attitude and experience of Aboriginal prisoners, it was revealed in the report, remained very much the same as it had always done. The confusion over identity because of the exchange of discs, noted by Forrest, was still creating havoc with tidy procedures, but this probably did not matter very much, since many had no idea why they were in prison, nor for how long. In one rather odd respect, the prison experience was rather less deterrent than was intended. The royal commissioner expressed the view that the beef which the prisoners ate probably increased their fondness for meat, and as a result led to more cattle killing. This report, which apart from the apparently insoluble question of chains was fairly liberal, drew a comment from the State Commissioner of Police, F. A. Hare, that the witnesses who had given evidence were the 'scum and riff-raff of the north'. As a result of this the royal commissioner was briefly suspended from office.[66]

A liberal attitude in respect of the treatment of Aborigines made its appearance rarely but persistently throughout the first thirty years of the twentieth century. The proposal to punish Aborigines by whipping, which was introduced in 1892, had its opponents.[67] One member during the debate said: 'It contains a principle that I feel I must oppose; it provides for a mode of punishment which has been generally discarded in almost every civilised country.'

In 1907 there was a debate in the Legislative Council on the subject of the imprisonment of Aborigines, which, characteristically, was abortive.[68] It was proposed, in the course of a long and passionate speech by Pennefather, that plantations should be established in the north-west of the state, where Aboriginal prisoners could work. Although he was clearly motivated by sympathy for the plight of the chain-gangs on northern roads, he cunningly pointed out rather more palatable advantages: 'I do not wish to urge the question so much on the ground of the humanitarian principle as from the utilitarian aspect.'

He went on to describe how the chains interfered with work. He proposed that the prisoners could be confined within palisades. His fellow representative from the north, Sholl, attacked him savagely, claiming that he knew nothing about the north, natives or prisoners. Several members were distressed about the fact that Western Australia was regarded as more cruel in its treatment of native prisoners than any of the other Australian states. In the state's defence it was stated that the natives preferred being chained at the neck to being chained by the ankle or the hands. And further that each man carried only ¾ of a pound of chains on his body. There was the usual consensual agreement that for a variety of reasons prison was not effective for Aborigines: 'After these natives have been in prison, they are far more desperate, more cunning, and more determined than they are in their native state in the bush, and they defy the white man.' Eventually an amended motion was passed which asked the government to investigate the possibility of establishing plantations as Pennefather suggested. Nothing came of it.

In 1921 the question of chaining prisoners was raised again in the Legislative Assembly. The premier was asked:

On whose advice was the order given to chain natives in the north-west gaols? Is he aware that the last 3 escapees got away with the

chains on? Will he cancel the order to chain during the excessively
hot weather, and in the meantime ascertain from those in charge of
northern gaols what necessity there is for the alteration.

The premier replied that native prisoners in the north had always
been chained, and pointed out that chaining had been decided
upon as the most humane method by the 1904 Royal Commission.
It appeared that the neck chains by this time had, in accordance
with the recommendations of that Royal Commission, been replaced by ankle chains.[69]

The position was as bad some fifteen years later, in 1935, when
another Royal Commission discussed the treatment of Aboriginal
prisoners.[70] But the tone of that report was very much less liberal
than that of the 1904 report. The royal commissioner was C. H. D.
Moseley, a stipendiary magistrate from Perth, who expressed the
opinion that 'they seemed perfectly comfortable in their chains.'
And the growing complaint that chaining causes 'the greatest
misery and degradation' was described by him as 'well intentioned,
but extravagant'.[71] In his approval of chaining he was supported
by the Reverend Love, the superintendent of Kunmunya, who
disagreed only to the extent that he believed 'a neck chain the
most humane way of restraining native prisoners'.[72] Moseley did
not believe that imprisonment was a punishment or a deterrent,
and recommended whipping instead 'in the presence of as many
of the tribes as possible'. Further, he wished for the establishment
of an island settlement like that on Palm Island in Queensland:

> In these cases there need be no fear of inflicting undue hardship by
> removing a man from his own country. He probably has no par-
> ticular country; if he has, he has done little or nothing to justify his
> being left in it, and, for the sake of others, he should be removed.[73]

Considering how relatively recently this report was issued, it must
rank as probably the most illiberal of all the reports on Aboriginal
imprisonment.

If there is any need to demonstrate that prisons are a reflection
of developments in the wider society, the subject-matter of the
three Royal Commissions into Western Australian prisons illustrate
this commonplace very well. The first Royal Commission, of 1899,
was a reflection of the classic reformers' concern about the treatment of prisoners. The second, in 1911, was substantially prompted

by staff dissatisfaction with conditions of service, once again reflecting the growth of labour as a political force in the community. The subject of the third Royal Commission, in 1972, was to be the alleged ill-treatment of Aboriginal prisoners.

7

The Modern Period (1)

New problems—Introduction of probation and parole—Parole as a penal concept—Alcoholism—Response of the prison system—Expansion—Beginning of change—Non-uniformed professionals

In the early 1960s the Western Australian prison system entered a period of change and development against a penal background which was very different in many respects from that of the previous thirty years. The main difference was change in the structure of the prison population: an increase in the percentage of younger offenders in the prisons, and a corresponding, sometimes overlapping, increase in the numbers of Aboriginal prisoners. This combination led to a change in the overall attitude of prisoners to their incarceration. Prisoners, it appeared, were less amenable to the traditional assumptions about prison life, challenging those aspects of it which had always been regarded as inevitable, such as a willingness to 'do time quietly' and to regain freedom as quickly as possible. This was almost certainly linked to the increase in the numbers of young prisoners, since these, like young people generally, are more prone to challenge adult dogma—whether it is expounded by staff or fellow prisoners.

Similarly, the increase in the numbers of Aboriginal prisoners tended to disturb the classic equilibrium, which had evolved from a quintessential shared assumption about daily living in prisons, common to staff and prisoners. This 'disturbance' had two dimensions. One of these, which as we have seen caused the early administrators to ponder the effectiveness of imprisoning Aborigines, still remained. This questioned the relevance of notions of 'training' and 'treatment' for people who stand, in major respects, outside the usual cultural framework within which such programmes are developed and promulgated. The second was of more recent vintage. This was an increasing degree of awareness, however slight, of the most important change in political alignment in recent years: the development of a consciousness of race as an issue which transcends what seem in Western democracies to have become rigid political affiliations. Whether in countries such as England or Australia race can disturb the balance of political power in any

146

major sense is debatable. What is likely to happen, generalizing from other more precocious situations, is that increasingly the prison will become a focal point for the resentment of minority races over the way in which society is organized.

The picture was complicated by a considerable increase in the numbers in prison. The daily average rose steadily throughout the decade and continued to do so into the 1970s. In 1963-64 the daily average was 856.42, of whom 818.49 were males (136.89 Aborigines), and 37.93 females (21.31 Aborigines).[1] The 1966-67 saw an average of 1016.69, of whom 969.54 were males (237.49 Aborigines), and 47.15 females (30.15 Aborigines).[2] By 1968-69 this had risen to 1175.57 males (314.39 Aborigines), and 64.47 females (49.41 Aborigines),[3] and continued to rise, until in 1972-73 the daily average was 1416.94.[4] Before analysing in detail the problems created by these trends, and the attempts to deal with them, it is necessary to outline the major changes in treatment of offenders which took place after 1960. Although these affected the

Table 7.1

Daily averages (males)

Year (ended June 30)	Aborigines	Non-Aborigines	Total
1961	99.29	526.69	625.98
1962	106.44	572.94	679.38
1963	130.12	647.05	777.17
1964	136.89	681.60	818.49
1965	189.78	647.53	837.31
1966	202.25	621.55	823.80
1967	237.49	732.05	969.54
1968	272.83	847.04	1119.87
1969	314.39	861.18	1175.57
1970	313.23	857.13	1170.36
1971	368.88	864.12	1233.00
1972			1306.84
1973			1211.48
1974			989.21
1975			913.43
1976			895.26

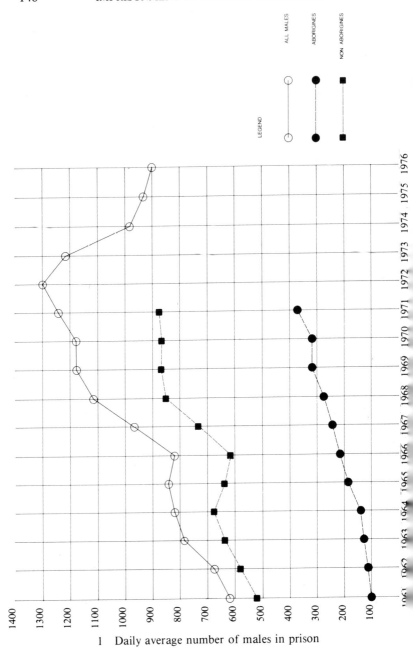

1   Daily average number of males in prison

whole penal system, the consequences for the prison system were profound.

The point has frequently been made in this account that the genesis of change in a penal system is difficult to pinpoint. The most important developments in the administration of criminal justice in Western Australia in this period were the enactment of a law to introduce probation as a means of dealing with adult offenders, the preservation of the concept of indeterminacy through the introduction of a parole scheme, and the attempt, at last, to remove alcoholics from the normal prison routines. This was an overdue, albeit hesitant, attempt to 'decriminalize' alcoholism. After so many years of torpor in the penal system, why did the developments take place?

The pattern of events at the time illustrate a general characteristic of penal history. This is that the enactment of legislation or the introduction of new systems is not necessarily the result of a calculated analysis of variations in the nature of the problem of criminality, or an evaluation of rival methods of dealing with it. Rather, especially in recent years, innovation in penal treatment is a result of the perusal of national and international practice which has been given a superficial validity by proponents of several ideologies.

The inspiration for changes in the law in respect of penal methods in Western Australia did not come from an awareness of the changing composition of the criminal, or more specifically the prison population. The changes were drawn from a welter of international assumptions about the best methods of dealing with crime, which were an amalgam of reformers' care for the oppressed, a distaste for imprisonment and a persistent faith in the successful outcome of a search for the 'scientific' treatment of the criminal.

The Offenders Probation and Parole Act of 1963 is a good example of this proposition.[5] One of the more remarkable features of the treatment of offenders in Western Australia is that until 1963 there was no statutory provision for adult probation in the state. In other countries, notably New Zealand and England, this option had been open to the courts for many years. This is not because probation as a means of disposing of offenders is indubitably successful, but because it is a tempting alternative to imprisoning people, which becomes increasingly attractive when the prospect of support from, and supervision by a probation officer seems to

Table 7.2

Daily average (females)

Year (ended June 30)	Aborigines	Non-Aborigines	Total
1961	15.88	14.57	30.45
1962	19.57	15.94	35.51
1963	20.20	19.57	39.77
1964	21.31	16.62	37.93
1965	25.00	14.62	39.62
1966	26.08	12.97	39.05
1967	30.13	17.02	47.15
1968	55.27	12.92	68.19
1969	49.41	15.06	64.47
1970	49.48	15.32	64.80
1971	62.23	19.57	81.80
1972			72.96
1973			83.26
1974			62.85
1975			42.72
1976			41.50

make further excursions into crime less likely. Parole, the other half of this important Act, while it appears akin to probation, is in basic respects entirely different. The only common denominator, theoretically, is that the offender is helped to survive in the community by a sympathetic counsellor. There the similarities end.

The actual organization of a parole system is straightforward enough. Generally the pattern is that a man is sentenced to a period of imprisonment, during which he can be released on parole. In Australia, and specifically in Western Australia, there tends to be provision for the sentencing judge to set a minimum sentence which must be served before a prisoner can be considered. This practice is usually a concession to the concern of judges over the handing over to administrators of their classic judicial authority. When the prisoner is eligible for consideration for parole, his case is usually at first reviewed at a local level, either by an individual reporting officer or by a committee. These local views, which are

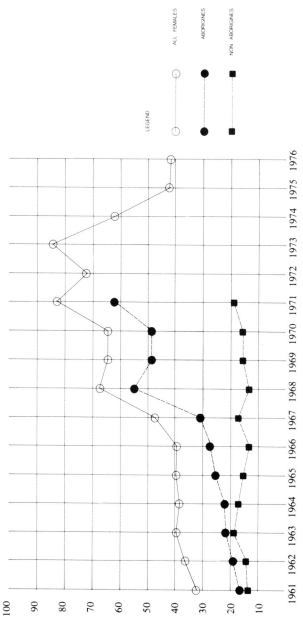

LEGEND

ALL FEMALES

ABORIGINES

NON ABORIGINES

2 Daily average number of females in prison

in no sense authoritative, are then communicated to a central Parole Board, which in Western Australia consists of five members, a judge, who is chairman, the Director of Corrections and three others. If a prisoner under consideration is male, or the matter is 'general', the three are to be male. If the prisoner is female, then two of the three are to be female, the third being one of the men appointed under the previous regulation.[6] An interesting aspect to the establishment of parole in Western Australia is that it was proposed in the parliamentary debates leading to the passing of the Act that a prison officer should serve on the Parole Board. The amendment which would have caused this to happen was defeated by just one vote.[7]

This is the simple and typical structure which was set up in Western Australia in accordance with a world trend which had its source in the Lombrosian positivism. This was based on a belief that more attention should be paid to the criminal than to the crime. This 'scientific' approach was in the twentieth century harnessed to the liberal reformers' classic distrust of court sentencing procedures. The outcome has been the belief that a calm evaluation of a person by penal experts, over a long period must by definition be more accurate and more to the point, more just, than the capricious and erratic sentencing procedure after a court hearing, in very artificial circumstances, which last minutes, or possibly hours. The argument for a parole system in such a context is difficult to resist. Yet generally, the concept of parole is under attack.

Many of the complaints about the operation of parole systems throughout the world stem from their organizational defects. The questions with which everyone is concerned as soon as parole is mooted are: Who will make the selection of prisoners to be released? And upon what criteria will such selection be made? The two questions are intertwined, but may be examined separately.

The constitution of the Parole Board in Western Australia as described above is typical. What is fairly unusual however, is the provision in the Act for the establishment of a Department of Probation and Parole which is distinct from the Department of Corrections. There are several sound reasons for this. One is that a clear division between prison and parole ought to demonstrate to prisoners that any hostility or prejudice they may feel they suffer at the hands of prison staff, at any level, cannot be translated into a blocking of parole. Another advantage is related: it is that when a prisoner feels aggrieved that he has not gained parole, then he cannot blame prison staff. Selection for parole, when thus taken out of the institutional arena, may be regarded by both groups as the work and responsibility of somebody else. This is in marked contrast to, say, the concept of indeterminacy in the English borstal system, where selection for promotion and ultimately release is made by staff closely connected with the inmate. As a result the period during which selection is made and announced excites a considerable amount of tension in the institution.

The Western Australian system, with parole responsibility being removed from the Department of Corrections, the latter nevertheless retaining responsibility for welfare, has certain disadvantages. The first of these is the problem of effective communication between staff of the two departments, especially between junior staff at an institutional level. In England parole supervision is undertaken by probation officers who also have responsibility for welfare/social work within the prison. Thus structurally, in the case of England the potential for collaboration and co-operation is high, since the roles of parole officer and prison welfare officer are interchangeable. Some Australian states, New South Wales for example, have included parole as part of the overall Corrections Department. In this way there is increased probability of effective communication, the failure of which is a source of great discontent amongst all associated with parole.

There is another possible weakness in the merging of the two professional areas of parole and probation with a concomitant exclusion of prison-based social work, as in Western Australia. The arguments for such merging are that the contents of the jobs are similar, since a department containing both, offers a more elaborate promotional structure, and there will be more variety at work. Offsetting these benefits is the reality that parole/after-care work is the most difficult and most dispiriting area of penal social work. It is likely therefore, and natural, that where a parole officer has a 'mixed' case load, he will concentrate on those people who are less sophisticated and more responsive to help and encouragement than the complex ex-prisoner. There is also a tendency amongst social workers to regard prison work or after-care as having low status because of its difficulties. This view is encouraged by a usual reluctance on the part of social workers to be involved with what they construe as the coercive aims of prisons. It was this last factor which caused concern and debate amongst probation officers in England when it was announced in the early 1960s that they were to expand their after-care activities, and were also to take responsibility for welfare/social work in the prisons.[8]

There undoubtedly exists a division between those who work in the prisons, and those who work in the community, which is a consequence of the facts discussed above. But the English penal services have tried to overcome this division by the establishment of a group of officers who make prison and after-care work a speciality. This enables them to concentrate on the peculiar problems presented by their clients, and to develop an expertise which both infuses the work with interest and raises its status. After a period in this area they may, of course, return to more traditional work.

The main penal lesson to be drawn from what has been said so far is that if a parole system is not part of an overall Corrections Department, there are likely to be problems of communication, the existence of which must be admitted, and the solution of which must be a priority. The natural barriers to communication, where a general responsibility for prisoners and ex-prisoners is shared between departments, are strengthened by a tendency to avoid difficulties of parole supervision by concentrating on other, equally important but undoubtedly more congenial activities. This latter possibility can be countered by the construction of a unit for working with parolees only.

The root of dissatisfaction with the concept of parole does not basically lie in the particular way in which it is administered. Its defect is inherent in indeterminacy in a prison sentence. Once again, it should be stressed that in theory indeterminacy has a high face value. It is in its practice that it fails. Indeterminacy fails and is frequently unjust, because the criteria for release are unintelligible not only to the prisoners but to the staff and to those making the final selection.

There is first of all the problem of deciding what, if any, the relationship is between behaviour in prison and the possibility of success on parole. It is a commonplace of practical penal experience that the 'model' prisoners may well turn out to be the least successful in conditions of freedom, since it is the absence of those qualities, notably aggression, which enables people to cope with society, which makes him a placid prisoner. The man who gives the staff no trouble is likely to be manifesting not judicious self-control but the condition which has been called 'institutional neurosis'.[9] This condition, common to institutional life, penal or free, is induced by a need for the crushing of individual identity and the cultivation of conformity.

Yet, the prisoner anxious for parole may fairly claim that if his prison behaviour is to be ignored, on what criteria is he to be judged? Prison 'behaviour' as a criterion is in prisoners' experience notoriously akin to Morton's fork. If he is 'well-behaved', it could be that he is hiding his 'real feelings', and if he is 'badly behaved', then he is clearly not 'ready' for release. But what else is there, apart from his daily performance in prison, upon which he can be judged?

Answers vary in different countries. In some, notably in America, political considerations are important, either in the literal sense, or in the broader sense of trying to gauge community reaction to the news that a given prisoner is to be released. This latter consideration, which *may* be deemed appropriate, indubitably operates in most, and probably all parole systems. The point here is not that it is an unreasonable criterion, although that is debatable, but that it is not usually admitted to be a criterion at all, and is entirely outside the control of the prisoner. Any suggestion therefore that co-operation with those agents who are trying to 'reform' him will auger well for his possible parole, is untrue. And there are other factors which may be taken into account, over which he has little or no control. The most important of these are his home situation and employment prospects. There has developed, in a penal system which includes indeterminacy, a culture in which prisoners manipulate such factors. They engineer prospects of family reconciliation, which have no chance of materializing, and arrange for letters in which jobs are professed in 'firms' which barely exist if at all.

The basic reason for the resentment, and perfectly natural manipulation of the parole system by prisoners, is that the criteria are not set out. Proof of this lies in the fact that in Western Australia, as is usual, prisoners who have been rejected for parole are not, as a procedure, given the reasons for the decision. Not only is there no explanation, but there is no appeal built into the structure. The point has been made throughout this account when indeterminacy has been discussed, that any process of selection necessitates rejection, and is therefore productive of bitterness. But a parole system has no chance whatever of even appearing moderately just, unless certain critical features are present.

The first of these is the establishment of clear explicable criteria upon which decision will be based. These should be open, subject to scrutiny and susceptible to debate. The next is that the prisoner should be seen frequently throughout his sentence by his parole officer, who should discuss frankly, exactly what the position is at any given time. The officer should also establish close links with the prison staff—although how far prison behaviour should be a factor may be debated—a conclusion should be reached, and once again disseminated as a matter of public information. The parole officer should, further, have influence in the decision making process, and should be expected to give an account of the reasons for a decision to the prisoner. Failure to do this not only leads to frustration, but is, simply, unjust. A preliminary to this, however, is the establishment of a specialized parole unit, preferably within a prison department. The lessons of the old Indeterminate Sentences Board have great relevance in this respect. Although not a part of the prison department, it had, as we have seen, very close association with it. Further, it was concerned only with a narrow segment of the penal process, and had the interest and the time to interview prisoners with whom they were concerned. Above all, the working of a parole system must be constantly re-examined.

Another important attempt being made at the same time to cope with a chronic problem, which was also influenced by worldwide discussion, was the Convicted Inebriates Rehabilitation Act of 1963.[10] The main feature of this legislation was the establishment of an advisory board which was to be given the task of overseeing, advising on and assisting in the clinical treatment and the rehabilitation of what were termed convicted inebriates. The Act allowed the court, under certain conditions, to place inebriates in an institution specially set aside for them. The Advisory Board could, amongst other things, recommend variation of the sentence. The people dealt with under the Act were sent to Karnet, the new establishment in the Serpentine district opened on 29 March 1963, which catered for sixty. Nine years later, in 1971, another institution, Byford, was established for alcoholics.[11] In the 1970s the problem of alcoholism has been viewed as a matter which needs more imaginative treatment than crude imprisonment. Increasingly, other ways of dealing with the problem are being discussed.

Alcoholism is a major problem in many modern communities, and Australia is no exception. It is a condition which has always been the cause of many people being imprisoned, either because of the definition of the effects of alcohol as criminal, such as being incapable, or because of its concomitant stimulation to commit, for example, acts of theft. In Western Australia this problem has been added to by the propensity of many of the Aboriginal population for alcohol. This propensity, linked to high visibility to the police, makes them especially vulnerable to arrest. Whether because of increased drinking, or because of this vulnerability, it was observed in the Annual Report for 1971 that there was a 'notable increase' in the number of Aborigines convicted of drunkenness and sent to prison.

The increased reluctance, formally expressed in law, and informally administered in the courts, to submit alcoholics to traditional prison routines is likely to cause a reduction in the numbers of prisoners in Western Australia. Already preliminary figures for 1975 and 1976 demonstrate that such a reduction is taking place. Whether such a pattern will be maintained depends on a number of factors, which are imponderable in the light of present knowledge and information. One of these is the extension or reduction of the work of the legal aid service for Aborigines which, it is generally accepted, has succeeded in reducing the numbers of prison sentences imposed. In the long term what is important is more control over drinking, as a consequence of improvement in the conditions of life in poorer sections of the community, and the development of treatment techniques which can cure individual alcoholics.

The last is the most problematic of all. The opinion is increasingly being expressed that therapeutic skills in respect of alcoholism, or more generally mental illness, have only limited success.[12] In many cases the prospect of curing the alcoholic condition is very bleak and requires the presence of conditions which are usually absent: the determination to be cured (the absence of such determination being a primary cause of the initial condition), and a supportive and understanding domestic situation.

Yet the hope is that 'treatment' will be available and effective. There is some danger that the optimism generated by the decriminalization of alcoholic offences will lead to a deterioration in the quality of the care provided for alcoholics. Oddly perhaps, the record of prison systems in the case of such people is by no means utterly bad, and in one respect is good. What prisons have always done for alcoholics is to clean them, feed them and give them a chance to recuperate, if only for a short period. In this respect prison has been an asylum. If alcoholics are not to be sent in future to prison, then society must ensure that there is a realistic alternative which will at least perform the modest task set out above. This is especially true in the case of the most incorrigible, dejected alcoholic. The latter is in some danger in modern treatment-oriented society, of being categorized as an addict, or being propelled into a treatment setting, and then being pronounced as beyond help, while resources are deployed to support more hopeful people such as the young drug taker. The legislation and the efforts designed to stop the imprisonment of alcoholics in Western Australia in the last fifteen years should be seen as the beginning of a process rather than a solution.

These two major changes in criminal justice in Western Australia, probation and parole, and the inebriates legislation, certainly affected the prison system profoundly. But the main problems after 1960 were associated with the increase in the number in prison, and with the changing backgrounds and behaviour of prisoners. The situation in recent years has had effects on the three major groups concerned, the policy makers, the prison staff and the prisoners themselves. We will now review the response of each of these to what was one of the most difficult and challenging periods in the history of Western Australian prisons. Since detailed situations change rapidly, in the main we will concentrate on the broad, persisting issues.

The rise in the number of prisoners led inevitably to overcrowding. The first act by the administration was to plan the expansion of existing facilities to cope with this. In 1964 Geraldton became a 'common gaol', the ancient term which meant that it was administered by prison staff, not by the police,[13] and there was a proposal, which never materialized, that a new prison should be built in the town.[14] In 1966 a new comptroller-general, C. W. Campbell, was appointed, and in the same year the prison at Albany, the first maximum-security building to be built in the state for a century, was completed.[15] In 1967 Geraldton prison was expanded to include the buildings of an adjacent empty hospital,[16] and the police lockup at Kalgoorlie, in the goldfields, became a common gaol. The year 1968 saw the establishment of Brunswick Junction as an open prison in premises vacated by the railways.[17] In 1970 another new prison was opened, at Bunbury,[18] and a large empty hospital at Wooroloo became a prison. Also in 1971, as had already been mentioned, Byford was taken over.

The most creditable and desirable aspect of all this expansion was the opening of a prison for women, called Bandyup, in the Perth metropolitan area in 1969.[19] From the opening of the first prisons in the colony the treatment of the female prisoner had been a subject of criticism. In 1881 it was recounted how the female prisoners were 'of the most abandoned class and utterly depraved' and how the accommodation in Perth gaol was totally unsuitable for them.[20] Throughout the nineteenth century the women were generally confined in the same prisons as the men, although they were kept separate from them. This was necessary because of the problem of transporting them to a central institution, because their sentences were short, and because they were, as they always have been, a relatively small proportion of the prison population. In 1875 for instance, 1153 men and 194 women were committed to prison.[21] Twenty years later, in 1895, the respective figures were 1464 and 153,[22] and in 1935, 2033 white men and 149 white women were sent to prison.[23]

Since the beginning of the twentieth century most women imprisoned in Western Australia have been kept at Fremantle. When people complained about Fremantle, their concern included the plight of women. It will be recalled how Hann, especially, tried to improve their environment, but this remained unsatisfactory. Nothing, however, was done to alter the situation until the opening of Bandyup, when at last the women finally left Fremantle. While the new prison was being set up, the female prisoners in the state were taken out of prison uniform.[24]

The initiative in respect of building in recent years has also led to a resurrection of the hope, expressed for a hundred years, that a prison could be built to replace Fremantle. To this end in 1971 land was selected in the Canning Vale district, and a long and novel process was begun to plan and design both the institution and its regime.[25] This involved extensive consultation with many people, including members of the prison service, which in itself is a remarkable action. The final report is a long provocative, interesting document, which to be intelligible should be studied in detail.[26] For our purpose it is sufficient to note that it is of relevance to any prison system contemplating a building programme, and that it is an illustration of a promising development of consultation which is generally alien to the prison tradition. As has happened before, however, the building has been halted because of the economic situation in 1975.

Plain recital of this expansion conceals some important facts about the prison system. It should be noted that the increase in the number of establishments has led to a considerable growth in the numbers of places for prisoners in open conditions. This is a process which continued with the opening of Wyndham in 1975 and, most important perhaps, with the initiation of a work release scheme. This is a programme whereby selected prisoners live in prison department property and are paid like any other workmen. The money earned contributes to their keep, assists their families and is saved. The scheme began in Bristol, England, in 1952, and despite the occasional inevitable calamity is one of the most constructive developments in modern penology. The Western Australian scheme was mooted in 1969,[27] and by 1973 five hundred prisoners had been through the scheme.[28] The new Prison Regulations of 1974, Part V, set out the most recent framework within which this is allowed. Under these regulations not only is work release possible, but a prisoner may be released:

(1) to attend hospital for medical treatment;
(2) to seek employment;
(3) to be in attendance on his family on occasions of family illness or bereavement, or
(4) for his welfare or the welfare of the family.

The development of open prisons, on the scale on which this has taken place, has had two beneficial results. The first is that a much larger proportion of prisoners have been allocated to open prisons than had been possible hitherto. A comparison with other Australian states made in 1969/70 shows (Table 7.3) that Western Australia had a much higher proportion in open conditions.[29]

The second benefit in the extension of open provision has been that the premises taken over are not purpose-built as prisons. This can, naturally, be inconvenient, but the paramount advantage of this situation is that the premises can be evacuated without a great deal of trouble, since the capital investment has been small. This

Table 7.3

Daily averages in open prisons

State	Daily average-minimum security	Percentage of total daily average
Queensland	92	7.98
New South Wales	851	21.52
Victoria	658	28.82
Tasmania	72	20.57
South Australia	133	14.92
Western Australia	592	51.11

is a point of general importance to prison administrators, since the nineteen-century practice of building prisons which were seemingly designed to last for ever, and which certainly allowed for no change of philosophy, is a massive burden for modern systems. Fremantle is a very good example. The open prisons are of special value in Western Australia because, as has been mentioned, the state is still susceptible to regional expansion and contraction as a result of exploration, and this fluid situation, together with the economic instability which accommodates it, seems to provoke criminal activity. Prisons become necessary, but as a social situation changes, the need disappears. In both eventualities the authorities are able to open a prison and close it again at little expense.

The most striking fact associated with this open prison policy is that it has supported maintenance of a tradition of community work by prisoners. In many of the Western Australian towns in which prisons are located, a great deal of work for old people, children and other groups is carried out by prisoners. This is, indubitably, more enjoyable and more constructive than what remains usual prison employment based on ageing workshops, in which too many prisoners try to spin out jobs which are repetitive and often pointless.

There was an important shift in the balance of prisons in the state in the 1960s. In discussing the inter-war years, reference was made to the small number of common gaols and a correspondingly large number of police gaols, which still, of course, were the responsibility of the prison department. By 1971 the policy of staffing more prisons with professional prison staff had resulted in there being thirteen common gaols and only six police gaols.[30]

This extension of the system was the framework within which many other changes and developments took place. One of these, which was a consequence of the opening of a wider range of institutions, was the institution of programmes of classification and assessment in an attempt to develop appropriate regimes for different categories of offenders. The first classification board was set up in 1963,[31] and in 1966 an assessment centre was established in Fremantle,[32] which was subsequently moved into the old female prison. The creation of such units in no way ensures that every prisoner is sent to a regime which, in detail, suits him, but the existence of a classification system, and constant re-examination of facilities in particular prisons, at least makes this possible.

The next, long overdue step was the introduction of staff training. Beginning in 1967, with a two-week training course in Fremantle,[33] the training organization was moved to Wooroloo in 1970,[34] where basic and promotional courses are regularly held. Like so much innovation in prison systems, the introduction of training emerges as the beginning of a process, not its end. The problems associated with training will be discussed later.

In addition to education for officers there was an expansion in the facilities for prisoner education. Education at Fremantle had always been present in some form, but by 1968 the school there had a total of three teachers.[35] It was also announced at the same time that the female prisoners were now having half-day education a week. This was certainly not much, but it is another interesting comment on the depressed status of the female prisoners that before that time there was no education for them. At the present time educational facilities for prisoners in the state vary from place to place. In some prisons, such as Bunbury, a full-time professional teacher is employed, in others, such as Pardelup, correspondence courses are available, while in many establishments, including Bandyup, it is possible to attend courses in educational centres in the community.[36]

The most significant development of all during the period under review has been the growth in the Department of Corrections of what are variously called 'professional', 'specialist' or 'expert' members of staff. Since such terms are ambiguous, they excite a discussion about their meaning which blocks analysis of what the people concerned actually do. Perhaps a more useful categorization is 'non-uniformed staff'. The introduction of the latter is common to all modern prison systems, the differences between one and any other being the timing of the introduction and the way in which the units in which they work are structured in relation to the overall establishment. In the main it may be stated that there are two reasons for the introduction of these grades. First, it is a reflection of the increase in professions, which is the most significant feature of occupational patterns in this century. It is also due to the prison administrators' wish to extract from any area of professional expertise any available help in the solution of what increasingly seem to be inordinately difficult problems.

This process had already begun, albeit in a very rudimentary, nuclear form in the nineteenth century, when prisons generally drew upon the specialist services of the classic professionals: the doctor and the priest. In the twentieth century, as teaching has become more 'professional' and psychology and social work have emerged as disciplines, people trained in them have become increasingly involved in prison work.

The beginning of this trend in Western Australia can be detected in the late 1950s, when it was reported that a welfare officer was at work in Fremantle.[37] In 1960 a 'parole' officer was appointed,[38] presumably to help with the supervision of discharged reformatory prisoners, and soon afterwards an Adult Probation and Welfare Service was instituted by the prisons department.[39] In the last years of the Indeterminate Sentences Board this service investigated applications for transfer to the reformatory prison. In 1968 there were five welfare officers, whose work was supplemented by prison officers, working part-time on welfare matters at Albany, Pardelup, Kalgoorlie, Geraldton and Broome.[40]

In 1969 the development of non-uniformed departments received a considerable boost when the Forensic Division of the Mental Health service was transferred to the prisons department.[41] This transfer involved one psychiatrist, a social worker and four psychologists. This division, which had been established in 1965 with one psychiatrist and a social worker, was reorganized in 1972 to establish a Training and Treatment Branch, which comprised three sections: Psychology and Research, Social Work and Welfare,

CELL..EBRITIES
INCARCERATED
(UNLIMITED)

⚹ P R E S E N T S ⚹

A Crown Theatre
Centenary celebration
EXTRAVAGANZA ! !

F E A T U R I N G

⚹ **A GALAXY OF GORGEOUS GIRLS**

⚹ **SCINTILLATING MUSIC**

⚹ **ALL STAR VOCALISTS**

And a **HOST** of **GRUESOME WITTICISMS**

🐦 🐦 🐦 🐦

10   Programme devised by prisoners to celebrate the centenary of
Fremantle Prison

and Staff training.[42] During 1971-72 this branch contained thirty-four personnel. The assistant director, W. Kidston, noted an intention to concentrate especially on the work and training of the uniformed staff, pointing out that 'This emphasis has developed from a firm commitment to the belief that the most important single unit in the Department is the uniformed officer.'[41] The extent of these developments in recent years is best gleaned from the organizational description of the department.[44]

Since these changes are so recent, it would be premature to try and evaluate their effect. What is clear is that the period from 1966 onwards has been distinguished by two major policies which together constituted a turning point in the administration of Western Australian prisoners. The first has been the infusion into the prison system of 'outsiders'. After the resignation of Hann, for the next fifty years all appointments at senior levels in the prison service were made from within. The debate about what is called in England direct entry to the senior ranks from outside, in prison and police services, is persistent and heated. A 'unified' service, where all appointments are made from the rank below has the apparent virtue of being fair. But services which adhere to this policy tend to stagnate and also to find difficulty in filling the most senior posts. At the present time several police and prison services are introducing or reintroducing direct entry to senior grades, or a system of expedited promotion, which is not very different. Included amongst these are the English police forces, and the prison services of New South Wales and Victoria.

The English prison service has always appointed outsiders to senior ranks, although this has never precluded the promotion of junior staff. It is logical to assume that the fusion of the best of the latter and carefully selected outsiders with alternative experience into the senior grades broadens the attitude of a prison service and provokes reassessment of aims and structures. It is certainly the case that the experimentation which after 1930 made the English prison service a model for many prison systems, was a consequence of direct entry into the governor grades, which was encouraged by the most remarkable prison commissioner of all time, Sir Alexander Paterson, himself a direct entrant.[45]

The appointment of C. W. Campbell in 1966 heralded an important change in this regard. Although he had experience of residential institutions, he had not been a prison officer. After his appointment most of the personnel who were appointed to key positions in the evolving non-uniformed departments were outsiders. These included two psychiatrists, Rollo and Hill, Assistant Director Kidston, chief psychologist Boyes and senior social worker Smith.

The second major change in policy has been a consequence of the first. The aims of the department have been broadened, as is evidenced by a change of title to Department of Corrections, with the head now titled Director of Corrections.[46] Imminent in this process has been the development of links with the community, most notably in respect of education. The Annual Report for 1968-69 contains a very significant statement, which is that the University of Western Australia was cooperating with the development of staff training. This was the first mention of the university in an annual report, and heralded the development of links which have been educative for the university, and have at the same time made it intelligible as an educational establishment to large numbers of prison staff. The chairman of the Training Board, which co-ordinates and supervises staff education, is a member of the staff of the University of Western Australia. It is of the greatest significance that the appointment of a university professor, R. W. Harding, as the first chairman, was greeted enthusiastically by the Prison Officers' Union.[47]

There are several other examples of this attempt to open the system to new influences and ideas. Those welfare officers who were unqualified were encouraged to undergo training.[48] In 1974 six uniformed officers were sent to Nedlands Secondary Teacher Training College as full-time students, to follow a course to qualify as recreation officers. The whole period was clearly one of considerable activity.

8

The Modern Period (2)

Deterioration in behaviour—The 1968 riot—The 1973 Royal Commission—Hearing and recommendations—Prison officers—Training—Relationships between uniformed and non-uniformed grades —Summary

These recent developments took place against a fairly turbulent background. We have shown how the prison population increased, and have mentioned the opinion, expressed in Annual Reports, that behaviour had deteriorated. Several episodes are perhaps symptomatic of this. The first, already noted, was the birching of a prisoner, which had not been done for many years,[1] and second was the shooting and killing of a prisoner who was trying to escape from Fremantle.[2] The most serious incident occurred in June 1968, when for the first time since 1929 there was a riot in Fremantle. The reason ostensibly was dissatisfaction over food, but the department expressed the view that overcrowding was the cause. As a result 100 prisoners were transferred from Fremantle to other prisons.[3]

The trouble began with some prisoners complaining that the meat in the evening meal was bad. Those who had complained were given an alternative meal. The next day, at midday, the bulk of the prisoners refused to go on parade and stayed in the exercise yards. There existed an inmates' representative committee in the prison, and this group presented a list of requests. These were all concerned with food and suggested improvements. The superintendent's promise to investigate the complaints did not satisfy the prisoners in one of the yards, and after expressing dissatisfaction with the inmates' committee, the prisoners asked that the administration should see representatives selected by them. This was agreed. The requests made by this group were different and included an immediate demand that all the prisoners should be given single cells. This kind of demand, clearly, could not be met, and the outcome was a trial of strength between staff and prisoners.

Additional staff, some armed, were called in to maintain order, and in addition police officers patrolled the area around the prison. In the evening prisoners began to destroy equipment and hurled some of it at staff. Attempts by the prisoners to break out of the

THE ORGANISATIONAL

CH

DEPARTME

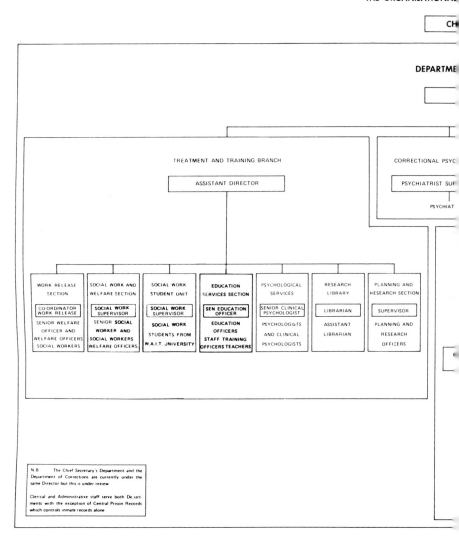

TREATMENT AND TRAINING BRANCH

ASSISTANT DIRECTOR

CORRECTIONAL PSYC

PSYCHIATRIST SUP

PSYCHIAT

WORK RELEASE SECTION	SOCIAL WORK AND WELFARE SECTION	SOCIAL WORK STUDENT UNIT	EDUCATION SERVICES SECTION	PSYCHOLOGICAL SERVICES	RESEARCH LIBRARY	PLANNING AND RESEARCH SECTION
CO-ORDINATOR WORK RELEASE	SOCIAL WORK SUPERVISOR	SOCIAL WORK SUPERVISOR	SEN EDUCATION OFFICER	SENIOR CLINICAL PSYCHOLOGIST	LIBRARIAN	SUPERVISOR
SENIOR WELFARE OFFICER AND WELFARE OFFICERS SOCIAL WORKERS	SENIOR SOCIAL WORKER AND SOCIAL WORKERS WELFARE OFFICERS	SOCIAL WORK STUDENTS FROM W.A.I.T. UNIVERSITY	EDUCATION OFFICERS STAFF TRAINING OFFICERS TEACHERS	PSYCHOLOGISTS AND CLINICAL PSYCHOLOGISTS	ASSISTANT LIBRARIAN	PLANNING AND RESEARCH OFFICERS

N.B.   The Chief Secretary's Department and the Department of Corrections are currently under the same Director but this is under review

Clerical and Administrative staff serve both Depart ments with the exception of Central Prison Records which controls inmate records alone

11   The organizational stru

OF THE DEPARTMENT

RY

RECTIONS

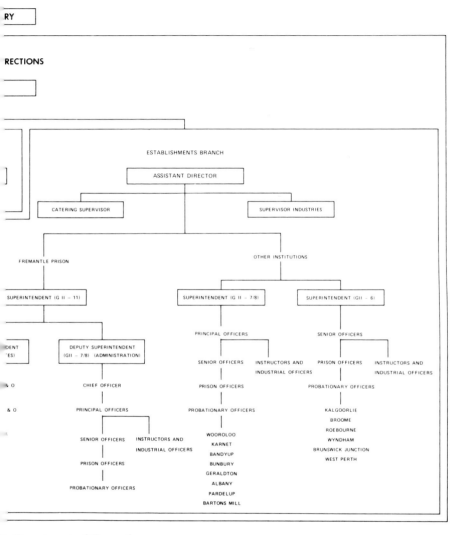

ESTABLISHMENTS BRANCH

ASSISTANT DIRECTOR

CATERING SUPERVISOR

SUPERVISOR INDUSTRIES

FREMANTLE PRISON

OTHER INSTITUTIONS

SUPERINTENDENT (G II – 11)

SUPERINTENDENT (G II – 7/8)

SUPERINTENDENT (GII – 6)

DENT
ES)

DEPUTY SUPERINTENDENT
(GII – 7/8) (ADMINISTRATION)

PRINCIPAL OFFICERS

SENIOR OFFICERS

& O

CHIEF OFFICER

SENIOR OFFICERS

INSTRUCTORS AND
INDUSTRIAL OFFICERS

PRISON OFFICERS

INSTRUCTORS AND
INDUSTRIAL OFFICERS

& O

PRINCIPAL OFFICERS

PRISON OFFICERS

PROBATIONARY OFFICERS

SENIOR OFFICERS

INSTRUCTORS AND
INDUSTRIAL OFFICERS

PROBATIONARY OFFICERS

KALGOORLIE
BROOME
ROEBOURNE
WYNDHAM
BRUNSWICK JUNCTION
WEST PERTH

PRISON OFFICERS

WOOROLOO
KARNET
BANDYUP
BUNBURY
GERALDTON
ALBANY
PARDELUP
BARTONS MILL

PROBATIONARY OFFICERS

Department of Corrections

yards were contained by the discharge of firearms, since there was a real danger of mass escape. Further discussion with the prisoners in each of the yards led to their agreeing to return to their cells. The episode had lasted about twelve hours, and considering the potential in the situation for injury, it is remarkable that so few people were hurt. Five prison officers and a police officer were struck by missiles and three prisoners received bullet wounds. Damage to the prison was extensive.

After transferring some prisoners, others were charged with offences associated with the riot, and a number of additional security precautions were instituted, such as the erection of an additional guard post. The overcrowding was not completely eliminated, and the easing of the situation at Fremantle caused some pressure in those prisons receiving the transfers. The Prison Officers' Union, conscious of the vulnerability of its members, advocated an open inquiry.[4]

The next crisis occurred in 1972, when as a result of allegations of ill-treatment there was a Royal Commission into incidents in Fremantle, which reported in 1973. The Prison Officers' Union played a large part in bringing this about, threatening industrial action if nothing was done to investigate the complaints. The kernel of the allegations was that some members of the prison staff had ill-treated certain prisoners, and that Aboriginal prisoners were subjected to discriminatory treatment. An especially unpleasant aspect of this latter allegation was the suggestion that prison officers encouraged or allowed assaults by white prisoners on black. The Commission, held by a judge, R. E. Jones, sat for twenty-eight days, heard ninety-nine witnesses and produced 2059 pages of transcript.

The task facing the commissioner was really quite formidable. He had to try to sort out fact from fiction, which in a prison context is almost impossible. As has been discussed, this generic quality in prison life makes accurate description of events in a prison extremely unlikely. Jones claimed that he encountered an additional difficulty, which was the inability of several of the Aboriginal prisoners to articulate their evidence. The first group of complaints were those made by prisoners against other prisoners. These were substantiated. The next group were allegations of brutality by staff, and a complaint against the medical officer that he did not 'sufficiently attend' a prisoner. The latter charge 'was not substantiated',[5] and on the whole neither were the complaints against the staff. Some of the complaints in the commissioner's opinion were true, some were untrue, and some were exaggerated or distorted.[6] Typical of these were situations where the commissioner was convinced that an officer had hit an inmate, but not as hard as was alleged, or, in one case, with a bunch of keys.[7] The aftermath of a strike by prisoners in August 1972 was the most tortuous episode which the commissioner had to unravel. This had been provoked in part by the curtailing of privileges and the increasing frequency of strip searches, which are what their name suggests. Prisoners are made to undress completely while each item of clothing is searched. It is a degrading and humiliating experience, which allegedly was a consequence of a dramatic escape the previous month—to which we will return.

When the strike was over, the ringleaders were removed to a segregation unit, and it was what allegedly happened there that was the subject of complaint. It was suggested that violence had been used in escorting the prisoners, that the latter were violently searched, that mattresses and blankets were not provided, that prisoners were kept without clothes and that they were given cold showers.[8] Jones described the evidence as 'very often unsatisfactory', but concluded that first there was an 'unnecessary degree of force', which did not amount to 'deliberate brutality', but which was explicable because of 'the natural indignation at the behaviour of some of the inmates during the disturbances in the yard'.[9] Next, that no violence was used during searching. Thirdly, it appeared that although blankets were provided, mattresses were not given out until the second night. All the prisoners except one were kept unclothed for a whole night which 'was quite against regulations and against proper procedure'. The prisoners had been given cold showers, only one towel was provided, and they had been made to run to and from the shower. Finally, the commissioner rejected categorically 'allegations of deliberate brutality by punching or kicking—"bashing"—of the complainants'.[10] No doubt the certainty that some prisoners colluded in the manufacture of evidence was a contributory factor in this decision,[11] although 'the evidence of the respondent officers, with some notable exceptions was not convincing'.[12]

What was probably the most serious charge against a member of staff was proved to the satisfaction of the commissioner. This was that an officer, who came across an escaping prisoner, coolly, deliberately and unlawfully shot him with a pistol, wounding him in the chest.[13] The officer claimed that the prisoner refused to halt when ordered, but the commissioner, after hearing the prisoner's version of how he had stood still, and after studying the geography of the incident, did not believe the officer.

A major concern of the commissioner was the alleged discrimination, general and particular, against Aborigines. The behaviour of a voluntary social worker, 'whose role in the bringing of these allegations was crucial', is discussed by Jones.[14] The particular charges alleged that certain officers incited white prisoners to assault blacks. Each of the five white inmates' allegations that they had first-hand experience of this was rejected by the commissioner. The evidence of one, he observed, could only be described as 'preposterous'.[15]

The commissioner's general observations on race relationship in Fremantle Prison are of considerable interest. He conceded that in the early part of 1972 'there was undoubtedly a general feeling of interracial tension throughout the prison'.[16] But he believed this was merely an isolated episode. He examined the record of punishments for fighting in the period from July 1971 to November 1972 and discovered that fifty-five of the prisoners charged were Aborigines and fifty were white. A close look at the breakdown revealed that there was no detectable racial pattern in these confrontations.[17] Reviewing the policy, instituted in 1965, of abolishing the special 'native party', and other historic features of prison discrimination, he found a great deal to commend in the policy of the department and in the behaviour of staff.

Jones recognized that there were racial incidents but he was satisfied that they were rare and inevitable, considering, in his view, that 'we have in Western Australia—and in the whole of Australia for that matter—a king sized problem in this respect.'[18] Far from there being any evidence of systematic discrimination by staff, or general inter-racial hostility, Jones stated: 'It is hard indeed to avoid the conclusion that the prison population of Fremantle prison is far more racially integrated than is the general population outside'.[19]

Before dealing with the recommendation of the Royal Commission, one incident discussed in the report should be recorded, although it is only marginally related to its major themes. This was the most remarkable escape in the history of the Western Australian prison system. The detailed account, which is set out in the report, reads rather like a plot of a spy film.[20] Briefly, the story began with the appointment of certain prisoners to the position of 'disc jockeys', in which role they played requests for prisoners via a prison radio system. Two of these 'jockeys' were 'trusties' and electrical repair men. The freedom they enjoyed, as is always the case, was a valuable preliminary to their escape attempt. In 1971 they were sent to relocate several telephones in the prison hospital. They promptly 'tapped' the line, and ran a line across the prison to the cell from which they played music for the prisoners. They already had headphones, and by using bits and pieces, including parts of an alarm-clock, constructed a dialing mechanism. The addition of a switch mechanism meant that they were now in contact with the outside. Many people were contacted, notably the voluntary social worker who has been mentioned.

They then became involved, with official approval, in the tracking and recording of weather balloons operated by the French Government. Two prisoners then *made* a device to monitor the signals from the balloons, and persuaded the administration to give them a cell for their work, to which they promptly ran a telephone line. Next, a hole was cut in the ceiling underneath a bank of lights. When everything was ready, one early morning they went through the ceiling and the roof. There were still two hazards to overcome. One was an officer on a nearby tower, who was armed. The ringleader had discovered that there was a direct line between the main gate and each gun tower. He now tapped this line, and rang the officer in the nearest tower, saying: 'Gate here. Some suspicious activity has been observed down near the back of the carpenters' shop. Keep a close eye on it for the next few minutes.'

The officer naturally enough moved away to do as he had been ordered. As he did so, the escapers made a wire bridge from the roof to the wall, crossed it and descended the 9 metres to the ground by means of a piece of line specially brought for the purpose. The whole performance ranks amongst the most ingenious of prison escapes.

The royal commissioner's recommendations were really quite far reaching.[21] In summary they were:

(1) That the policy of racial integration should be continued.

(2) That there should be more supervised recreation for inmates.

(3) That summer time lock-up should be put back from 4.30 p.m. to 5.30 p.m.

(4) That more officers should supervise prisoners in the yards.

(5) That there should be a mobile reserve of officers who could be called upon in emergency.

(6) That the necessary finance should be provided to employ additional staff for the preceding purpose.

(7) That procedures of staff selection should be varied slightly, so that senior staff would be consulted about such selection.

(8) That there should be a sufficient number of welfare officers concerned with all prisoners irrespective of race, who should not be ex-prison officers, and should be in the Department of Community Welfare.

(9) In respect of security, prison 'broadcasting' should be controlled by the staff, the 'trusty' system needed tightening up, and a general alarm system should be installed.

(10) With regard to administration, the post of superintendent should not be confined to serving staff or the most senior of those, another deputy should be appointed, there should be two assistant chief officers, security grades should be increased in status and number, and a principal officer should be in charge of divisions at all times.

(11) Prison regulations should be rewritten, displayed and obeyed.

(12) Trafficking by officers 'should be the subject of a rigorous internal investigation immediately'.

These recommendations are a mixture of the desirable and the undesirable, mostly the former. Thus more and constructive recreation is a good aim, as is the perpetuation of the policy, at least as a statement of intent, of racial integration. The 'mobile reserve' on the other hand has been used in other systems, and indeed still is, but it is a boring duty since most of the time little is happening. Even if combined with constant searching, it is not likely to encourage the imaginative approach to work which officers can and should develop. Our earlier discussion of parole and of the dangers of dividing responsibility between departments must lead to a conclusion that, contrary to the report's recommendation, welfare officers should be firmly kept in the Department of Corrections.

Nor is there any reason why after training, prison officers should not make good welfare officers. The advantages of direct entry to senior positions have already been discussed. One regrettable but inevitable set of recommendations concerns the freedom of prisoners, and the modest amount of freedom they had in running their affairs. The abuse of this freedom in several respects is a constant theme in the report, and is unfortunately a commonplace of prison experience when efforts are made to allow inmates an amount of self-government however modest.

The last recommendation, in respect of trafficking, is rather strange, since this was not discussed at all. It is true that one prisoner alleged that he could name officers who were trafficking.[22] Counsel for the Prison Officers' Union requested that this be done, but the matter was not pursued. In the light of the force of the final recommendation it is a pity that this was not taken up and evidence produced and dealt with if necessary.

The response of the Department of Corrections to this wide-ranging and diverse group of recommendations has been variable.[23] Some were accepted, apparently unequivocally, and where appropriate, were implemented. These included the maintenance of the principle of racial integration in the prisons, rather than a return to separation, and some expansion of recreational facilities, including more television sets, an improved library, and the placement of a small number of uniformed officers on specialized courses on recreation. In addition the control of internal broadcasting was taken back by the staff, a second deputy superintendent's post was established at Fremantle, prison Rules and Regulations have been rewritten and, moreover, distributed to prisoners in booklet form.

Another group of recommendations have been partly implemented. Thus, there was an increase in staff, but they were not necessarily deployed in the way the commissioner recommended. Some are rostered to supervise the grills leading on to the yards, but they are not stationed on the back overlooking that area as recommended. Nor, as was also recommended, has a 'mobile reserve' been established, since this latter recommendation would involve extra expenditure, the allocation of which was outside the scope of the department. Another example of a part-implementation is that concerning 'trusties'. They now have to carry a pass, but nevertheless they can still move about unescorted.

The future of a third group of recommendations may be characterized as uncertain. Included in this category are the putting back of summer 'locking up' time, the establishment of a principal officer in charge of divisions at all times, and, perhaps most controversial of all, the possibility of an appointment as Superintendent of Fremantle from *outside* the department. Two eastern states, New South Wales and Victoria, introduced 'direct entrants' into the senior ranks in the prisons in 1975.

Finally, certain recommendations were rejected. These included that which stated that welfare officers should 'preferably not be ex-prison officers'. The majority are, and the department expressed its satisfaction with that fact. The mysterious proposal for a 'rigorous internal investigation' into trafficking was also rejected, with an observation that the question of trafficking by staff is under constant attention.

The years since 1960 have in many respects been difficult for the uniformed prison officers. The overcrowding and the several strikes and riots have been very much their concern, since obviously they carry out the daily routine. Not only the crises, but the major changes which have been introduced have affected them too. The increased stress, because of overcrowding and, officers were to allege, bad behaviour, led to demands from officers for heavier punishment. The persistence of these demands led to a remarkable success in 1964, when a Prison Acts Amendment Bill was presented to parliament.[24] This Bill, which 'has been presented, in the main, because of the strong representations made . . . by the Gaol Officers "Union",' proposed the reintroduction of the 'cumulative sentence'. This is the process whereby a prisoner convicted of an 'aggravated', which is to say serious, prison offence, could be sentenced to six months' additional imprisonment. This practice, which at the present time is common in Australian prison systems, had been condemned by the Royal Commission of 1899 and abandoned. In 1964 the Member of the Legislative Assembly for Swan, while approving of heavier punishment for prisoners who assaulted staff, opposed the measure.[25] He quoted extensively from the debates surrounding the Prison Act of 1903, in which concern was expressed about excessively-severe punishment for prison offences. His proposal that the period be reduced from six to three months was rejected, and after the chief secretary's reiteration of the pressure from staff he asked: 'Will you always do what the Gaol Officers' Union wants?'

Despite considerable opposition in the Legislative Council the measure was passed and the cumulative sentence was re-established in Western Australian prison administration.[26]

In two important respects, however, the prisoner's position when charged with a prison offence is very different from that of the turn of the century. Today he is allowed to engage a lawyer to defend him, a process which has been facilitated by the availability of legal aid. Furthermore, if the prisoner is dissatisfied with the outcome, then he has a right to complain, like anyone else, to the Parliamentary Commissioner for Administrative Investigations (the Western Australian 'Ombudsman').

The creation of an elaborate training programme too has created a certain amount of anxiety. The evolution of an acceptable, intelligible training programme for prison staff is a very difficult task, and it has been complicated in Western Australia by the creation of promotional courses. After considerable debate, some of it conducted in the columns of the *Western Australian Prison Officers' Union Newsletter*,[27] the officers voted to accept such courses. This means that promotion from officer to senior officer, and on to principal officer, is now substantially a consequence of success on these courses.

This fact in itself is still hotly debated. The dispute is common in prison systems—and in similar organizations, such as mental hospitals or schools—where goals are not precisely laid down, and appropriate training for a better performance at work is therefore difficult to establish. The main difficulty is that in work situations which are about human relationships, the skills needed *may* be enhanced by experience, or they *may* be enhanced by training. There cannot, however, be any certainty that either can combat the personality traits, good or bad, which are brought to a work situation. A man who cannot fly aeroplanes can be taught to do so and can become a pilot. There is a close and measurable correlation between his training and his job performance. In prison work, or teaching, or psychiatric nursing no such correlation has yet been demonstrated.

Apart from the argument as to whether courses should be linked with promotion, and apart from the complex question of the nature and content of such courses, which has been discussed elsewhere,[28] a curiosity of prison-staff training in modern societies is the swift onset of a fantasy about what the courses are trying to achieve. It is common, throughout the world, for staff undergoing training to see the process as an insidious attack on their beliefs. The very creation of training seems to prove to uniformed staff that either their attitudes are wrong and need 'correcting', or that their knowledge is defective and needs increasing. The fact that the courses contain academic subjects, notably drawn from the social sciences, confirms the suspicion that 'brainwashing'—the word most commonly used—is going on. The usual experience of officers attending courses in sophisticated prison systems is that this is not the case, and that attendance at courses may be enjoyable as well as educative. To the officer who has not attended, such a change of attitude on the part of those who have is proof that the process of brainwashing has been successful.

All these complicated responses to training, which in Western Australia for a short time led to a staff ban on courses, have to be dealt with. Since the inception of training, and especially since the creation of a Training Board, with a wide representation and of which staff approved,[29] those responsible for training have been aware of the difficulties. Like so many prison 'problems', because they are inherent in the prison situation, they cannot be entirely resolved. Attitudes to training can only be coped with, and from time to time modified. One forthright comment from a prison officer is worth quoting in full, since it offers an effective summary of how training, which is so appealing as an idea for the improvement of prison systems, creates as many problems as it solves:

> Have any of you ever wondered how the lecturers on the courses do this brainwashing without actually doing it in the open? It must be sort of filtered between the lines, because when the Senior and Principal Officers return from courses they break their necks to tell everyone 'They tried to brainwash us but it didn't work', but it's quite clear that something has rubbed off because even a rusty screw can see a remarkable change in the people concerned. Such minor details like: going soft on inmates—no respect or backing for fellow officers and no regard for Union rules, Constitution or Award etc.[30]

The most traumatic aspect of recent change in the prison system, as far as officers have been concerned, has been the introduction of non-uniformed professionals into the system. Officers' apprehension about this process is once again shared by prison staff in other countries. It is an apprehension which, if not dealt with seriously, can harden into resistance and opposition. The experience in Western Australia has general lessons for all modern prison systems.

The basis of the attitude to specialist staff lies in the fact that they are introduced, in the wake of a reformative commitment, to 'help' prisoners. This tends to make officers uneasy. This uneasiness does not, as despairing reformers tend to believe, spring from officers' dislike of prisoners, or disgust because the latter are likely to meet better times. A prison service certainly has its share, but not a monopoly of cruel and sadistic staff. But the caution which characterizes officers' attitudes to non-uniformed professionals is too common and too universal to make credible an explanation which depends on assumptions about a mass-personality trait, and a bizarre one at that, which is found in every prison officer.

The more likely explanation is more rational. The attempt to introduce reformative regimes, of which the introduction of non-uniformed staff is a major component, brings real problems for officers. Generally such a regime involves an increase in freedom for prisoners, with a corresponding increase in the difficulty of supervising their activities. Thus for the prison officer reform increases the likelihood of escape, assault or other disturbance, which is not only stressful, but focuses the attention of the community on him. Today there is a belief amongst many officers, most especially in America perhaps, that the community is hostile to prisons and will quickly criticize, or worse, ridicule what is going on in them. This process of estrangement is symbolized by the growth of radical pressure groups in society—Prisoners Action in Australia, Preservation of the Rights of Prisoners in England—which are more critical than older organizations, such as the various Howard societies. In a report of the Australian Federation of Prison Officers' meeting in 1974 the Tasmanian statement was: 'all States are experiencing their particular difficulties with strikes, *assaults on officers and the ever-increasing interference by outsiders who do not understand the problems* as we do.'[31]

Officers take the view that in some vague way the psychologists, teachers, social workers and others who join the prison service are associated with these critics. The non-uniformed staff, generally, have a high degree of education, and so far as the officer is concerned, this education leads to condemnation of prisons. They cannot resist the feeling that their menial, routine, tasks, such as locking and unlocking, are regarded by non-uniformed staff with contempt. This feeling is exacerbated by the strong links which are developed between non-uniformed staff and prisoners individually or collectively.

This close association, which after all is the very essence of professional activity, has two effects on the officers' attitudes. The first is that he suspects that the professional and the prisoner may be in some way combining against him. It is likely to occur to him that he is the subject of their conversation, and no amount of reassurance that this is not so, is likely to convince him. The second effect is that, as training and treatment become major aims in the prisons, the traditional custodial goals are depressed. Since his work is associated with those goals, his status diminishes. This is usually followed by a demand that the officer be involved in the new reformative regime. This demand has been powerfully voiced in England by the Prison Officers' Association, and may be considered a responsible role for an officers' union.[32] If some concession is not made to this demand, then the officer becomes a messenger collecting prisoners and delivering them to the non-uniformed staff. He will resent this and will ultimately sabotage any arrangements which perpetuate it.

One consequence of the introduction of specialists is a new allocation of resources, which is invariably a source of resentment. Prison staff are well accustomed to being told that money and other resources are in short supply. The continuing use of Fremantle is the most prominent example in Western Australia. When non-uniformed staff are recruited, it appears to officers that resources which are in short supply, are deflected to the newcomers. They resent not only the fact that the newcomers are treated well, but that ultimately the prisoners benefit, while the officers' position remains unsatisfactory. Prison officers' magazines and newsletters throughout the world constantly complain about this, and Western Australia is no exception. Examples are plentiful, such as the following from a member of the staff in Fremantle:

> Eventually we have been able to make some headway with the long awaited maintenance of our antiquated Gun Posts. Number 3 post has just been temporarily renovated and rumour has it that work may commence on a complete replacement by mid-October. Mean-

while our Psychologist friends will shortly be taking up residence in
two new suites of interview offices. These have been recently built
at untold expense with all the refinements; that is except air con-
ditioners but these are probably on order. One of these would be
nice perched on top of the wall in replacement of the disgusting
structures called Gun Posts, but then it would be a waste of time.
The guns are only manned 24 hours a day.[33]

The point has been stressed that the relationship between uniformed and non-uniformed staff is the most urgent question in
modern prison systems. Western Australia is no different, nor is
the relationship in the service worse than anywhere else. As has
also been stated, it is impossible to solve the problem once and for
all because it derives from so many causes, including the confusion
over the aims of a prison system. Since there is no evidence of an
end to this confusion, the conflict will remain. However, two
actions may contribute to a slight easing of tension.

One is a consideration of the possibility that the non-uniformed
staff could be of assistance to officers. Two brief examples may
be given. Because of the new links between education and promotion, teachers might consider in what ways they might possibly
be able to help uniformed officers overcome deficiencies in formal
education. Or again, social workers might make it clear that if an
officer in difficulty wishes to avail himself of their skills, he is
welcome to do so. Teachers or social workers may argue that their
business is with prisoners, but a refusal to recognize the constraints
imposed on professional activity in prison by the existence of
officers dooms that activity.

The most hopeful method of avoiding an irreparable division
between the two groups is to encourage dialogue in which differences can at least be aired if not buried. This is especially important as non-uniformed departments grow and make the overall
administration of the prison service more complex. Growth and
fragmentation into semi-independent units hinders effective communication, and this has to be countered with studied attempts to
encourage exchange. This has been done in Western Australia in a
setting known as a 'Search Conference', when staff of all kinds
were brought together to examine the nature of their differences.
This encouraging development is currently being analysed and
documented. The reported reaction of the uniformed staff appeared favourable.[34]

This whole issue is one of an unavoidable confusion of the goals of a prison system, which emanates from the community, and is at last, left as a daily problem to be pondered by prison staff, especially uniformed officers. The particular issue of conflict between custodial and reformative aims, in the context of Western Australian prisons, has very recently been subjected to a scholarly analysis by T. A. Williams.[35] Although this study is of great value to those concerned with a local situation, its general discussion is relevant to all modern prison systems. To attempt to summarize it would be less than just to its depth and complexity. It is necessary, however, to note that in Australia, where so little has been written about prisons, this study is of signal importance and should be widely known.

This account of imprisonment in Western Australia has shown that many of the problems and developments in its history have been part of those trends in penal reform which, because of the strength of international communication amongst people who are interested, are an important, if under-reported, part of social history. The abolition of separate confinement is an example of a process which in the face of international experience and conclusion could not be halted.

At times the state has been in advance of other states and other countries, as when Hamel and Pardelup were opened, and when in very recent years such a large proportion of prisoners were allocated to open conditions. There is much too, in the history of the system which is unusual and sometimes unique. The tradition of prisoners being employed on community work is perhaps the most outstanding example.

Since the mid-1960s, as we have shown, the Western Australian prison system has undergone radical change during a period when the problems facing staff were arguably greater than they had ever been. Some of our conclusions must be provisional, since the events described are recent and difficult on that account to put into perspective. These problems are not likely to diminish. As more minor and first offenders and alcoholics are kept out of prison, and as sentences lengthen because of an evident growth of very serious crime, the prison population will develop a very different complexion from that of forty years ago. It is likely too that the racial issue, despite the royal commissioner's optimism in 1973, is likely to be prominent. Nor is the community any more likely to take an intelligent interest in the complexities of prison work than it has previously. In the light of such prognoses the Western Australian prison system will no doubt have to work hard to maintain such initiative as it has displayed in recent years— quite a challenge.

APPENDIX 1

'The Establishment'

Fremantle Prison—'The Establishment', as it was called when it was an imperial institution—has featured prominently in this account of imprisonment in Western Australia. Since, despite its purpose, it has always been one of the most important buildings in the state, and since it will inevitably one day be evacuated, it is appropriate now to set out some of its many interesting features. This is especially necessary, because its future, when it is no longer a prison, is bound to be uncertain. It is to be hoped that conservation has reached such a degree of maturity in Western Australia that demolition will be resisted, and that the building will instead fulfil a useful and pleasanter function in the future.

The up-hill approach to the prison became known as the 'tramway', because of the wooden rails which were laid down to carry small trucks laden with rubble and stone from the excavations made in the hillside on which the buildings were established. The tramway is now called Fairbairn Street. Even a superficial examination of the prison makes clear that the excavations that were made were considerable. At the top of the hill is the focal point of any prison: the gate. Here it is that staff assemble, going on and off duty, where they reintegrate as a group and where they re-emphasize their unity. It is at the gate too that the public get their impression of the prison, and for this reason the gatekeeper is one of the most important officers in a prison. One of the first acts in compiling a list of rules was to set out special instructions for the gate officer, which were periodically elaborated and stressed.[1]

The gateway itself, in common with Victorian practice, is an elaborate, and probably in its day an impregnable edifice. On either side of the gate are the guard-houses from which the military could deploy to strategically-positioned slits set in an inner wall to quell disturbance. On the central archway, above the gate, is a clock-tower, at the pinnacle of which is a clock made in London in 1854 by the famous firm Thwaite & Reid. On either side of the gate are very good examples of Victorian architecture in the form of houses for the chaplain, superintendent, stipendiary magistrate and surgeon. These were occupied until very recently, and have

184

now been put to other uses. The officers' quarters, which are still occupied by prison staff, were built in Henderson Street, just below the prison.

Between the gatehouse and the main prison is a wrought iron gate, designed by Captain Wray and made by Sergeant Nelson, both sappers, in about 1856. Both names are inscribed upon it. Inside the prison yard, in the immediate foreground, is the Anglican chapel, on the front of which is a crown with the letters V.R. and the date 1855. The interior of the chapel is plain, strongly made (especially the roof), and has a gallery, typical of the period, in which officers and their families sat when attending services. The first confirmation service was held on 20 May 1858. There is also a Roman Catholic chapel in the prison.

Religion naturally played an important part in the life of prisoners and staff. One of the duties of the officers was to say grace at the beginning and end of meals. As stated in the Superintendent's Order Book, 'it is strictly required that the recital of such graces should be done in a reverent manner, and with a slow distinctive voice. The hurried and slovenly manner in which this duty has been frequently performed gave the Superintendent great displeasure.'[2]

Denominational differences created a certain amount of difficulty in the prison. One chaplain, Reverend O'Neil, urged the Roman Catholic prisoners to demonstrate in support of a demand for more feast days. He was consequently suspended and there was a riot of the Roman Catholic prisoners. The refusal from time to time of prisoners to take religion seriously annoyed the authorities. In 1898 Superintendent George complained that prisoners were registering as Roman Catholics because the latter had fewer services.[3] Until in recent years in most countries attendance at religious services was made voluntary, the manipulation by prisoners of religious oddities of this kind was a commonplace of prison administration.

The prison itself is divided into cell blocks known as 'divisions'. Apart from the introduction of conveniences such as electricity, these blocks are in most respects the same as when they were built. There is one notable exception: the progressive enlargement of cells, which was instigated by the Royal Commission of 1898-99. When the prison was built, the bulk were only kept in the prison at night, but when the prison was used to incarcerate prisoners all the time, a concern, which so far has been ineffective, began to be expressed about the unsuitability of the buildings for the purpose.

In number 4 division are two of the most remarkable prison cells in the world. The first of these is a cell on the walls of which are a series of pencil drawings. They depict biblical scenes and classical portraits beautifully executed by a very skilled convict draftsman. Unfortunately he did not leave his name. Although, some of the drawings have been erased by an enthusiastic cleaner (also anonymous), a lot remains. A few feet away is another cell, which was reinforced with metal studs and wood, apparently in an attempt, on this occasion successful, to prevent further escapes by 'Moondyne Joe'. The whole prison is surrounded by a gun patrol. Although this is now mounted on the walls, prior to 1926 guards were positioned on the ground.

When a Victorian prison officer joined 'the Establishment', he not only guaranteed to be of good behaviour himself, but he guaranteed the good behaviour of his family. The officers' families were very much a part of the prison. On one occasion two families were ordered to leave quarters immediately because their wives had been 'guilty of creating a disturbance, disgraceful to them, and discreditable to the establishment'. In the event of misbehaviour the officers' rations as well as his pay could be stopped. Not only could his rations be stopped, but the rations of his family could be suspended. The mutual identification of officers and prisoners under such rigorous supervision is evidenced by the reluctance of officers to flog their charges. By 11 December 1851 it was necessary for the comptroller-general to direct that the officers should carry out flogging in rotation, and that the chief warder should arrange for the flogger to practise for ten minutes on a sack filled with seaweed.[4] Staff continued to be reluctant, and in 1854 the duties devolved onto the gatekeeper. In 1863 a paid 'scourger' was employed. Corporal punishment was severe. In 1854 the ringleaders of a minor riot were sentenced to be given 100 lashes each.[5]

There is within the prison a hospital block which for a period at the end of the century became the imperial invalid depot. There is also a series of workshops where bootmaking, tailoring and printing are carried out. This workshop activity, it will be remembered, was considerably extended at the beginning of the present century as a consequence of the Royal Commission. There are the usual exercise yards. 'The cage' which resembled a segmented orange for exercising prisoners undergoing separate treatment was demolished in 1911-12.[6]

On a lighter note, there is a concert hall which was once the hospital condemned by the Royal Commission of 1898-99. In 1924 a gallery was added to this concert hall so that female prisoners could attend performances without being seen by the male prisoners. There is a tendency for prison officials everywhere, in dealing with visitors, to display the kitchen. The kitchen in Fremantle Prison is especially interesting, since bread is still baked in old Scottish ovens with wood fires. There is also a complex system of underground, convict-built wells, tunnels and reservoirs, which in 1888 were attached to a steam pump to supply water both to the prison and to part of the town of Fremantle. Since the closure of the Round House and Fremantle Gaol in 1888 all executions have taken place in 'the Establishment'. The execution chamber, now rapidly becoming a thing of the past, remains intact.

The point which it is worth reinforcing about a prison with the historic associations of Fremantle is, that while it has been productive of more misery than human happiness, it is inevitably an important part of the social history of the state. Probably the building which has been most productive of human misery in the world is the Tower of London. This fact, however, does not justify its demolition. The unhappiness of Fremantle Prison is as much a part of the human experience of Western Australia, as are the more dramatic, congenial episodes in its history.

Heads of the Western Australian Prison System

Comptrollers-General of Convicts

1850   E. Y. W. Henderson
1856   H. Wray
1858   E. Y. W. Henderson
1863   Captain C. F. Newland, Royal Navy
1866   G. E. Hampton (Acting Comptroller-General)
1867   H. Wakeford
1872   W. R. Fauntleroy

Superintendent of Convicts

1878   J. F. Stone

Sheriffs and Inspectors of Prisons
(The first time that all the state prisons were put in the charge of one individual.)

1886   J. B. Roe
1901   O. Burt

Under-Secretary and Comptrollers-General of Prisons

1912   F. D. North
1921   H. C. Trethowan
1930   F. J. Huelin
1944   W. L. Wilson
1945   H. T. Stitfold

Comptrollers-General of Prisons

1950   A. Mackillop
1959   A. H. Waterer
1965   E. G. Cant
1966   C. W. Campbell

Director, Department of Corrections

1966-77   C. W. Campbell
1977   W. Kidston

APPENDIX 3

Site of Convict Prison at Fremantle

[2 Edwardi VII No 7]

The First Schedule

Fremantle Lot CD, contents 39 acres 1 rood, more or less. Bounded on the *South-West* by a line about 3 chains 60 links in length, extending in a direction East 34 degrees 52 minutes South along South Terrace from the South-West end of Henderson Street, then by a line about 6 chains 55 links in length in direction East, 50 degrees 7 minutes South along South Terrace aforesaid, and by a line about 4 chains in length, extending East 64 degrees 39 minutes South along South Terrace, to a prolongation of the North-West side of Arundel Street; on the *South East* by about 10 chains 95 links of said prolongation, extending North 50 degrees 7 minutes East, then by a line about 3 chains 52 links in length, extending North 5 degrees West, and by a line about 10 chains 60 links in length, extending East 5 degrees North; on the *East* by a line about 13 chains 52 links in length, extending North 5 degrees West; and on the *North* by a line about 10 chains 60 links in length, extending West 5 degrees South, then by a line about 5 chains 38 links in length, extending South 65 degrees 45 minutes West, then by a line about 2 chains 74 links in length, extending South 27 degrees West, then by about 3 chains 56 links of the South-West side of Queen Street, extending West 27 degrees North, and finally by the South-East side of Henderson Street aforesaid, extending South 27 degrees West to South Terrace aforesaid—all bearings and boundaries here given being true or thereabouts, and an iron boundary mark being fixed at every angle or corner of the land herein described.

The Second Schedule

A Grant, dated 23rd January, 1889, from Her late Majesty Queen Victoria to the Commissioners of the Presbyterian Church in Western Australia, of Fremantle Town Lot 1360.

189

A Grant, dated 11th June, 1894, from Her late Majesty Queen Victoria to the Mayor, Councillors, and Burgesses of the Town of Fremantle, of Fremantle Town Lot 1372.

A Grant, dated 16th April, 1896, from Her late Majesty Queen Victoria to Elias Solomon and William Frederick Samson, of Fremantle Town Lot 1375, in trust for a place of worship for the members of the Jewish Church.

A Grant, dated 3rd August, 1897, from Her late Majesty Queen Victoria to the Mayor, Councillors, and Burgesses of the Town of Fremantle, of Fremantle Town Lots 1376 and 1380.

A Grant, dated 28th July, 1899, from Her late Majesty Queen Victoria to the Mayor, Councillors, and Burgesses of the Town of Fremantle, of Fremantle Town Lot No. 1386.

Abbreviations

A.R.	Annual Report
BL	Battye Library [State Reference Library of W. Aust.]
B.P.P.	*British Parliamentary Papers*
CSF	Colonial Secretary's Office Records, outward correspondence
CSO	Colonial Secretary's Office Records
CSR	Colonial Secretary's Office Records, inward correspondence
V. & P.	Western Australia, *Minutes, Votes and Proceedings*
W.A.*P.D.*	Western Australia, *Parliamentary Debates* (Hansard)
W.A.P.O.U. Newsletter	*Western Australian Prison Officers' Union Newsletter*

Notes

1 Early imprisonment

1. Despatch to Governor Stirling by Secretary of State Goderich 1833, quoted J. S. Battye, *Western Australia: A History from its Discovery to the Inauguration of the Commonwealth* (London, Oxford University Press 1924), p. 50.
2. J. S. Battye, *Western Australia: A History,* pp. 59-60.
3. Battye, p. 59.
4. Ibid. p. 62.
5. Ibid. p. 62.
6. This information about the Albany settlement is taken from uncatalogued material in the archives of the Albany Historical Society.
7. J. E. Thomas, *The English Prison Officer Since 1850: a study in conflict* (London, Routledge and Kegan Paul 1972), p. 11. For a history of the English hulks see William Branch Johnson, *The English Prison Hulks . . .* (London, Christopher Johnson 1957).
8. CSO R/1828-9, vol. 1 pp. 151, 159, BL.
9. Swan River Papers, vols 3, and 4 p. 65, BL.
10. CSO R/1830, p. 114, BL.
11. CSR 7/132, pp. 132-3, BL.
12. CSO R/1830, p. 132, BL.
13. Fremantle Harbour Trust, PR 2378 (roneo), BL.
14. CSF 4/36, BL.
15. S. & B. Webb, *English Prisons under Local Government* (London, Longmans 1927), p. 110.
16. 5 & 6 Will. IV C 38 (1835) An Act for effecting greater Uniformity of Practice in the Government of the several Prisons in England and Wales; and for appointing Inspectors of Prisons in Great Britain.
17. For an account of this period in English prison history see S. & B. Webb, *English Prisons under Local Government.*
18. Battye Research Notes, ref. 65222 RN 107/108, BL.
19. For an account of its place in the development of penal treatment for young offenders see L. W. Fox, *The English prison and Borstal systems . . .* (London, Routledge & K. Paul 1952), chap. 19.
20. 6 Vict. No 8 (1842) An Act to Regulate the Apprenticeship and otherwise to provide for the Guardianship and Control of a certain class of Juvenile Immigrants.
21. During his guardianship Schoales kept a letterbook, which is a valuable source of information: Letterbook of Superintendent of Juvenile Emigrants 7 Dec. 1843-12 Sept 1847, BL.
22. Schoales's Letterbook, p. 4.
23. Battye Research Notes, 5 Nov. 1849, ref. 65222 RN 108, BL.
24. Rica Erickson, *Old Toodyay and Newcastle* (Perth, Toodyay Shire Council 1974), p. 95.
25. Schoales's Letterbook, p. 1.

26. Ibid. 8 April 1844.
27. Erickson, *Old Toodyay and Newcastle,* pp. 44-6.
28. 6 & 7 Will. IV C 30 (1836) An Act to repeal so much of two Acts of the Ninth and Tenth Years of King George the Fourth as directs the Period of the Execution and the Prison Discipline of Persons convicted of the Crime of Murder. Adopted by 7 Vict. 13 (1844) An Act for adopting certain Acts of Parliament passed in the third and fourth, the fourth and fifth, the fifth and sixth, and the sixth and seventh years of the reign of His late Majesty King William the Fourth; and also certain Acts of Parliament passed in the first and second, the second and third, and the fifth and sixth years of the reign of Her present Majesty Queen Victoria, respectively, and applying the same in Administration of Justice in Western Australia in like manner as the other Laws of England are applied therein.
29. 12 Vict. No 7 (1849) An Ordinance for the Regulation of Gaols, Prisons and Houses of Correction in the Colony of Western Australia, and for other purposes relating thereto.
30. Webb, *English Prisons under Local Government,* p. 118.
31. *British Parliamentary Papers, Crime and Punishment, Transportation,* 1837, vols 2, 3, 4 (Irish University Press Series 1968-).
32. J. T. Burt, *Results of the System of Separate Confinement as administered at the Pentonville Prison* (London, Longman & co 1852).
33. 14 Vict. No 6 (1850) An Ordinance to provide for the due Custody and Discipline of Offenders Transported to Western Australia; and of Offenders sentenced therein to Transportation.
34. 19 Vict. No 8 (1856) An Ordinance to substitute other punishment in lieu of Transportation.
35. 24 Vict. No 1 (1860) An Ordinance to amend the Ordinance 19th Victoria, No. 8, of 1856, to substitute in certain cases other punishment in lieu of Transportation.
36. Ibid. and 21 Vict. No 12 (1858) An Ordinance to extend and enlarge the Provisions of an Ordinance passed in the twelfth year of the reign of Her present Majesty, intituled "An Ordinance for the Regulation of Gaols, Prisons, and Houses of Correction in the Colony of Western Australia, and for other purposes relating thereto".
37. 21 Vict. No 1 (1857) An Ordinance to make additional provisions for Convict Discipline in Western Australia.
38. 43 Vict. No 4 (1879) An Act to make additional provisions for Prison Discipline in Western Australia.
39. 51 Vict. No 5 (1887) An Act to amend the Law in respect of the employment of Prisoners sentenced to hard labour.
40. 17 Vict. No 7 (1854) An Ordinance for the suppression of violent Crimes committed by Convicts illegally at large.
41. 32 Vict. No 9 (1868) An Ordinance to make better Provision for the Suppression of Violent Crimes committed by Convicts.
42. *V. & P.* 1882, Annual Report 1881.
43. Report of the Commission to Inquire into Certain Departments in the Public Service 1878, *V. & P.* 1878, p. 399.
44. *V. & P.* 1880 No 7, p. 1, quoted T. Saunders, Development of the Prison

System (thesis, Graylands Teacher Training College), p. 14, BL ref. 7326.

45. *V. & P.* 1882 No 30, quoted T. Saunders, Development of the Prison System, p. 15.

46. W. Aust. Blue Book 1887, p. 164, quoted T. Saunders, p. 15.

47. Blue Book 1888, p. 179, quoted T. Saunders, p. 15.

48. Blue Book 1890, p. 190, quoted T. Saunders, p. 15.

49. Correspondence respecting the transfer to the colony of the Imperial Convict Establishment, *V. & P.* 1884, paper 22.

50. Annual Report 1886, *V. & P.* 1887.

51. *V. & P.* 1881, vol. 2 paper 6: Report on Rottnest for 1880.

52. CSO Records 1882-84, 4 March 1882, BL.

53. CSO Records, 7 Oct. 1882, BL.

54. *V. & P.* 1894, paper 3.

55. *V. & P.* 1895, vol. 1 paper 12.

56. CSO 2269/1901/5 and CSO 2269/1901/3, BL.

2 *British Convicts in Western Australia*

1. Report from the Select Committee on Transportation 1861, *British Parliamentary Papers, Crime and Punishment, Transportation,* session 1837-61, vol. 3 (Irish University Press Series 1968). Evidence Q976ff.

2. A discussion of this period may be read in J. S. Battye, *Western Australia: A History.*

3. Battye, p. 175.

4. Ibid. p. 186.

5. Ibid. p. 200.

6. *Perth Gazette* 2 Jan. 1847.

7. Correspondence and papers relating to convict discipline and transportation 1849, in *B.P.P. Crime and Punishment, Transportation,* vol. 9 pp. 245ff.

8. Ibid.

9. A scholarly account of transportation is in A. G. L. Shaw, *Convicts and the Colonies* (London, Faber and Faber 1966).

10. Shaw, Appendix.

11. Ibid. p. 270. For a biography of Maconochie see J. V. Barry, *Alexander Maconochie of Norfolk Island: a study in penal reform* (Melbourne, Melbourne University Press 1958).

12. Select Committee on Transportation 1838, in vol. 3 of *B.P.P. Crime and Punishment, Transportation.*

13. Correspondence and papers, etc. (vide note 7 supra), pp. 251ff.

14. J. E. Thomas, 'Killed on duty: an analysis of the murders of English prison staff since 1850', *Prison Service Journal* (England), No 7 (new series), July 1972.

15. Convict Journal V12, BL. See also W. B. Kimberley, *History of Western Australia: A narrative of her past together with biographies of her leading men* (Melbourne, F. W. Niven 1897), vol. 1 p. 155.

16. Du Cane is the subject of G. A. Hasluck's *Royal Engineer: life of Sir Edmund Du Cane* (Sydney, Angus and Robertson 1975). There is a biographical note

on Henderson in *Australian Dictionary of Biography,* vol. 4 ed. by Douglas Pike (Melbourne, Melbourne University Press 1972).

17. See text p. 28.

18. For a detailed information see J. E. Thomas, *The English Prison Officer Since 1850: a study in conflict.*

19. Select Committee of the House of Lords to enquire into an Act to substitute punishment in lieu of transportation 1856, in *B.P.P. Crime and Punishment, Transportation,* vol. 4 Q848.

20. W. Porter, *History of the Corps of Royal Engineers* (London, Royal Engineers 1889-1915), p. 356.

21. Ibid. p. 354.

22. Porter ibid., quoted D. Roberts, *Victorian origins of the British welfare State* (New Haven, Yale University Press 1960), p. 157.

23. Porter ibid., is wrong in his statement that Du Cane and Crossman arrived together in January 1852. See G. A. Hasluck's *Royal Engineer,* p. 8.

24. For a discussion of Du Cane's contribution to prison administration see J. E. Thomas, *The English Prison Officer Since 1850,* chaps 1-6.

25. G. A. Hasluck, *Royal Engineer,* p. 16.

26. Lords Select Committee on Transportation 1856 (vide note 19 supra), Q 844ff.

27. An account of all aspects of the shipping of convicts to Australia is in C. Bateson, *The Convict Ships 1787-1868,* 2nd edn (Sydney, A. H. & A. W. Reed 1974).

28. Ibid. p. 298.

29. Ibid. p. 307.

30. Ibid. pp. 309-10.

31. C. Gertzel, The convict system in Western Australia 1850-1870 (BA honours thesis in history, University of Western Australia), p. 8.

32. These regulations are held in the Battye Library. This rule is entitled 'Regulations for Holders of Tickets of Leave', p. 7, Reg. 30, BL.

33. Superintendent's Order Book, Fremantle. Catalogue SO9, BL.

34. The full account, from which this summary is drawn is in the *B.P.P. Crime and Punishment, Transportation,* session 1864-69, vol. 16, Convict Discipline, Western Australia, pp. 241ff. (Hereafter noted as Convict Discipline, Western Australia).

35. Battye, *Western Australia: A History,* p. 254.

36. Select Committee on Transportation 1861 (vide note 1 supra), pp. 427ff.

37. Ibid. p. 44 Q2025.

38. See H. Willoughby, *British Convict in Western Australia* (London 1865), p. 32, quoted J. S. Battye, *Western Australia: A History.*

39. A. Hasluck, *Unwilling Emigrants* (Melbourne, Oxford University Press 1959), Appendix.

40. Select Committee of the House of Lords 1856 (vide note 19 supra), Q872.

41. Select Committee on Transportation 1861 (vide note 1 supra), question 1609 is an example.

42. Ibid. Q874.

43. C. Bateson, *The Convict Ships 1787-1868,* p. 396. A. Hasluck gives the number as 589, *Unwilling Emigrants,* p. 138. There is some doubt about the number aboard the *Robert Small.*

44. Superintendent's Order Book, Fremantle Catalogue SO3, BL.

45. Select Committee on Transportation 1861 (vide note 1 supra), Q1014.
46. Ibid. Q1357.
47. See S. S. O'Luing, *Fremantle Mission* (Anvil Books 1965).
48. F. Broomhall, The Veterans: a history of the Enrolled Pensioner Force in Western Australia 1850-1880 (East Perth 1975), pp. 166-7.
49. O'Luing, *Fremantle Mission,* pp. 65-6.
50. An account of his escape is in J. J. Roche, *Life of John Boyle O'Reilly . . .* (London, T. Fisher Unwin 1891).
51. Superintendent's Order Book, Fremantle. Catalogue SO9, BL.
52. A detailed account, from which this summary is taken, is S. S. O'Luing's *Fremantle Mission.* For assessments of various aspects of the affair see J. Watson (ed.), *Catalpa. 100 Years Ago . . .* (Nedlands, University of Western Australia 1976).
53. Select Committee of the House of Lords to enquire into an Act to substitute punishment in lieu of transportation 1856, *B.P.P. Crime and Punishment, Transportation,* vol. 4 Q863.
54. Ibid. Q855.
55. A brief account of his life was given in the *Civil Service Journal,* 20 July 1929, p. 76, BL. See also J. B. O'Reilly, *Moondyne: a story of convict life in Australia* (London, G. Routledge & Sons ltd 1889).
56. From Select Committee on Transportation 1861 (vide note 1 supra), QQ1598, 1601 et passim.
57. Convict Discipline, Western Australia (vide note 34 supra), p. 429.
58. From Select Committee on Transportation (vide note 1), Q976ff.
59. Ibid. Q87.
60. Ibid. QQ1592 and 1593.
61. Convict Discipline, Western Australia (vide note 34), p. 155ff.
62. All the correspondence is at Convict Discipline, Western Australia (vide note 34 supra), pp. 185ff.
63. Convict Discipline, Western Australia (vide note 34), pp. 182-3.
64. Shaw, *Convicts and the Colonies,* p. 358.
65. Uncatalogued material in Albany Historical Society archives.
66. Calculations about the numbers of convicts sent to Western Australia vary. Shaw gives a figure of 9635, Battye a figure of 9721. Gertzel states that 9721 set off from England and 9669 landed. However, in the table at the conclusion of Gertzel's work the figure is given as 9668. Bateson calculates 9636. Shaw, *Convicts and the Colonies,* p. 356, Battye, *Western Australia: A History,* p. 246, Gertzel, The convict system in Western Australia 1850-1870, p. 6, Bateson, *The Convict Ships 1787-1868,* p. 380.
67. Gertzel, The convict system in Western Australia 1850-1870, p. 9.
68. Convict Discipline, Western Australia (vide note 34), pp. 240-1.
69. W. B. Kimberley, *History of Western Australia: a narrative of her past together with biographies of her leading men* (Melbourne, F. W. Niven 1897), p. 193.
70. Erickson, *Old Toodyay and Newcastle,* p. 205.
71. A. Trollope, *Australia and New Zealand,* vol. 1 (London, Chapman and Hall 1876), p. 97.
72. Select Committee on Transportation 1861 (vide note 1), QQ1706 and 1708.

73. Uncatalogued material in Albany Historical Society archives.

74. Select Committee of the House of Lords to enquire into an Act to substitute punishment in lieu of transportation 1856 (vide note 19), QQ992-993.

75. Western Australia, Parliament, *Parliamentary Debates* (Hansard), 29 July 1903, vol. 23 p. 225 col. 2.

76. Uncatalogued material in Albany Historical Society archives.

77. For a full account of this important group see F. Broomhall, The Veterans: a history of the Enrolled Pensioner Force in Western Australia 1850-1880.

78. Battye, *Western Australia: A History,* p. 465.

79. Roche, *Life of John Boyle O'Reilly,* p. 70.

80. Trollope, *Australia and New Zealand,* p. 126.

81. Select Committee on Transportation (vide note 1 supra), Q1399.

82. E. Millet, *An Australian Parsonage; or the Settler and the Savage in Western Australia,* p. 332.

83. Battye, *Western Australia: A History,* p. 459.

3   *The Royal Commission 1898-1899*

1. For an account see *Attica: the official report of the New York State Special Commission* (New York, Bantam Books 1972).

2. Report of the Inquiry into Prison Escapes and Security 1966 (the Mountbatten Report), *British Parliamentary Papers, Colonies, Australia,* vol. 8, 1969, cmd 3175.

3. For detailed account of the causes, courses and consequence of the Gladstone investigation see J. E. Thomas, *The English Prison Officer Since 1850; a study in conflict,* chap. 6; and L. W. Fox, *The English prison and Borstal systems,* chaps 3 and 4. The Gladstone Committee is bulky and is divided into three parts: 1 Report from the Departmental Committee on Prisons 1895, cmd 7702; 2 Observations of Prison Commissioners on Recommendations of Departmental Committee 1895; 3 Minutes of Evidence taken by the Departmental Committee on Prisons, with Appendices and Index, 1895, cmd 7702-1.

4. *Western Mail* 6 Aug. 1892, p. 15.

5. *Inquirer and Commercial News* 20 Oct. 1893, p. 18.

6. Ibid. 23 July 1897, p. 9. For other press coverage see: *Inquirer and Commercial News* 30 July 1897, p. 11, 6 Aug. 1897, p. 3; *West Australian* 28 Apr. 1898, p. 7, 5 Jan. 1898, p. 4.

7. See for example Hansard, 26 Aug. 1897, vol. 10 p. 310 col. 2.

8. For an account see C. Péan, *The Conquest of Devil's Island* (London, Max Parrish 1953).

9. J. Bastin & J. Stoodley, 'F. C. B. Vosper, An Australian Radical', *University Studies in History,* vol. 5 no. 1 (University of Western Australia Press 1967).

10. Annual Report 1897, *V. & P.* 1898.

11. Hansard, 6 July 1898, vol. 12 p. 302 col. 2ff.

12. Annual Report 1897, *V. & P.* 1898.

13. 15 & 16 Eliz. II C 80 Criminal Justice Act 1967, sect. 65.

14. Hansard, 28 Sept. 1898. vol. 13 p. 2020 col. 1.

15. These and other details of members of the commission may be seen in G. C.

Bolton & Ann Mozley, *The Western Australian Legislature 1870-1930* (Canberra, Australian National University Press 1961).

16. *Report of the Commission appointed to inquire into the Penal System of the Colony* (Perth, Govt Printer 1899).
17. Royal Commission 1899, First Report, p. 1.
18. Royal Commission Evidence Q40.
19. Ibid. Q53.
20. Ibid. Q322.
21. See e.g. Final Report, pp. 1-3, and Evidence QQ239, 564, 479 and 562.
22. These figures are taken from the prison reception book in Geraldton Prison. The book is located in the prison.
23. Royal Commission Evidence Q353.
24. For example Evidence Q371.
25. Royal Commission Evidence Q137A.
26. Ibid. Q496.
27. Ibid. Q839ff.
28. First Report, p. 4.
29. Royal Commission Evidence Q370.
30. Ibid. Q797.
31. Ibid. Q798.
32. First Report, p. 4.
33. Final Report, p. 11.
34. Royal Commission Evidence QQ479, 562 and 678.
35. See Convict Report (England) 1864 *British Parliamentary Papers,* pp. 11, 88, and Hansard (England) 23 Feb. 1864.
36. Final Report, p. 11.
37. Royal Commission Evidence Q180.
38. Final Report, p. 9.
39. Second Report, p. 2.
40. Ibid. p. 3.
41. Ibid. p. 2.
42. Ibid. p. 2, and Evidence Q903.
43. Royal Commission Evidence Q875.
44. First Report, p. 3.
45. Second Report, p. 2.
46. Ibid.
47. Royal Commission Evidence Q899.
48. Ibid. Q104.
49. Final Report, p. 12.
50. Final Report, p. 14.
51. Royal Commission Evidence Q751.
52. Ibid. Q764.
53. Ibid. Q390.
54. Ibid. Q106.
55. Ibid. Q107.
56. For an account of Tallack see G. Rose, *The Struggle for Penal Reform: the Howard League and its predecessors* (London, Stevens & Sons 1961).
57. Royal Commission Evidence, QQ 608 and 645.

58. John Howard's major work is *The State of the Prisons in England and Wales, with Preliminary Observations, and on Account of some Foreign Prisons,* 2 parts (Warrington 1777-80).
59. Royal Commission Evidence, pp. 58-9.
60. Ibid. Q649.
61. For Bentham's theory see 'Principles of Penal Law' in Jeremy Bentham, *Works,* edited by Sir John Bowring (Edinburgh, Tait 1843-59). An illustration of masks in use may be seen in H. Mayhew & J. Binney, *The Criminal Prisons of London and scenes of Prison Life* (London 1862; reprinted Frank Cass 1968). For a lengthy discussion of the separate system see U. R. Q. Henriques, 'The rise and decline of the separate system of prison discipline', *Past and Present,* no. 54, February 1972.
62. Final Report, p. 6 (note).
63. Ibid. p. 7.
64. For an account of the aftermath see J. E. Thomas, *The English Prison Officer Since 1850,* chaps 7 onwards.
65. Final Report, p. 5.
66. Cesare Beccaria's best-known work is *An Essay on Crimes and Punishments,* English translation 1767 (London, J. Almon 1767); see especially p. 13ff.

4   *1900-1920: 'need for reform'*

1. Pigott, Hansard, 1 Sept. 1903, vol. 23 p. 738 col. 1.
2. *Morning Herald* 11 Nov. 1901, p. 4 col. 9.
3. J. Bastin & J. Stoodley, 'F. C. B. Vosper, An Australian Radical', *University Studies in History,* 1967, vol. 5 no. 1 p. 52.
4. Annual Report 1899, *V. & P.* 1900.
5. A.R. 1917, *V. & P.* 1918.
6. A.R. 1901, *V. & P.* 1902.
7. A.R. 1900, *V. & P.* 1901.
8. *Civil Service Journal* 20 July 1929, p. 7.
9. *Morning Herald* 3 Apr. 1902, p. 4.
10. Annual Report 1901, *V. & P.* 1902.
11. A.R. 1902, *V. & P.* 1903.
12. Hansard, 28 July 1903, vol. 23 p. 166 col. 1.
13. Hansard, 29 July 1903, vol. 23 p. 223 col. 1. See also 11 Aug. 1903, vol. 23 p. 405 col. 2.
14. Hansard, 1 Sept. 1903, vol. 23 p. 731 col. 1.
15. See entries for respective members in G. C. Bolton & Ann Mozeley, *The Western Australian Legislature 1870-1930.*
16. Hansard, 1 Sept. 1903, vol. 23 p. 734 col. 2.
17. Hansard, 12 Nov. 1903, vol. 24 p. 2037 col. 2.
18. Hansard, 18 Nov. 1903, vol. 24 p. 2197 col. 2.
19. Hansard, 3 Nov. 1902, vol. 24 p. 1825 col. 1.
20. *Government Gazette* 8 Jan. 1904, p. 77.
21. Ibid. 15 July 1904, p. 1869.
22. Hansard, 1 Aug. 1905, vol. 27 p. 529 col. 2.

23. Hansard, 31 July 1907, vol. 31 p. 566 col. 1.
24. Hansard, 19 Dec. 1907, vol. 32 p. 1973 col. 2.
25. Hansard, 11 Dec. 1908, vol. 34 p. 886 col. 1.
26. Hansard, 29 Jan. 1909, vol. 35 p. 1780 col. 1.
27. Hansard, 6 Oct. 1909, vol. 36 p. 858 col. 2.
28. Hansard, 28 Nov. 1911, vol. 41 p. 474 col. 1.
29. J. H. Clapham, *An Economic History of Modern Britain* (Cambridge: Cambridge University Press 1932), p. 455.
30. Private letter received from the Librarian, Battye Library, 23 Sept. 1975. We are indebted to P. D. Wilson, Queensland State Archivist for guidance in respect of the newspaper reports discussed in this section.
31. *West Australian,* editorial 10 May 1911.
32. Ibid.
33. Ibid.
34. Ibid.
35. Hansard, 26 Sept. 1918, vol. 58 p. 453 col. 1.
36. Annual Report 1908, *V. & P.* 1909.
37. *West Australian,* editorial 10 May 1911.
38. Ibid.
39. *West Australian* 10 May 1911.
40. Ibid.
41. Hansard, 6 Dec. 1911. vol. 41 p. 680 col. 1, and 22 Oct. 1913, vol. 47 p. 1895 col. 2.
42. J. S. Battye, *The Cyclopedia of Western Australia,* vol. 1 p. 524.
43. Ibid. under Hann H.
44. See bibliography entries under Drew J. M.
45. Annual Report 1912, *V. & P.* 1913.
46. Both the 1902 rules and the 1913 rules may be seen in the *Government Gazette* issues: the former in the edition of March 28, 1902 at p. 1225, and the latter in Sept. 12, 1913 at p. 3439.
47. Annual Report 1904, *V. & P.* 1905.
48. Ibid. and A.R. 1914, *V. & P.* 1915.
49. Annual Report 1908, *V. & P.* 1909.
50. A.R. 1905, *V. & P.* 1906.
51. A.R. 1897, *V. &. P.* 1898.
52. Hansard, 6 Dec. 1906, vol. 30 p. 3474 col. 2.
53. Hansard, 28 July 1908, vol. 33 p. 17 col. 1.
54. Hansard, 5 Aug. 1908, vol. 33 p. 180 col. 1.
55. Hansard, 22 Jan. 1909, vol. 35 p. 1599 col. 1.
56. Hansard, 7 Sept. 1909, vol. 36 p. 171 col. 2.
57. Annual Report 1911, *V. & P.* 1912.
58. J. M. Drew, *Penological Reform in Western Australia* (Perth, Govt Printer 1916), p. 4.
59. Annual Report 1912, *V. & P.* 1913.
60. C. Gertzel, The convict system in Western Australia 1850-1870, p. 8.
61. Annual Report 1912, *V. & P.* 1913.
62. A.R. 1913, *V. & P.* 1914.
63. Drew, *Penological Reform in Western Australia,* p. 8.

64. See R. W. Chamberlain, *There is No Truce. A Life of Thomas Mott Osborne, prison reformer* (London, G. Routledge & Sons 1936).
65. Annual Report 1914, *V. & P.* 1915.
66. See the respective Annual Reports for these years.
67. Annual Report 1915, *V. & P.* 1916.
68. *West Australian* 4 Apr. 1918.
69. *West Australian* 5 Apr. 1918.
70. Annual Report 1918, *V. & P.* 1919.
71. Amendment No. 32, 1918.
72. See entry in Bolton & Mozeley, *The Western Australian Legislature 1870-1930*.
73. Hansard, 19 Sept. 1918, vol. 58 p. 379 col. 2.
74. Hansard, 24 Sept. 1918, vol. 58 p. 409 col. 1.
75. Hansard, 26 Sept. 1918, vol. 58 p. 448 col. 1.
76. Ibid.
77. Hansard, 5 Feb. 1918, vol. 56 p. 270 col. 1.
78. Hansard, 12 Feb. 1918, vol. 56 p. 357 col. 1.
79. Hansard, 17 Sept. 1918, vol. 58 p. 343 col. 1.
80. Hansard, 1 Oct. 1918, vol. 58 p. 475 col. 2.
81. Hansard, 3 Oct. 1918, vol. 58 p. 554 col. 2.
82. See entry in Bolton & Mozeley, *The Western Australian Legislature 1870-1930*.
83. Hansard, 17 Oct. 1918.
84. Hansard, 29 Oct. 1918.

5 *1920-1960: The Regressive Years*

1. Annual Report 1919, *V. & P.* 1920.
2. A.R. 1920, *V. & P.* 1921.
3. A. R. 1919, *V. & P.* 1920.
4. Ibid.
5. A.R. 1925, *V. & P.* 1925.
6. A.R. 1924, *V. & P.* 1925.
7. A.R. 1933, *V. & P.* 1934.
8. A.R. 1922, *V. & P.* 1923.
9. A.R. 1927, *V. & P.* 1927.
10. See for example letters from J. McGivern, Prison Superintendent, to the *Western Australian Prison Officers' Union Newsletter* March 1974 and Oct. 1973.
11. Hansard, 7 Oct. 1924, vol. 70 p. 1152 col. 1.
12. Hansard, 3 Aug. 1926, vol. 74 p. 25 col. 2.
13. Hansard, 6 Aug. 1925, vol. 72 p. 125 col. 1.
14. Hansard, 26 Aug. 1925, vol. 72 p. 536 col. 1.
15. Hansard, 2 Sept. 1925, vol. 72 p. 657 col. 1.
16. Annual Report, *V. & P.* 1923.
17. A.R. 1921, *V. & P.* 1921.
18. A.R. 1924, *V. & P.* 1924.
19. A.R. 1923, *V. & P.* 1923.
20. A.R. 1924, *V. & P.* 1924.

21. Ibid.
22. See for example A.R. 1925, *V. & P.* 1925.
23. A.R. 1926, *V. & P.* 1926.
24. A.R. 1924, *V. & P.* 1924.
25. *Women's Co-operation,* 9 Oct. 1924, pp. 15-16.
26. Hansard, 6 Aug. 1925, vol. 72 p. 125 col. 1.
27. This account is taken mainly from J. M. Drew, *Prison Reform in Western Australia—The Pardelup Prison Farm* (Perth, Govt Printer 1928).
28. Drew, ibid.
29. Annual Report 1928, *V. & P.* 1928.
30. Official Visitors Book, Pardelup Prison, kept in the prison.
31. Drew, *Prison Reform in Western Australia—The Pardelup Prison Farm,* p. 6.
32. For an account of the English borstal system see R. Hood, *Borstal re-assessed* (London, Heinemann 1965).
33. *Prison Officers' Magazine* (England), Dec. 1967.
34. Hansard, 28 Aug. 1945, vol. 115 p. 381 col. 1.
35. Ibid. col. 2.
36. See Hansard, 29 Aug. 1945, vol. 115 p. 412 col. 1, and 30 Aug. 1945, vol. 115 p. 457 col. 1.
37. Hansard, 6 Nov. 1945, vol. 116 p. 1661 col. 2.
38. Annual Report, *V. & P.* 1929.
39. Regulations relating to the management and control of the prisons of Western Australia (23 Aug. 1940), *Government Gazette* 1940, vol. 2 p. 1543.
40. Annual Report 1942-43. Those printed Reports which were not published and to which reference is made in the text, are available in the W. Aust. State Archives, BL.
41. Hansard, 3 Oct. 1945, vol. 115 p. 968 col. 2.
42. Hansard, 28 Sept. 1949, new series vol. 125 p. 1595 col. 1.
43. Hansard, 5 Dec. 1950, n.s. vol. 127 p. 2508 col. 1.
44. Hansard, 8 Apr. 1954, n.s. vol. 137 p. 74 col. 1.
45. Annual Report 1950.
46. A.R. 1953-54.
47. A.R. 1963-64.
48. A.R. 1953-54.
49. A.R. 1957-58.
50. A.R. 1959-60.
51. A.R. 1954-55.
52. A.R. 1957-58.
53. A.R. 1961-62.
54. A.R. 1958-59.
55. A.R. 1962-63.
56. A.R. 1958-59.
57. A.R. 1958-59.
58. A.R. 1949.
59. A.R. 1961-62.
60. A.R. 1963-64.
61. Hansard, 9 Sept. 1953, vol. 134 p. 501 col. 2.
62. Hansard, 30 Sept. 1953, vol. 134 p. 872 col. 1.

63. Hansard, 16 Sept. 1953, vol. 134 p. 626 col. 1.

6 *The Imprisonment of Aborigines*

1. Annual Report 1883, *V. & P.* 1884.
2. Report on Rottnest, *V. & P.* 1889.
3. Annual Report 1908, *V. & P.* 1909.
4. A.R. 1901, *V. & P.* 1902.
5. Pardelup Prison's Official Visitors Book.
6. P. Hasluck, *Black Australians: A Survey of Native Policy in Western Australia, 1829-1897* (Melbourne, Oxford University Press 1942).
7. See T. E. Gaddis, *Birdman of Alcatraz; the story of Robert Stroud* (New York, Random House 1955).
8. 4 & 5 Vict. No 21 (1841) An Act to constitute the Island of Rottnest a legal Prison.
9. Reports from the governors of the Australian colonies and other papers relating to the condition of the Aboriginal population 1844, *British Parliamentary Papers, Colonies, Australia,* vol. 8 (Irish University Press Series 1969), p. 375.
10. Ibid. p. 387.
11. W. Sommerville, *Rottnest Island: its history and legends, its discovery and development, natural beauties, fauna and flora* (Perth, Rottnest Board of Control 1948), p. 49.
12. CSO 1848, Chief Clerk's Report 25 Sept. 1848, BL.
13. He was appointed to the Round House in 1831. CSF 4/98, BL.
14. P. Hasluck, *Black Australians,* at note 6 p. 13.
15. CSO Records 1848, Chief Clerk's Report 25 Sept. 1848, BL.
16. CSO Records 1848, letter from Armstrong 18 March, BL.
17. CSO Records 1848, letter from Vincent 9 Oct., BL.
18. Quoted Hasluck in *Black Australians,* at note 6 p. 82.
19. Reports from the Governors of the Australian colonies and other papers relating to the condition of the Aboriginal population 1844, *B.P.P. Colonies, Australia,* vol. 8 at note 9 p. 409.
20. Ibid. p. 420.
21. Ibid. p. 428.
22. Ibid. pp. 432-3.
23. Ibid. p. 433.
24. Ibid. p. 428.
25. *Western Australian Government Gazette* 4 Sept. 1846, no. 65, and 18 Sept. 1846, no. 66.
26. Hasluck, *Black Australians,* at note 6 p. 83.
27. *Inquirer* 4 Jan. and 10 Jan. 1866.
28. Sommerville, *Rottnest Island,* at note 11 p. 71.
29. Hansard, 4 Sept. 1897, vol. 1 p. 150 col. 1.
30. A. Trollope, *Australia and New Zealand,* vol. 1 pp. 91, 109.
31. Ibid. p. 89.
32. Report of the Commission to inquire into the administration of certain departments in the public service 1878, *V. & P.* 1878.

33. Hansard, 18 June 1878, vol. 3 p. 71 col. 1.
34. Hansard, 29 Aug. 1881, vol. 6 p. 334 col. 2.
35. Ibid.
36. Pamphlets 040 840 series xcvi, W. Aust. Archives, BL.
37. Report of the Commission to Inquire into the Treatment of Aboriginal Native Prisoners of the Crown in this Colony and certain other matters 1884 (the Forrest Report), *V. & P.* 1885.
38. *Government Gazette* 2 Jan. 1883.
39. Hansard, 6 Aug. 1883, vol. 8 p. 158 col. 2.
40. Hansard, 10 Aug. 1883, vol. 8 p. 199 col. 1.
41. Hansard, 25 July 1883, vol. 8 p. 77 col. 2.
42. Hansard, 2 Aug. 1883, vol. 8 p. 133 col. 2.
43. Hansard, 4 Sept. 1883, vol. 8 p. 460 col. 1.
44. The Forrest Report, at note 37.
45. L. C. Timperley, *Reminiscences of Life on Rottnest 1883-1890.*
46. Annual Report for Rottnest 1897, *V. & P.* 1898.
47. Hansard, 25 Aug. 1886, vol. 11 p. 52 col. 1.
48. Hansard, 2 Aug. 1887, vol. 12 p. 278 col. 2.
49. Hansard, 30 Dec. 1887, vol. 13 p. 121 col. 1.
50. Hansard, 15 Feb. 1892, vol. 2 p. 532 col. 1.
51. Hansard, 15 Feb. 1892, vol. 2 p. 532 col. 1.
52. Hansard, 6 Feb. 1892.
53. Hansard, 29 Jan. 1892, vol. 2 p. 398 col. 2.
54. Hansard, 22 Aug. 1895, vol. 8 p. 674 col. 2.
55. Hansard, 6 Jan. 1893, vol. 3 p. 572 col. 2.
56. The 1899 Royal Commission 3rd Report, pp. 14-15, in *Report of the Commission appointed to inquire into the Penal System of the Colony, V. & P.* 1899 (also published separately at Perth, Govt Printer 1899).
57. Hansard, 22 Aug. 1895, vol. 8 p. 674 col. 2.
58. Royal Commission into the administration of the Aborigines Department, and the employment and treatment of the aboriginal and half-caste subjects of the State 1904 (the Roth Report), *V. & P.* 1904.
59. Ibid. p. 18(c).
60. Ibid. Minutes of Evidence Q1020ff.
61. Ibid. Minutes of Evidence Q241.
62. Ibid. Minutes of Evidence Q243.
63. Ibid. p. 20ff.
64. Ibid. p. 19ff.
65. Ibid. p. 21ff.
66. A. W. Gill, Aspects of the West Australian Police Force 1887-1905, 1973-74, BL.
67. Hansard, 2 Feb. 1892, vol. 2 p. 428 col. 1. See also debate on Aboriginal Offenders Act Amendment, Jan. 1898.
68. Hansard, 7 Aug. 1907, vol. 31 p. 667 col. 1.
69. Hansard, 7 Nov. 1921, vol. 65 p. 1588 col. 2.
70. Royal Commission appointed to investigate, report and advise upon matters in relation to the condition and treatment of Aborigines 1935.
71. Ibid. p. 22 para. 4 col. 2.

72. Ibid. p. 23 para. 4 col. 1.
73. Ibid. p. 15 para. 1(e) col. 1-2.

7 *The Modern Period (1)*

1. Annual Report 1963-64.
2. A.R. 1966-67.
3. A.R. 1968-69.
4. A.R. 1972-73.
5. 12 Eliz. II No 23 (1963) An Act relating to the Release of Offenders on Probation or Parole. A major study of probation services in Australia, New Zealand and the United Kingdom is being undertaken by Stephen White of University College, Cardiff, Wales (see Bibliography). Of special relevance is his detailed analysis of the process by which the Western Australian Act of 1963 was passed.
6. Ibid. para. 21.
7. Hansard, 11 Sept. 1963, vol. 164 p. 461 col. 1.
8. For discussion of this change see *The Organisation of After-Care* by Advisory Council on the Treatment of Offenders (1963), and J. E. Thomas, *The English Prison Officer Since 1850,* chap. 6.
9. See R. Barton, *Institutional Neurosis* (Bristol, John Wright and Sons 1959).
10. 12 Eliz. II No 63 (1963) An Act to make better provision for the Rehabilitation of Convicted Inebriates and for incidental and other purposes.
11. Annual Report 1971-72.
12. See for example T. S. Szasz, *Ideology and insanity: essays on the psychiatric dehumanization of man.* (Harmondsworth, Penguin Books 1974).
13. Annual Report 1964-65.
14. A.R. 1965-66.
15. A.R. 1956-57.
16. A.R. 1967-68.
17. A.R. 1968-69.
18. A.R. 1970-71.
19. A.R. 1969-70.
20. A.R. 1881, *V. & P.* 1882.
21. W. Aust. Blue Book 1875.
22. Ibid. 1895.
23. A.R. 1935.
24. A.R. 1966-67.
25. A.R. 1971-72.
26. F. Emery, M. Emery & Cy de Jago, *Hope within walls* (Canberra, Australian National University Centre for Continuing Education 1973).
27. A. R. 1968-69.
28. A.R. 1972-73. The law enabling this is 18 Eliz. II No 74 (1969) An Act to amend the Prisons Act, 1903-1964 to make provisions for the grant of leave to certain prisoners.
29. Department of Corrections, *Structures and functions of the Department of Corrections, Western Australia* (Research Section, Dept of Corrections, Perth).

Reprinted 1975.
30. A.R. 1970-71.
31. A.R. 1962-63.
32. A.R. 1966-67.
33. Ibid.
34. A.R. 1969-70.
35. A.R. 1967-68.
36. A detailed account is given in *Structure and functions of the Department of Corrections,* at note 29 pp. 6ff.
37. Annual Report 1957-58.
38. A.R. 1960-61.
39. A.R. 1961-62.
40. A.R. 1967-68.
41. A.R. 1969-70.
42. A.R. 1971-72.
43. Ibid.
44. *Structure and functions of the Department of Corrections,* at note 29 p. 1.
45. See J. E. Thomas, *The English Prison Officer Since 1850,* chap. 8.
46. The Prisons Act, 1903-1971. 20 Eliz. II No 43 (1971) An Act to amend the Prisons Act, 1903-1969 to change the title of Comptroller General of Prisons to Director of the Department of Corrections.
47. *W.A.P.O.U. Newsletter* Apr. 1973.
48. Annual Report 1971-72.

8   *The Modern Period (2)*

1. Annual Report 1962-63.
2. A.R. 1966-67.
3. A.R. 1967-68.
4. *Western Australian Prison Officers' Union Newsletter* May 1973.
5. Royal Commission appointed to investigate: Various allegations of assaults on or brutality to prisoners in Fremantle Prison: and of discrimination against aboriginal or part-aboriginal prisoners therein: and upon certain other matters touching that prison, its inmates and staff 1972 (the Jones Report), *V. & P.* 1973.
6. Ibid. p. 42.
7. Ibid. For example pp. 54, 79.
8. Ibid. p. 145.
9. Ibid. pp. 146ff.
10. Ibid. p. 147.
11. Ibid. pp. 126-7.
12. Ibid. p. 126.
13. Ibid. pp. 98ff.
14. Ibid. pp. 165ff.
15. Ibid. p. 154.
16. Ibid. p. 157.
17. Ibid. p. 160.

18. Ibid. p. 160.
19. Ibid. p. 159.
20. Ibid. pp. 80ff.
21. Ibid. pp. 173ff.
22. Ibid. p. 6.
23. This information on departmental response to the recommendations was supplied to me by the Director of Corrections privately in 1975.
24. Hansard, 15 Sept. 1964, vol. 167 p. 945 col. 2.
25. Hansard, 17 Sept. 1964, vol. 167 p. 1037 col. 1.
26. 13 Eliz. II No 22 (1964) An Act to amend the Prisons Act, 1903-1963, and the Prisons Act Amendment Act, 1963.
27. See for example the editions of June 1973, Nov. 1973, pp. 4 and 7ff; Oct. 1973, p. 1; and especially 'The dilemma of a superscrew' in May 1973.
28. See J. E. Thomas, 'What Kind of Training?', *Adult Education* (England), March 1971, vol. 43 no. 6, and 'Training Schemes for Prison Staff: An analysis of some problems', *Australian and New Zealand Journal of Criminology,* Dec. 1972, vol. 5 no. 4.
29. *W.A.P.O.U. Newsletter* June 1973.
30. Ibid. Aug. 1975 p. 25.
31. Ibid. Dec. 1974 p. 2.
32. See Thomas, *The English Prison Officer Since 1850,* pp. 202ff.
33. *W.A.P.O.U. Newsletter* Sept. 1975, p. 18.
34. Ibid. Dec. 1974 p. 10.
35. T. A. Williams, Custody and Conflict: An organisational study of role problems and related attitudes among prison officers in Western Australia (PhD thesis, University of Western Australia 1974).

Appendix 1: 'The Establishment'

1. Superintendent's Order Book, Fremantle, SO1, BL.
2. Ibid. SO1, SO4. See also Kimberley, *History of Western Australia,* p. 175.
3. Annual Report 1898.
4. Superintendent's Order Book Fremantle, SO1, BL.
5. Ibid. SO3.
6. There is a photograph of the cage in the *Civil Service Journal* 20 July 1929.

Bibliography

RELEVANT STATUTES

ENGLISH STATUTES

Compiled in: J. M. Lelly (ed.), *The Statutes of Practical Utility, being the Fifth Edition of "Chitty's Statutes"*, London, Sweet and Maxwell, Stevens and Sons 1895; *The Public General Acts of the United Kingdom of Great Britain and Ireland,* London, The Queen's Printer; *The Statutes: Revised Edition,* London, George Edward Eyre & William Spottiswoode 1876; *The Public General Statutes,* London, George E. B. Eyre & William Spottiswoode 1866; *The Public General Acts and the Church Assembly Measures,* London, Law Journal Reports; *The Statutes of the Realm,* London, Dawsons of Pall Mall 1963. [Full titles of the Acts are given in Notes.]

16 Geo. III C 43 (1776) 'Hard Labour' or 'Hulks Act'. Continued by 18 Geo. III C 62 (1778) and 19 Geo. III C 54 (1779). Authorized the use of hulks.

19 Geo. III C 74 (1779) Penitentiary Act. Established a government prison.

4 Geo. IV C 64 (1823) Gaol Act. A turning point in government intervention in local prisons.

5 & 6 Will. IV C 38 (1835) Prisons Act. Authorized the use of government inspectors.

13 & 14 Vict. C 39 (1850) Convict Prisons Act. Established the convict prison services.

40 & 41 Vict. C 21 (1877) Prisons Act. Brought every prison in England under central government control.

61 & 62 Vict. C 41 (1898) Prison Act. Introduced reforms consequent upon the Gladstone Report.

WESTERN AUSTRALIAN STATUTES

Compiled in: *Western Australia, Statutes of the Realm adopted by Ordinances and Acts of Council,* ed. by J. C. H. James, London, Spottiswoode & co 1896; *The Statutes of Western Australia,* Melbourne, M'Carron, Bird & co 1883; *The Statutes of Western Australia,* ed. by J. C. H. James, London, Spottiswoode & co 1896; *The Acts of the Parliament of Western Australia,* Perth, Govt Printer, 1902-; also volumes of W. Aust. *Parliamentary Debates* (Hansard). [Full titles of the Acts are given in Notes.]

6 & 7 Will. IV C 30 (England 1836) Execution of persons convicted of murder. Adopted by 7 Vict. 13 (1844).

4 & 5 Vict. No 21 (1841) Constituted the Island of Rottnest a legal prison.
12 Vict. No 7 (1849) For the regulation of gaols etc.
14 Vict. No 22 (1850) To vest site of Fremantle Prison in trustees.
14 Vict. No 6 (1850) Provided for the due custody and discipline of offenders transported to Western Australia.
16 Vict. No 18 (1853) Made further provision for the custody and discipline of offenders transported to Western Australia.
17 Vict. No 7 (1854) For the suppression of violent crimes committed by convicts illegally at large.
18 Vict. No 1 (1855) Regulated the forms to be observed by pardoned convicts leaving the colony.
19 Vict. No 8 (1856) Substituted other punishment in lieu of transportation.
21 Vict. No 1 (1857) Made additional provisions for convict discipline in Western Australia.
21 Vict. No 12 (1858) Extended and enlarged the 1849 Act.
24 Vict. No 1 (1860) Amended No 8 of 1856.
32 Vict. No 9 (1868) Made better provision for the suppression of violent crimes committed by convicts.
43 Vict. No 4 (1879) Made additional provisions for prison discipline.
51 Vict. No 5 (1887) Amended the law in respect of prisoners sentenced to hard labour.
55 Vict. No 6 (1892) To permit the conditional release of first offenders in certain cases.
58 Vict. No 10 (1894) Authorized transfer or removal of colonial prisoners.
1 & 2 Edw. VII No 3 (1902) Established lock-ups as police gaols and amended gaol Acts.
2 Edw. VII No 7 (1902) Repealed 14 Vict. No 22.
3 Edw. VII No 14 (1903) Consolidated and amended the law relating to prisons. This is the principal statute affecting present-day administration.
9 Geo. V No 32 (1918) Amended the Act of 1903. Introduced reformatory prisons.
9 Geo. V No 32 (1918) Amended the Criminal Code. Set the pattern for indeterminacy.

RECENT AMENDMENTS TO PRISONS ACT OF 1903

11 Eliz. II No 36 (1962) Established institutions for convicted inebriates.
12 Eliz. II No 22 (1963) Contained necessary modifications of legislation.
12 Eliz. II No 23 (1963) Established probation and parole.
12 Eliz. II No 63 (1963) Made better provision for the rehabilitation of convicted inebriates.
13 Eliz. II No 22 (1964) Made adjustment to earlier legislation.

18 Eliz. II No 74 (1969) Granted leave to prisoners.
20 Eliz. II No 43 (1971) Changed the title of Comptroller-General of Prisons to Director of the Department of Corrections.

OFFICIAL PAPERS AND REPORTS

1 WESTERN AUSTRALIA

Annual Reports of the Gaol, Prison and Department of Corrections, Western Australia, in W. Aust. Parliament, *Minutes, Votes and Proceedings.* [Referred to as A.R. in Notes.] Since these are short and may be easily found, page numbers are not generally included.

Australia, Parliament. *Historical Records of Australia: Governors' Despatches to and from England.* Series 1. Library Committee 1914-25. Covers years 1788-1848.

Blue Books, Western Australia. From 1837.

Western Australian Department of Corrections. Structures and functions of the Department of Corrections, Western Australia. New edn compiled and put out by Psychol. and Res. Sect. of Western Australian Department of Corrections under Prison Establishments and Facilities, Oct. 1975.

Reports on Rottnest Prison. W. Aust. *Minutes, Votes and Proceedings.*

Western Australia, Parliament. *Parliamentary Debates* (Hansard). [Referred to as Hansard in Notes.]

Western Australia. *Minutes, Votes and Proceedings.* [Referred to as V. & P. in Notes.]

Western Australian Government Gazette and *Government Gazette of Western Australia.*

Royal Commissions which are of special interest to this study:

Commission to Inquire into Certain Departments in the Public Service 1878, W. Aust. *V. & P.* 1878.

Commission to inquire into the treatment of Aboriginal prisoners of the Crown in this colony and certain other matters (the Forrest Report) 1884, W. Aust. *V. & P.* 1885.

Royal Commission appointed to inquire into the penal system of the colony 1899 (the Jameson Report), W. Aust. *V. & P.* 1899; also published separately as Western Australia, *Report of the Commission appointed to inquire into the Penal System of the Colony,* Perth, Govt Printer 1899.

Royal Commission into the administration of the Aborigines Department and the employment and treatment of the aboriginal and half-caste subjects of the State 1904 (the Roth Report), W. Aust. *V. & P.* 1904.

Royal Commission into the administration and conduct of Fremantle prison and matter incidental thereto 1911 (the Pennefather Report). This report is published in *West Australian* 10, 1911.

Royal Commission appointed to investigate, report and advise in relation to the condition and treatment of aborigines 1935 (the Moseley Report), W. Aust. *V. & P.* 1935.

Royal Commission appointed to investigate: Various allegations of assaults on or brutality to prisoners in Fremantle Prison: and of discrimination against aboriginal or part-aboriginal prisoners therein: and upon certain other matters touching that prison, its inmates and staff 1972 (the Jones Report), W. Aust. *V. & P.* 1973.

Civil Service Journal. Centenary 20 July 1929 (copy in BL).

2 ENGLAND

British Parliamentary Papers. Irish University Press Series.
Shannon: Irish University Press 1968- .
Especially the volumes:
1. *Crime and Punishment. Transportation,* vols: 3 (1968), 4 (1969), 9 (1969), 16 (1971).
2. *Colonies. Australia,* vol. 8 (1969).
   And of these volumes especially:
   Reports from the governors of the Australian colonies and other papers relating to the condition of the Aboriginal population.
   Royal Commissions on the Penal Servitude Acts 1863 and 1879.
   Report from the Select Committee of the House of Lords on the present state of discipline in gaols and houses of correction 1863.
   Report from the Departmental Committee on Prisons 1895, cmd 7702 (the Gladstone Report).
   Minutes of Evidence, Departmental Committee on Prisons, with Appendices and Index 1895, cmd 7702-1.
   Observations of Prison Commissioners on recommendations of Departmental Committee 1895.
   Reports of the Directors of Convict Prisons, Commissioners of Prisons, and the Prison Department 1851-1974.
   The organization of after-care. Advisory Council on the Treatment of Offenders 1963.
   Report of the Inquiry into Prison Escapes and Security 1966, cmd 3175 (the Mountbatten Report).

3 OTHER

Attica: the official report of the New York State Special Commission. New York: Bantam Books 1972.

Bibliography   211

UNPUBLISHED SOURCES

Albany Historical Society archives (unclassified), and in the possession of
the society.
Western Australian State Archives in the Battye Library, Perth, W. Aust.:
1. Colonial Secretary's Office Records.
2. Letterbook of Superintendent of Juvenile Emigrants (Schoales's
   Letterbook) 7/12/1843-12/9/1847.
3. Battye Research Notes, ref. 65222 RN 107/108.
4. Superintendent's Order Book Fremantle, ref. SO9, SO3, SO1.
5. Annual Reports of Western Australian Prisons 1929-60. Reports
   that were made but not published during this period are in the
   W. Aust. State Archives.
Prison Reception Book, Geraldton Prison. Kept at the prison.
Official Visitors Book, Pardelup Prison. Kept at the prison.
Fremantle Harbour Trust, PR2778.
Swan River Papers.
Broomhall F. The Veterans: a history of the Enrolled Pensioner Force in
   Western Australia 1850-1880. 2 vols. East Perth 1975-76. Copy in Reid
   Library, University of Western Australia.
Gertzel C. The convict system in Western Australia 1850-1870. BA
   honours thesis in history, University of Western Australia 1949.
Gill A. W. Aspects of the West Australian Police Force 1887-1905, 1973-
   74. Copy in the Battye Library.
Paterson A. The principles of the borstal system. Private circulation 1932.
Saunders T. Development of the Prison System. Thesis, Graylands
   Teacher Training College. BL ref. 7326.
White S. Probation Officers and Pre-sentence Reports in Australia, New
   Zealand and United Kingdom 1976.
Williams T. A. Custody and Conflict: An organisational study of role
   problems and related attitudes among prison officers in Western Aus-
   tralia. PhD thesis, University of Western Australia 1974.

BOOKS, PAMPHLETS AND ARTICLES

Australian Dictionary of Biography. Melbourne: Melbourne University
   Press 1966- .
Barry J. V. *Alexander Maconochie of Norfolk Island: a study in penal
   reform.* Melbourne: Melbourne University Press 1958.
Barton R. *Institutional Neurosis.* Bristol: John Wright and Sons 1959.
Bastin J. & Stoodley J. 'F. C. B. Vosper, An Australian Radical', *Uni-
   versity Studies in History,* 1967, vol. 5 no. 1. University of Western
   Australia Press.

Bateson C. *The Convict Ships 1787-1868.* 2nd edn. Sydney: A. H. & A. W. Reed 1974.

Battye J. S. *The Cyclopedia of Western Australia.* 2 vols. Adelaide: Hussey & Gillingham 1913.

Battye J. S. *Western Australia: A History from its Discovery to the Inauguration of the Commonwealth.* London: Oxford University Press 1924.

Beccaria Bonesana, Marquis C. *An essay on Crimes and Punishments* [*Dei delitti e delle pene . . .*]. English translation 1767. London: J. Almon 1767.

Bentham, Jeremy. *Works.* Edited by Sir John Bowring. Edinburgh: Tait 1843-59.

Binney J. see Mayhew H.

Bolton G. C. & Mozeley, Ann. *The Western Australian Legislature 1870-1930.* Canberra: Australian National University Press 1961.

Burt J. T. *Results of the System of Separate Confinement as Administered at the Pentonville Prison.* London: Longman & co 1852.

Chamberlain R. W. *There is No Truce. A Life of Thomas Mott Osborne, prison reformer.* London: G. Routledge & Sons 1936.

Clapham J. H. *An Economic History of Modern Britain.* Cambridge: Cambridge University Press 1932.

Clark C. M. H. *A History of Australia.* 3 vols. Melbourne: Melbourne University Press 1962-73.

de Jago C. see Emery F.

Devoy J. *Recollections of an Irish Rebel.* Shannon: Irish University Press 1969.

Drew J. M. *Penological Reform in Western Australia.* Perth: Govt Printer 1916.

Drew J. M. *Prison Reform in Western Australia—The Pardelup Prison Farm.* Perth: Govt Printer 1928.

Du Cane E. F. *The Punishment and Prevention of Crime.* London: Macmillan 1885.

Du Cane E. F. 'The decrease of crime', *Nineteenth Century,* March 1893.

Emery M. see Emery F.

Emery F., Emery M., de Jago Cy. *Hope within walls.* Canberra: Australian National University Centre for Continuing Education 1973.

Erickson R. *Old Toodyay and Newcastle.* Perth: Toodyay Shire Council 1974.

Fox L. W. *The English prison and Borstal systems: an account of the prison and Borstal systems in England and Wales after the Criminal justice act, 1848, with a historical introduction and an examination of the principles of imprisonment as a legal punishment.* London: Routledge & K. Paul 1952.

Gaddis T. E. *Birdman of Alcatraz; the story of Robert Stroud.* New York:

Random House 1955.

Gruenhut M. *Penal Reform. A comparative study.* Oxford: Oxford University Press 1948.

Hasluck A. *Unwilling Emigrants.* Melbourne: Oxford University Press 1959.

Hasluck A. *Royal Engineer: life of Sir Edmund Du Cane.* Sydney: Angus and Robertson 1975.

Hasluck P. *Black Australians: A Survey of Native Policy in Western Australia, 1829-1897.* Melbourne: Oxford University Press 1942.

Henriques U. R. Q. 'The rise and decline of the separate system of prison discipline', *Past and Present,* no. 54, February 1972.

Hood R. *Borstal re-assessed.* London: Heinemann 1965.

Howard J. *The State of the Prisons in England and Wales, with Preliminary Observations, and an Account of some Foreign Prisons.* 2 parts. Warrington 1777-80.

Johnson, William Branch. *The English Prison Hulks . . .* London: Christopher Johnson 1957. Rev. edn Phillimore & co ltd 1970.

Judge A. see Reynolds G. W.

Kimberley W. B. *History of Western Australia: A narrative of her past together with biographies of her leading men.* Melbourne: F. W. Niven 1897.

McLachlan N. 'Penal Reform and Penal History' in Bom-Cooper L. (ed.) *Progress in penal reform.* Oxford: Oxford University Press 1975.

Mayhew H. & Binney J. *The Criminal Prisons of London and scenes of Prison Life.* London 1862. Reprinted Frank Cass 1968.

Millett E. *An Australian Parsonage; or the Settler and the Savage in Western Australia.* London: Ed. Stanford 1872.

Morrison, Rev. W. D. 'The increase of crime', *Nineteenth Century,* June 1892.

Morrison, Rev. W. D. 'Are our prisons a failure?', *Fortnightly Review,* April 1894.

Neild J. *State of the prisons in England, Scotland and Wales . . . with . . . documents . . . and remarks, adapted to . . . improve the condition of prisoners in general.* London 1812.

O'Luing S. S. *Fremantle Mission.* Anvil Books 1965.

O'Reilly J. B. *Moondyne: a story of convict life in Australia.* London: G. Routledge & Sons ltd 1889.

Péan C. *The Conquest of Devil's Island* [*Conquêtes en terre de bagne*]. London: Max Parrish 1953.

Pears E. (ed.) International Penal and Penitentiary Congress [London 1872]. *Prisons and Reformations at home and abroad: being the Transactions of the International Penitentiary Congress, held in London . . . 1872, including official documents . . .* Ed. by Edwin Pears. London: Longmans, Green & co 1872.

Porter W. *History of the Corps of Royal Engineers.* 3 vols. London: Royal Engineers 1889-1915.

Prison Officers' Association (England). 'The Role of the Modern Prison Officer', *Prison Officers' Magazine,* November 1963.

Pugh R. B. *Imprisonment in medieval England.* London: Cambridge University Press 1968.

Reynolds G. W. and Judge A. *The Night the police went on strike.* London: Weidenfeld and Nicolson 1968.

Roberts D. *Victorian origins of the British welfare State.* New Haven: Yale University Press 1960.

Roche J. J. *Life of John Boyle O'Reilly . . . Together with his complete poems and speeches edited by Mrs. J. B. O'Reilly.* London: T. Fisher Unwin 1891. [USA printed.]

Rose G. *The Struggle for Penal Reform: the Howard League and its predecessors.* London: Stevens & Sons 1961.

Ruck S. K. (ed.) *Paterson on Prisons.* London: Frederick Muller 1951.

Shaw A. G. L. *Convicts and the Colonies.* London: Faber and Faber 1966. Reprinted Melbourne University Press 1977.

Sommerville W. *Rottnest Island: its history and legends, its discovery and development, natural beauties, fauna and flora.* Perth: Rottnest Board of Control 1948.

Szasz T. S. *Ideology and insanity: essays on the psychiatric dehumanization of man.* Harmondsworth: Penguin Books 1974.

Tallack W. *Defects in the Criminal Administration and Penal Legislation of Great Britain and Ireland with Remedial Suggestions.* London: Howard Association 1872.

Thomas J. E. *The English Prison Officer Since 1850; a study in conflict.* London: Routledge and Kegan Paul 1972.

Thomas J. E. 'What Kind of Training?', *Adult Education* (England), March 1971, vol. 43 no. 6.

Thomas J. E. 'Training Schems for Prison Staff: An analysis of some problems', *Australian and New Zealand Journal of Criminology,* December 1972, vol. 5 no. 4.

Thomas J. E. 'Killed on duty: an analysis of the murders of English prison staff since 1850', *Prison Service Journal* (England), No 7 (new series), July 1972.

Trollope A. *Australia and New Zealand.* Vol. 1. London: Chapman and Hall 1876.

Watson J. (ed.) *Catalpa 1876. 100 Years Ago . . . A special collection of papers on the background and significance of the Fenian escapes from Fremantle, Western Australia, Easter 1876.* Nedlands: University of Western Australia 1976.

Webb S. & B. *English Prisons under Local Government.* London: Longmans 1927.

Willoughby H. *British Convict in Western Australia.* London 1865.

NEWSPAPERS (Western Australian)

Women's Co-operation (Oct. 1924)
Daily News
Inquirer and Commercial News
Morning Herald
Western Mail
Perth Gazette later the
West Australian
Western Australian Prison Officers' Union Newsletter [referred to as *W.A.P.O.U. Newsletter* in Notes.]

Subject Index

217